Abolishing School Fees in Africa

LESSONS FROM ETHIOPIA, GHANA, KENYA, MALAWI, AND MOZAMBIQUE

Abolishing School Fees in Africa

LESSONS FROM ETHIOPIA, GHANA, KENYA, MALAWI, AND MOZAMBIQUE

A publication of The World Bank in collaboration with UNICEF

© 2009 The International Bank for Reconstruction and Development / The World Bank
1818 H Street, NW
Washington, DC 20433
Telephone: 202-473-1000
Internet: www.worldbank.org
E-mail: feedback@worldbank.org

A publication of The World Bank in collaboration with the United Nations Children's Fund (UNICEF)

The findings, interpretations, and conclusions expressed in this volume do not necessarily reflect the views of the Executive Directors of The World Bank or the governments they represent, the policies of UNICEF, the views of the Executive Director of UNICEF, or the governments who are Member States of the United Nations.

The boundaries, colors, denominations, and other information shown on any map in this work do not imply any judgement on the part of The World Bank or UNICEF concerning the legal status of any territory or the endorsement or acceptance of such boundaries.

ISBN: 978-0-8213-7540-2
eISBN: 978-0-8213-7541-9
DOI: 10.1596/978-0-8213-7540-2

Library of Congress Cataloging-in-Publication Data

Abolishing school fees in Africa: lessons from Ethiopia, Ghana, Kenya, Malawi, and Mozambique.
     p. cm.
  ISBN 978-0-8213-7540-2 (alk. paper) — ISBN 978-0-8213-7541-9 (electronic)
  1. Education, Elementary—Africa—Costs—Case studies. 2. School enrollment—Africa—Case studies. 3. Education and state—Africa—Case studies. I. World Bank.
  LB2829.3.A35A26 2008
  372.12'06—dc22

                                                                    2008013198

Contents

BOX

FIGURES

MAPS

TABLES

Foreword

I n the 1960s, as developing countries gained independence, investment in free basic education was one of the policies they used to build capacity and provide for more equitable participation in economic growth and politics. As education systems expanded and economies stagnated, however, the policy of free education was increasingly abandoned. This experience, shared by a wide range of countries, led to two hard lessons about economic barriers to schooling and their impact on the poor. The success or failure of current efforts to achieve the right to education for all by 2015 will depend in large measure on how well these lessons have been learned.

The first hard lesson came courtesy of the structural adjustment programs of the 1980s, when many countries implemented user fees as an alternative to tax-based financing of public services such as education. With hindsight, it became clear that insufficient attention was given to the impact of these fees and related costs on family budgets, on the spending choices of the poor, and on children's right to education.

By the late 1980s, evidence that user fees were having a negative impact on school participation was widespread. In 1987, the UNICEF study entitled *Adjustment with a Human Face: Protecting the Vulnerable and Promoting Growth*, by Cornea, Jolly, and Stewart, focused attention on the negative impact of fees and challenged the beliefs of many development practitioners.[1] The message was increasingly clear: user fees in education were working to stifle demand, particularly for the poorest and most vulnerable children, and leading to stagnating or even declining enrollment rates.

---

[1] Giovanni Andrea Cornea, Richard Jolly, and Frances Stewart. 1987. *Adjustment with a Human Face: Protecting the Vulnerable and Promoting Growth*. New York: Oxford University Press.

In the mid-1990s, often with the support of development agencies and nongovernmental organizations (NGOs), governments began to champion the elimination of user fees in primary education. Among the first countries to move in this direction were Malawi and Uganda. It was at this point that the second hard lesson became apparent. If poor children were the most vulnerable to the imposition of fees and the existence of other economic barriers, they could also, ironically, be the most vulnerable to unplanned or underplanned attempts to remove these barriers. Early efforts to remove fees showed the enormous power of such measures to increase enrollments, but they also showed how quickly the promise of these initiatives could be lost. Quality was compromised by dramatic increases in class size and a loss of school-level funding, far too frequently leaving the children of the poor no better off than before.

These experiences showed that as important as school fee elimination could be to facilitate the right to education and to universalize primary education, it must be carefully planned and widely negotiated if it is to make a positive and sustainable impact on school access and learning outcomes. In short, school fee abolition and similar measures to remove the economic barriers to schooling, such as conditional cash transfers, are unlikely to succeed unless they are part of a sustainable national education plan to ensure that the children they are targeting complete a good-quality primary education. This requires careful planning and implementation as well as major public investments. Most development agencies and NGOs agree with countries that the provision of additional teachers and materials will help to ensure that any surge in school enrollment does not weaken the quality of education or further disadvantage vulnerable populations. Also, long-term predictable financing—a key focus of the Education for All Fast Track Initiative—is regarded by all development partners as necessary to enable schools to replace lost income from abolished fees.

The cosponsors of this document—UNICEF (United Nations Children's Fund), the World Bank, and the Fast Track Initiative—believe that school fee abolition and related education responses can both draw on and contribute to broader poverty reduction and more equitable development efforts. As current economic instability places increased stress on poor families in developing countries around the world, these programs take on even greater importance in safeguarding and accelerating recent progress toward Education for All goals. Success in the future means learning the lessons from the past, from the countries themselves. It is our intent that this publication will help to serve this purpose and contribute to the process of dialogue and consensus building among parents, communities, teachers, and governments. After all, when some families can't afford to educate their children, hopes dim and futures are lost, and that is something no country can afford.

Robin Horn
Education Sector Manager
Human Development
World Bank

Cream Wright
Associate Director, Programs
Global Chief of Education
UNICEF

Robert Prouty
Acting Head
Education for All
Fast Track Initiative

Preface

This book constitutes one of the main outputs of the School Fee Abolition Initiative (SFAI). The initiative, launched in 2005 by the United Nations Children's Fund (UNICEF) and the World Bank, was designed to support countries in maintaining and accelerating progress toward universal primary education as outlined in the Millennium Development Goals and the Education for All (EFA) goals. Specifically, SFAI strengthens country efforts to eliminate school fees and/or implement targeted exemptions, subsidizations, and incentives to reduce education costs for the poor. The initiative has now grown into a broad partnership through the involvement of other key development partners and constituencies as well as research and academic institutions.

SFAI promotes access to quality basic education worldwide through three specific and interlinked goals. The first is to construct a knowledge base on school fee abolition in order to inform sound and sustainable policies, strategies, and interventions. SFAI recognizes that school fee abolition is a complex process that requires both the development of a credible database and the solid analysis that builds on lessons learned from experience. The second goal is to provide guidance and support to countries in planning and implementing school fee abolition policies. Engagement by SFAI partners is taking the form of both technical and financial assistance within the framework of ongoing national planning processes. The third goal is to advance the global policy dialogue on the financial barriers to education access and to build on existing EFA partnerships. The result will ensure a good understanding of the complexities involved in school fee abolition, facilitate the articulation of complementary roles, and create an environment for success.

In the course of discussions with partners, it was agreed to develop an operational guide on school fee abolition as a toolkit for action on the three goals. The guide was to draw not only from existing research on the issue but also from concrete lessons learned from country experiences. To this end, a workshop entitled "School Fee Abolition: Building on What We Know and Defining Sustained Support" was organized by UNICEF and the World Bank in Nairobi, Kenya, April 5–7, 2006. It brought together ministry of education representatives from six countries whose governments had already abolished fees (Ethiopia, Ghana, Kenya, Malawi, Mozambique, and Tanzania) and from three other countries that were planning to do so (Burundi, Democratic Republic of Congo, and Haiti), as well as bilateral and multilateral agencies, major international nongovernmental organizations, academic institutions, and other constituencies.

The Nairobi workshop took a pragmatic approach. It focused on the actual experiences of practitioners who planned and implemented school fee abolition policies. Of the six countries that had already abolished fees, five (Ethiopia, Ghana, Kenya, Malawi, and Mozambique) prepared and presented studies on their national experiences. Tanzania did not prepare a study but contributed to the presentations. Questions from representatives of the three countries that were in the process of planning school fee abolition enriched the analysis of the country studies in terms of strategies adopted, results obtained, challenges faced, and lessons learned.

The individual teams that participated in the research for and development of the country studies (see the acknowledgments section) continued the consultative process after Nairobi. This effort involved a broader range of ministry of education officials and diverse stakeholders. The studies were finalized by the end of 2006 by the five country teams after further analysis and systematization of the data in view of their prospective publication (in the present book). The studies therefore reflect only the data available to that date, with a few updates concerning certain education reforms and developments. Chapter 1 draws on the five studies to highlight the potential and various challenges of school fee abolition policies, and it provides a comparative overview on processes, challenges, and lessons learned.

The operational guide has also been finalized, after several other consultations with practitioners and partners. It is being published in 2009 jointly by UNICEF, the World Bank, the Association for the Development of Education in Africa, the UNESCO (United Nations Educational, Scientific and Cultural Organization) International Institute for Educational Planning (IIEP), and the EFA Fast Track Initiative.

The work on and around this publication, and the commitment through which it was produced, is a reflection of the value accorded by education stakeholders to the need for bold initiatives in accelerating progress toward universal primary education. It also reflects the imperative of basing such initiatives on rigorous evidence and sound planning in order to achieve sustainable results. We hope that the experiences and lessons summarized in this book will help national policy makers and their development partners move forward along these lines.

Acknowledgments

The five country studies in this book were conducted by five country teams made up of ministry of education officials, UNICEF and World Bank staff, development partners, researchers, and consultants. These individuals are acknowledged below. The positions indicated are those held at the time of the finalization of the studies in 2006, and the team members are listed in alphabetical order.

The **Ethiopia** chapter was written by Teklehaimanot Haileselassie (consultant) in collaboration with the following members of the country team: Kasu Abdi (Team Leader, Ministry of Education [MoE] Educational Program and Supervision Panel), Augustine Agu (Chief of Education Section, UNICEF Ethiopia), Maekelech Gidey (Project Officer, Education Section, UNICEF Ethiopia), Bruno Maes (Senior Program Officer, UNICEF Ethiopia), Yeshitla Mulat (Department Head, MoE Teachers' Education Development), Alemayehu Worku (Team Leader, MoE Project Preparation and Planning Panel), and Setotaw Yimam (Project Officer, Education Section, UNICEF Ethiopia). Additional support was provided by Ato Dereje Asfaw, Ato Tilaye Gete, Ato Abreha Hagos, and Zerihun Kebede (Education Bureau Heads of Oromia, Amhara, Tigray, and Addis Ababa, respectively) and by Woizero Almaz Beyene (Head, Educational Management Information System). The Ethiopia team thanks H. E. Ato Fuad Ibrahim, State Minister of Education, for his support during the initiation, write-up, and debriefing stages of the study. Isa Achoba (Monitoring and Evaluation Specialist, UNICEF Ethiopia) and Meklit Seido (Data Base Assistant, Monitoring and Evaluation Section, UNICEF Ethiopia) collaborated in the final review.

The **Ghana** chapter was written by Charles Otoo (Financial Controller, Ghana Education Service) in collaboration with the following members of the country team: Joseph Afrani (Director of Planning, Budgeting,

Monitoring and Evaluation, Ministry of Education, Science and Sports), Agnes Boadi-Siaw (District Director, Abura-Asebu-Kwamankese), Chris Koramoah (Accountant, Ghana Education Service), Michael Nsowah (Director General, Ghana Education Service), and Peter de Vries (Chief of Education Section, UNICEF Ghana). Charles Aheto-Tsegah (Acting Director of Planning, Budgeting, Monitoring and Evaluation, Ministry of Education, Science and Sports), Kwame Agyapong Apiadu-Agyen (Planning Officer, Ministry of Education, Science and Sports), and Jane Mwangi (Monitoring and Evaluation Specialist, UNICEF Ghana) collaborated in the final review.

The **Kenya** chapter was written by the following members of the country team from the Ministry of Education, Science and Technology: George Godia (Education Secretary), Waithaka Kabugu (Senior Assistant Director of Quality Assurance and Standards), Simon Karanja (Principal Economist), Simon Ole Kingi (Senior Assistant Director of Education), Karega Mutahi (Permanent Secretary), Miriam Mwirotsi (Director of Policy and Planning), Priscal Njiru (Secretary), Mary Njoroge (Director of Basic Education), Samuel Nthenge (Senior Economist), and Patricia Shitambasi (Secretary). Susan Kiragu (Monitoring and Evaluation Specialist, UNICEF Kenya), Aminata Maiga (Chief of Education Section, UNICEF Kenya), and Charles Obiero (Senior Economist/Statistician, Ministry of Education) collaborated in the final review.

The **Malawi** chapter was written by Esme Chipo Kadzamira (Centre for Educational Research and Training, University of Malawi) in collaboration with Nelson Kaperemera (Director for Basic Education, Ministry of Education [MoE]) and Simon Mphisa (Chief of Education Section, UNICEF Malawi). Additional support was provided by several MoE officials and education development partners in Malawi and by Catherine Chirwa (Project Officer, Education Section, UNICEF Malawi). The Malawi team thanks Joseph Matope, former Principal Secretary of Education, for lending his support to the development of the study. Mcknight Kalanda (present Director for Basic Education, MoE) collaborated in the final review.

The **Mozambique** chapter was written by Roger Avenstrup (consultant) in collaboration with the following members of the country team: João Assale (Deputy Director of Basic Education, Ministry of Education and Culture [MEC]), Stella Kaabwe (Chief of Education Section, UNICEF Mozambique), Manuel Lobo (Education for All Adviser to the Minister of Education), Xiaoyan Liang (Task Team Leader, World Bank), Antonio Mizé (Program Officer, Canadian International Development Agency), Manuel Rego (Director of Planning and Cooperation, MEC), Deirdre Watson (Project Officer, Education Section, UNICEF Mozambique), Cristina Tomo (Director of General Education, MEC), Jeannette Vogelaar

(Education Adviser, Dutch Embassy), and Paul Wafer (Education Adviser, Department for International Development [U.K.]). Anjana Mangalagiri (Chief of Education Section, UNICEF Mozambique), Kenji Ohira (Program Officer, Education Section, UNICEF Mozambique), Tomoko Shibuya (Education Specialist, Education Section, UNICEF Mozambique), and Stefano Visani (Monitoring and Evaluation Specialist, UNICEF Mozambique) collaborated in the final review.

Birger Fredriksen (Consultant on Education Development) and Dina Craissati (Senior Education Adviser, UNICEF New York) coedited the book. Birger Fredriksen guided and reviewed the initial writing of the five country studies. Dina Craissati led and coordinated the project.

The work on this publication was funded by UNICEF, the World Bank, and the Education for All Fast Track Initiative.

Abbreviations

ABE	alternative basic education
ASAL	arid and semiarid lands (Kenya)
ASE	Acçao Social Escolar (Social Action Fund—Mozambique)
Br	birr (Ethiopian currency)
₵	cedis (Ghanaian currency)
DDE	district directorate of education (Mozambique)
DFID	Department for International Development (U.K.)
DSS	Direct Support to Schools (Mozambique)
EC	Ethiopian calendar
EFA	Education for All
EMIS	Educational Management Information System
EP1/EP2	primary education: grades 1–5/grades 6–7 (Mozambique)
ESDP	Education Sector Development Program
ESG	secondary general education (Mozambique)
ESP	Education Strategic Plan
ESSP	Education Sector Strategic Plan
fCUBE	free compulsory universal basic education (Ghana)
FPE	free primary education
FTI	Fast Track Initiative
GABLE	Girls Attainment in Basic Literacy and Education (Malawi)
GDP	gross domestic product
GER	gross enrollment rate
GES	Ghana Education Service
GPRS	Growth and Poverty Reduction Strategy
HIV/AIDS	human immunodeficiency virus/acquired immune deficiency syndrome
KCPE	Kenya Certificate of Primary Education

KESSP	Kenya Education Sector Support Program
KNEC	Kenya National Examinations Council
K Sh	Kenya shillings (currency)
MDG	Millennium Development Goal
MEC	Ministry of Education and Culture (Mozambique)
MIITEP	Malawi Integrated In-service Teacher Education Programme
MK	Malawi kwacha (currency)
MoE	Ministry of Education (Ethiopia and Malawi)
MoESC	Ministry of Education, Sports, and Culture (Malawi)
MoESS	Ministry of Education, Science and Sports (Ghana)
MoEST	Ministry of Education, Science and Technology (Kenya)
Mt	meticais (Mozambican currency)
NARC	National Rainbow Coalition (Kenya)
NER	net enrollment ratio
OVC	orphans and vulnerable children
PARPA	Plano De Acção para a Redução da Pobreza Absoluta (Action Plan for the Reduction of Absolute Poverty— Mozambique)
PCR	primary completion rate
PSIA	Poverty and Social Impact Analysis
PTA	parent-teacher association
PTR	pupil-teacher ratio
SFAI	School Fee Abolition Initiative
SMC	school management committee
SPIP	School Performance Improvement Plan (Ghana)
TVET	technical and vocational education and training
UNESCO	United Nations Educational, Scientific and Cultural Organization
UNICEF	United Nations Children's Fund
UPE	universal primary education
USAID	United States Agency for International Development
US$	United States dollars (currency)
WEO	woreda education office (Ethiopia)

CHAPTER 1

Rationale, Issues, and Conditions for Sustaining the Abolition of School Fees

Birger Fredriksen

The School Fee Abolition Initiative (SFAI) seeks to accelerate progress toward quality education for all children by supporting policies that remove cost barriers, preventing parents from enrolling and maintaining their children at school. As explained further in the preface to this book, SFAI was launched by the United Nations Children's Fund (UNICEF) and the World Bank in 2005 as an instrument to ensure that existing Education for All (EFA) commitments were met. Its main objective is to provide guidance and support to countries planning to abolish school fees with respect to the development and implementation of such policies. SFAI helps countries answer the following two questions: What are the challenges faced when school fees are discontinued, and what are the options for overcoming these challenges in a sustainable manner, especially in low-income countries?

In many countries, recent efforts to reduce or abolish school fees are, in fact, second attempts. The first efforts were initiated many decades earlier but were abandoned or reversed under pressure of economic crises. In Ghana, for instance, primary school fees were first abolished in 1961; while in Kenya and Tanzania, fee abolition policies were introduced in 1974. These policies had a significant impact on enrollment and resulted in rapid gains toward the goal of universal primary education (UPE). Over time, however, the policies were largely abandoned, and many of the early gains reversed.

Many countries have reintroduced fee abolition policies during the past decade as part of the renewed international effort to achieve UPE by 2015. Many more countries may be expected to follow suit in the years to come. Since these countries confront many similar challenges in preparing for and implementing fee abolition, it is important to understand the lessons of past experience. To this end, the SFAI workshop organized in Nairobi April 5–7, 2006, aimed to harness the experience of six African countries (Ethiopia, Ghana, Kenya, Malawi, Mozambique, and Tanzania) that have introduced school fee abolition policies in recent years. The workshop was also attended by officials from three countries (Burundi, Democratic Republic of Congo, and Haiti) that planned to embark on fee abolition processes, as well as by bilateral and multilateral agencies, major international NGOs, academic institutions, and other constituencies.

Five of the six countries presenting their national experiences at the Nairobi Workshop also prepared papers summarizing their experiences (Tanzania did not prepare a paper). These papers (in revised form) constitute the following five chapters of this book. This chapter draws from those experiences to explain the value of fee abolition as a policy measure that helps maintain the momentum toward universal primary education, as well as to identify the potential pitfalls and challenges associated with its use. It provides a short comparative overview of the lessons learned from the national experiences presented in subsequent chapters, and attempts to answer the following questions:

- What are the rationale for and the challenges associated with school fee abolition?
- How did these five countries go about developing and implementing their school fee abolition policies, and what are the outcomes?
- What practical lessons do the country studies draw from their experiences?

To answer these questions, this chapter examines other countries' experiences in addition to the five case studies. Although the remaining chapters and much of the following discussion focus heavily on the region of Sub-Saharan Africa (SSA), most of the issues raised are relevant to all low-income countries that are considering the abolition of primary school fees.

SCHOOL FEE ABOLITION: WHAT ARE THE RATIONALE AND CHALLENGES?

Studies show that the large majority of the countries in Sub-Saharan Africa are at risk of not reaching universal primary school completion by 2015 (see Carceles, Fredriksen, and Watt 2001; UNESCO 2002, 2004, 2006, 2007; Bruns, Mingat, and Rakatomalala 2003). The *2008 EFA Global Monitoring Report*, for instance, lists São Tomé and Principe, the Seychelles, and Tanzania as the only countries to achieve the goal in 2005, and five additional countries (Benin, Lesotho, Madagascar, Malawi, and Zambia) as likely to achieve the goal by 2015 (see UNESCO 2007, 180).

Between 1960 and 1980, the region's gross enrollment rate (GER) grew from 45 percent to 80 percent, and enrollment, by some 260 percent, a level of growth not experienced by any other region at any time. Unfortunately, the next 20 years were marked by stagnation. The GER declined from 80 percent in 1980 to 72 percent in 1992 and did not regain its 1980 level until 2000. The 70 percent increase in enrollment during the 1980–2000 period barely matched the growth in the primary-school-age population during the same 20-year period, leaving the GER unchanged. A comparison between the two periods shows that progress in Sub-Saharan Africa toward the target of universal primary education by 1980, agreed on in Addis Ababa in 1961 by African political leaders, was far greater than the progress made toward the subsequent target of UPE by 2000, agreed on in Jomtien (Thailand) in 1990. While UPE was not attained by 1980, the number of students enrolled that year exceeded the enrollment target by 24 percent. However, the GER was only 80 percent in 1980 because the school-age population grew five times faster between 1960 and 1980 than projected in 1961 (93 versus 18 percent) (see Fredriksen 1981, 1983).

Significant enrollment growth in the region, resulting from rapid increases in access, resumed in the late 1990s at a level not seen since the 1970s. The GER reached 97 percent in the school year ending in 2005, up from 80 percent in 1999. This represents a 36-percent increase in enrollment in six years, at an annual rate of 5.2 percent (see UNESCO 2007, 290). Given the stagnation of the 1980s and 1990s, the main question about education development in Sub-Saharan Africa (including at the 2000 Dakar World Education Forum) has been: how to address education stagnation? The resurgence of growth in recent years, however, has changed this question. It is now: how to sustain and reinforce the renewed progress toward EFA?

The answer to this question is important with respect to SFAI success because of the vital role school fees play in determining the degree to which the growth momentum can be maintained.[1] It is also important from an equity and "right to education" point of view since the children who do not enter school or drop out before completing are increasingly children who—from an economic and social point of view—are the most vulnerable. Finally, the answer is important as SFAI has the ambition of being a "bold initiative," whereby school fee abolition becomes a catalyst for other basic reforms needed to reach equity in both access and quality learning opportunities for all.

To be successful, fee abolition must be accompanied by a number of other reforms. These reforms must ensure that fee abolition is financially sustainable over time; that its benefits reach the most vulnerable groups; and that it preserves and, indeed, improves education quality. Each of these three points is discussed below.

FINANCIAL SUSTAINABILITY

The increase in total primary school enrollment in the five case study countries in the year following fee abolition was 12 percent in Mozambique, 14 percent in Ghana, 18 percent in Kenya, 23 percent in Ethiopia, and 51 percent in Malawi. The increase in grade 1 enrollment far exceeded the total increase for all grades. Similar increases in enrollment in the year following fee abolition have occurred in many other countries; for example, Cameroon, 26 percent in total primary enrollment (59 percent in grade 1); Lesotho, 11 percent in total enrollment (75 percent in grade 1); Tanzania, 23 percent in total enrollment (43 percent in grade 1); and Uganda, 68 percent in total enrollment. This clearly demonstrates the importance of fee abolition and cost considerations in determining whether parents will be able to enroll and maintain their children at school.

However, past experience also shows that such gains have been difficult to maintain through economic crises. Several countries that are at risk of not reaching universal primary school completion by 2015 had reached a GER exceeding 100 percent in 1980 or even earlier. For example, in addition to the seven countries in Sub-Saharan Africa that have reached and maintained a GER above 100 percent,[2] at least nine countries exceeded this level at some point during the 1965–85 period but dropped well below 100 percent by the mid-1990s.[3] In other words, while one-third of the region's countries (about half of the children of primary school age) had reached a GER exceeding 100 percent in the early 1980s, by the mid-to-late 1990s, this had declined to seven countries (about 7 percent of the school-age population). Decreased enrollment rates show that the high priority given to basic education in the 1960s and 1970s was not sustained when economic problems started in the early 1980s. This could happen again, especially as countries address the strong pressure for expanding post-primary education, which results from the present rapid progress toward universal primary education. For one thing, the political voice of primary and secondary school graduates seeking access to the next education level is much stronger than the voice of those excluded from primary education, who predominantly belong to economically and socially vulnerable groups.

Many of the African countries that made strong progress toward universal primary education during the 1960s and 1970s did so after they abolished school fees, including three of the six countries participating at the 2006 Nairobi SFAI Workshop (Ghana, Kenya, and Tanzania). However, in all three cases the gains from the earlier fee abolition policy were undermined by lack of financial sustainability. To illustrate, the experiences of these three countries, as well as those of a fourth country (Zambia), which reached 100 percent GER in the early 1980s, are summarized as follows:

- *Ghana* gained independence in 1957; in 1961, primary school (six years) and middle school (four years) was made fee-free and compulsory.[4] Grade 1 enrollment increased from 139,000 to 231,000 in the first year, and total primary school enrollment increased from 664,332 in 1960 to 1,413,517 in 1965, a staggering 113 percent increase in five years, or 16.2 percent per year. This resulted in an increase in the GER from 59 percent in 1960 to 106 percent in 1965. While this high GER resulted from the enrollment of many overage pupils, it could be argued that Ghana in 1965 already had an enrollment capacity to cater to all children of primary school age. However, as economic conditions worsened, enrollment stagnated between 1965 and 1970, resulting in a decline in the GER, which in 1975 was only 72 percent and remained below 80 percent until 2000.
- *Kenya* experienced strong growth in enrollment after independence in 1963, with another surge in the 1970s following abolition of school fees in 1974 for grades 1 to 4, resulting in a near tripling of grade 1 enrollments. In 1978, fees were abolished in grades 5 to 7 as well. As a result, Kenya reached a GER of 104 percent in 1975, which stayed above 100 percent until 1989. It then declined during a period of economic stagnation to fluctuate at about 90 percent during the 1990s until 2002, when it jumped from 88 percent to 105 percent in 2004 and 112 percent in 2005 as a result of the abolition of school fees.
- *Tanzania* showed a GER in primary education of only 31 percent at independence in 1961 and remained as low as 35 percent in 1970.[5] Following a decision in 1974 to introduce free universal primary education by 1977 (advancing an earlier target date for 1989 set in the Third Five-Year Plan), the grade 1 apparent intake rate increased from 56 percent in 1974 to 98 percent in 1975, 110 percent in 1976, 111 percent in 1977, and 168 percent in 1978. It then declined to 97 percent in 1979, 83 percent in 1980, and 82 percent in 1982. The rate continued to decline to 75 percent in 1991 and 74 percent in 1999. This

downward trend reflects Tanzania's economic stagnation and decline during most of this period.[6] The sharp increase between 1974 and 1978 resulted in the GER reaching a peak of approximately 100 percent in 1981. The one-year enrollment increase between 1977 and 1978 was 32 percent for total primary school enrollment and 59 percent for grade 1 enrollment.[7]

- *Zambia* experienced an increase in GER from 59 percent at independence in 1964 to above 100 percent in the early 1980s; it then declined during the 1990s to 75 percent in 1999 and increased during the past few years to reach 111 percent in 2005.[8] The apparent intake rate in grade 1 hovered at 100 percent during the 1970–77 period, peaking in 1972 at 109 percent for boys and 102 percent for girls. A steady decline in the GER began in the early 1980s and continued in the 1990s; the absolute number of pupils enrolled in primary education declined between 1991 and 1995 and remained stagnant for the rest of the 1990s.

In all four cases mentioned above, a combination of worsening economic conditions, reduced education budgets, and reemergence of school fees led to the reversal of earlier gains of fee abolition. In the case of Tanzania, Williams (2006c, 10) notes:

As soon as UPE had been launched the situation of the country changed for the worse, with a serious economic crisis reflecting downturn in the world economy, exacerbated in Tanzania's case by the strain of the Uganda war. An early response to the economic difficulties was the decision to ask parents to contribute 20 shilling per school child—this was not easy to collect and the Ministry of Education reported that only 34 percent of the levies could be collected in 1980 and 39.5 percent in 1984. Despite the rate of non-payment when the fee was only 20 shilling, it was increased to 100 shilling in 1985. Later, in 1995, primary school tuition fees were formally reintroduced and a level of about 2,000 shilling per pupil was being charged by the end of the century. However, according to the Education Sector Review, only 51 percent of fee income was being collected in 2000.

Similarly, for Zambia, Volan (2003, 100–01) notes the following:

Throughout the 1980s and 1990s the economic crisis hit the education system hard. Primary schools have experienced a difficult time in trying to maintain coverage and standards. Today the state pays for teachers' salaries and a few books and nothing more. Teachers' salaries gradually constitute an increasing share of the education budget. Salaries took 77 percent of the budget in 1977. In 1980 the percentage rose to 88, and in 1985 to 96 percent. . . . In 1996, the monthly salary for a trained teacher was US$88.00 per month, while the starting salary for an untrained teacher was US$67.60. This is less than what university students are paid monthly to cover costs for their meals.

The sector has been forced to adopt various coping strategies. These measures include large class size (90 or more pupils per class), adopting multiple shifts and shortening length of contact time in order to allow additional groups of children to access. . . . In addition, quality of education declined due to inadequate textbooks and learning materials, lack of in-service teacher training, low morale of teachers, lack of inspection, physical dilapidation of classrooms and lack of professionalism and managerial experience of head teachers. [To help address the shortage in funding] . . . the Government was encouraging private initiative at all levels. The reliance on parental contribution was steadily increasing. . . . The introduction of cost sharing at the primary level in particular had a detrimental impact on the school attendance of poor, contributing to the declining GER in recent years.

In short, the financial sustainability of fee abolition is a critical issue. Among the five countries examined in this book, Malawi was unable to accommodate the enrollment surge because of the lack of financing, resulting in severe deterioration in learning conditions, disillusionment among parents and students, and high dropout rates. As the case studies on Ghana, Kenya, and Mozambique describe recent experiences, the longer-term impact is unclear. However, there are reasons to believe that these outcomes will be more positive than Malawi's or that the impact will be more lasting than in the cases of earlier fee abolition initiatives cited above for Ghana, Kenya, and Tanzania. Reasons for optimism include the following:

- The efforts are better planned and are included as part of sectorwide education development programs, which, in turn, are included in nationwide poverty-reduction programs and medium-term expenditure frameworks.
- There is stronger awareness—internationally and at the country level—of the key role of high-quality universal basic education in poverty reduction. The awareness has led to greater financial commitment at

both the national and international levels in support of basic education. For example, the programs for Ghana, Kenya, Lesotho, Mozambique, Tanzania, and Uganda were developed with strong technical and financial support from development partners.[9]

- There is also growing awareness in the countries and among their development partners that EFA cannot be attained without targeted programs for the special needs of those excluded from school or in the absence of concerted efforts to improve education quality.

- Finally, resumption of economic growth in an increasing number of African countries, combined with an increase in the share of GDP devoted to education, have considerably increased education budgets in Sub-Saharan Africa, from an average annual rate of growth of 2.3 percent during the period 1970–2000 to about 8.0 percent during the period 1999–2004.[10] Continued economic growth and prioritization of EFA are both crucial to the sustainability of fee abolition.

Still, as pointed out in Bray and Bunly (2005, 8) in the case of Cambodia:

> Ideals need to be tempered with reality, especially in poor countries. Although most governments would like to be able to provide fee-free primary education—and some, including Cambodia, even enshrine this in their constitutions—in many countries the practical realities of balancing the books require at least some contribution from households and communities.

Similar to Cambodia, the 2006 Constitution of the Democratic Republic of Congo—the country in Sub-Saharan Africa that probably relies the most on fees to finance its primary education system—stipulates that primary education shall be free and obligatory. That is why, as Bray and Bunly (2005, 9) point out, to mobilize resources for EFA financing, the Declaration of the Dakar World Education Forum called for new and revitalized partnerships at all levels, including those between governments and NGOs, the private sector, local communities, religious groups, and families. The challenge is to ensure that such arrangements do not place an inequitable burden on poor families or result in the exclusion of any children from school because of their inability to pay.

THE NEED FOR TARGETED PROGRAMS

In the context of Sub-Saharan Africa in 2006, on average, more than 90 percent of children enter school, two-thirds of whom reach the end of the primary cycle. Of these, at least half fail to master the expected basic skills. In this context, those who do not enter school, drop out prior to completing the primary cycle, or do not acquire basic skills are increasingly children who—from an economic and social point of view—are the most vulnerable.[11] They are predominantly from poor rural families, the majority are girls, many are disabled, and an increasing number are orphans because of the impact of civil strife and HIV/AIDS (see below).

For these children, the indirect and direct cost of education to families is often the single most important factor excluding them from school. Furthermore, these are children from families that do not have a strong political voice; they may not be heard when the demand for greater allocation of resources for post-primary education increases (because of the progress toward universal primary education) from those already enrolled. Therefore, to maintain the present growth momentum, it is necessary to have determined political leadership, resulting in targeted assistance to address both demand and supply factors hampering access and school retention for these children. There is a powerful ethical as well as development case for governments to provide the leadership required to ensure that no child is excluded from school because of inability to pay.

With respect to access, despite the encouraging increase in admission experienced in most of the region's countries in recent years, serious challenges remain, especially as children not yet enrolled are from marginalized groups, more difficult and costly to reach than children already at school. Within countries, access differs markedly according to family income, geographic location, and gender, in that order of importance, and examples abound.

- A study covering 12 Francophone countries shows that, on average, disparity in access between children from families in the first and fifth income quintiles is three to four times greater than disparity based on gender. Similarly, the disparity between urban and rural children is two to three times greater than by gender (Mingat 2003a). The combination of being poor, rural, and female means that girls account for about two-thirds of those who do not enter school. In some poor, rural areas no more than 10–15 percent of girls are enrolled.
- Data from Mozambique's case study show that, in 2004, the GER for the two upper grades of primary education (grades 6 and 7) ranged from 50 percent for the poorest 20 percent of the families to 87 percent for the richest 20 percent. Similarly, data from Malawi's case show that, in 1990, the net enrollment ratio was only 33 percent for children from the poorest quintile as compared to 75 percent for the richest.

However, in 1997, following fee abolition, the corresponding figures were 76 percent and 80 percent, respectively.

- In four northern provinces of Cameroon in 2001, the percentage of admission to primary education from families belonging to the poorest 20 percent was 31 percent for girls and 55 percent for boys in rural areas and 55 percent and 72 percent, respectively, for girls and boys in urban areas.[12] The corresponding figure for children belonging to the richest 60 percent in urban areas was 72 percent for girls and 84 percent for boys. In other words, the possibility of entering school in these four provinces ranged from 31 percent to 84 percent, depending on geographical location, gender, and income group (see World Bank/Pôle de Dakar 2003).

- Finally, a study by the United Nations Educational, Scientific and Cultural Organization Institute for Statistics (UNESCO-UIS 2005, 84–85) shows that of the 41 countries in Sub-Saharan Africa, 27 had more than 50 percent of children from the poorest quintile out of school, while this was the case in only two countries for children from the richest quintile. Only three countries had more than 80 percent of children from the poorest quintile enrolled, while this was the case in 19 countries for children from the richest quintile.

New obstacles to access have emerged in recent years, including the rapidly increasing number of children orphaned by war, civil strife, drought, or HIV/AIDS, especially in Africa. Largely driven by the increasing impact of HIV/AIDS, the number of orphans is projected to reach a staggering 45 million by 2010. According to UNICEF, about one-third of orphans in the region are of primary school age, constituting, on average, 12 to 15 percent of that age group (much higher in high-prevalence countries). The cost of reaching EFA will be heavily influenced by the need to cater to these and other disadvantaged children.[13]

Thus, in terms of access, the overarching challenge of attaining universal primary education in Sub-Saharan Africa, which, since independence, has focused on achieving a general increase in admission, must shift to focus on ensuring access for poor and disadvantaged children who are excluded from the system. To implement such a policy will require measures on both the supply side (the provision of schools with government-financed teachers in reasonable walking distance in sparsely populated areas, boarding schools, or other adapted solutions for children of nomadic families) and on the demand side (limiting direct and opportunity costs of sending children to school and special measures to help orphans and other vulnerable groups). The importance of supply factors is illustrated by the sharply increased access in many low-enrollment countries in response to increased provision (Burkina Faso, Ethiopia, Mali, and Niger).[14] However, as supply increases, the main constraint even in low-enrollment countries will shift toward demand factors. Increasingly, direct costs to parents will be the major obstacle to attaining universal access.

It is important in this connection to note that both indirect and direct costs are often higher in rural areas, where the majority of the poor live, than in the urban areas. First, with respect to indirect costs, rural children often have chores to do at home (for example, collect firewood, fetch water, mind younger siblings, herd livestock, or help in the fields); sending them to school often occasions significant opportunity costs to parents. Strategies to address these costs must be a more integral part of education sector planning. Even a well-endowed school will not retain children and ensure their learning if children are ill-nourished, have to work long hours at home, walk long distances to school, or live under conditions in which they cannot do their homework. As these factors are intimately related to the high level of absolute poverty in the region, they are relevant in determining which other interventions, beyond abolition of school fees, will be required to stimulate demand for education among the poorest population groups and especially from orphans. Strategies worth consideration in this context include targeted cash transfers to families, early childhood care and education, school feeding, and provision of water (either at the school or another accessible site). Such strategies frequently entail significant collaboration across sectors and highlight the need for school fee abolition strategies to be embedded within country-wide poverty alleviation and growth strategies.

Second, as regards direct costs, in some countries in addition to the costs of training materials, uniforms, and other school inputs, communities have had to establish and finance their own schools. This situation occurs in many sparsely populated areas where there are no public schools because of governments' severe budget constraints. In a very resource-constrained situation, government schools are more likely to be found in urban areas, both because teachers prefer to reside in such areas and because rural parents and children normally have a much weaker political voice than their urban counterparts. Illustrations are easy to find.

- Parents pay a major share of the cost of primary school teachers in many African countries. As indicated above, this especially happens in rural areas where lack of public schools often leads parents to establish "community schools" and hire and pay the teachers fully or partially. A study of 12 Francophone countries (Mingat 2004) found that, in 2002 or thereabouts, almost one-third of all primary school teachers, on average, were paid by parents, ranging from 4 percent in Niger to 68 percent in Chad. Often this means that the poorest rural communities finance their children's education, while better-off urban areas benefit from publicly financed teachers. Also, teachers paid by parents received only about one-quarter of the salary of government teachers. This, in turn, means that rural children have less-qualified teachers than children in urban areas. It also suggests that enrollment gains may be lost quickly in periods of localized economic downturn, as parents are unable to continue financing teachers. For example, this situation occurred in the Sikasso region of Mali in the late 1990s as a decline in the price of cotton directly affected parents' ability to recruit new teachers or to maintain teachers hired previously.

- In Cameroon (not included among the 12 countries above), despite the official elimination of school fees in 2000, low public funding has resulted in high private cost of education. The number of public primary school teachers paid by parents reached about 25 percent in 2002 (see World Bank/Pôle de Dakar 2003). These teachers are working mainly in rural areas. Adding the 23 percent of the total number of primary teachers who teach in private schools (only slightly subsidized), approximately half of the total number of primary school teachers are paid by parents. A survey shows that in 2001, parents' education expenses corresponded to 44 percent of total expenditures in primary education. In the Democratic Republic of Congo, households finance as much as 80 to 90 percent of expenditures in public sector–education institutions (see World Bank 2005a). Similarly, in Haiti, parents bear the responsibility for the majority of primary school financing, with a disproportionate burden in the poorest regions of the country.

THE NEED TO PROTECT QUALITY

All five case studies raise questions about the impact of fee abolition on the quality of education, both because the revenues from fees typically provided for learning materials and because resources must be shared among more pupils to cater to the enrollment surge. This results in crowded classrooms and increased pupil-teacher ratios (PTRs). Low quality was a serious concern before fee abolition and, without a funded strategy to address quality issues, the situation has often been more serious after the removal of fees.[15] While the case studies differ in many aspects, the question of quality features in all of them.

In the past, governments and aid agencies have given priority to improving access rather than to improving retention and learning outcomes, both prerequisites to achieving EFA. Yet the figures on retention and outcomes show that although admission remains an important concern, the main obstacle to attaining EFA has shifted to reducing dropouts and improving acquisition of basic literacy and numeracy skills. Both depend crucially on improving the quality of the learning process, which is likely to be the single most difficult challenge in reaching EFA.

To discuss the difficulties of defining "education quality" or the evidence for how "quality" affects retention and learning outcomes is beyond the scope of this book. However, from the point of view of choices open to low-income African countries for improving quality, the following points should be made about education inputs, management of resources, and the impact of school fee abolition.

Education Inputs. One determinant of the vast disparity in student achievements between rich and poor countries is the difference in availability of key education inputs. This is, in part, a result of economics: OECD countries spend about one hundred times more per child than do countries in Sub-Saharan Africa.[16] This is largely the result of different levels of teacher salaries, number of pupils per teacher, and nonsalary inputs. Education professionals differ on the relative importance of the contribution of different inputs to learning outcomes. Notwithstanding this caveat, in most of the region's countries, priority should be given to nonsalary inputs, that is, the type of inputs typically financed through school fees. First, while salary levels in Sub-Saharan Africa are very low in absolute terms, they are on average somewhat higher than in OECD countries and in other low-income countries when expressed in terms of GDP per capita.[17] Second, as discussed above, before increasing salaries of existing government-paid teachers, many countries should give priority to paying the teachers who are paid by parents through school fees. Since these teachers are paid much less than civil servant teachers, they are likely to have priority for any salary increases. Third, the number of pupils per teacher in Sub-Saharan Africa is three times that of high-income countries (in 2005, 45 as compared to 15). While some countries have very high pupil-teacher ratios that must be reduced, a PTR below 40:1 is unlikely to be cost effective in the present economic context in most Sub-Saharan African countries.[18] It is also interesting to note that large class size was an essential part of the "low-cost approach" many East Asian countries (for example, the Republic of Korea, Singapore, and Vietnam) followed to reach universal primary education quickly.[19]

In short, in terms of use of additional resources, priority should be given to ensuring that governments (a) do not leave the poorest communities to pay their own teachers and (b) provide the resources for essential nonsalary inputs such as textbooks, teacher manuals, better in-service training, and support for teachers. Over the past few years, UNICEF has devoted considerable energy to helping countries, especially in West and Central Africa, define the content and costs of an "Essential Learning Package."[20]

Management. As emphasized in the case studies, success of school fee abolition requires that well-functioning and transparent mechanisms be put in place for managing the resources made available to local authorities and schools. These mechanisms provide yet another occasion for using SFAI to improve efficiency in allocation and management of existing education resources. There is, in fact, a large variation between Sub-Saharan African countries, as well as between schools within countries, in learning outcomes for the same resource endowment per student (Mingat 2003b). Therefore, while it is urgent to make more resources available to local authorities and schools to replace fees and finance quality inputs, this needs to be coupled with more attention to converting these inputs into learning outcomes by improving management at both the system and the school level.

At the system level, priority must be given to more effective allocation and use of teachers to reduce the variation in pupil-teacher ratios across schools and to reduce absenteeism among teachers. At the school level, priorities include more effective use of the school year[21] and of the school day; revision of existing, often outdated, teaching practices (including more student-oriented pedagogy and more use of mother tongue instruction); and closer involvement of parents and communities in school management. These types of measures consume a relatively small part of the education budget, but require better management capacity and accountability for outcomes at both the system and school levels.

The negative impact of a high average pupil-teacher ratio can be somewhat reduced by decreasing the variation in class size across and within schools. For instance, if some classes have 15 students and others have 65, the average pupil-teacher ratio may be 40, but the negative impact will be far greater than if all classes have 40 students per teacher. This is particularly true because in almost all low-income countries, the largest class size is in grade 1. The key strategy for reducing the variation in class size is the use of multigrade classrooms to avoid very low class size in some sparsely populated areas. This, in turn, will require training of teachers and headmasters, careful monitoring, and availability of supplemental materials.

Impact of Fee Abolition on Quality. Two points on the sustainability of fee abolition and the impact of the enrollment surge on quality should be stressed. First, the EFA objective is to reach quality education for all by 2015. Fee abolition is an important instrument for realizing this goal.

Therefore, the large surge after fee abolition must be seen as very positive since this instrument has proved effective in removing an important barrier to education, especially for vulnerable groups. However, sound planning is vital so that the surge is handled in a sustainable manner rather than considered a problem. Second, as the case studies show, while total income from fees generally constitutes a small part of total education resources, enrollment of children from poor households is very sensitive to even small fees. Therefore, from an equity point of view, the main quality impact of school fees is often highly regressive since fees prevent access for poor children, thereby limiting overcrowding in schools and providing a greater share of public resources per student for those who can afford school.

Because the quality of education plays a key role in the success of fee abolition, the question arises, How can SFAI increase awareness of the urgent need to meet the challenge of quality? The focus of school fee abolition policies in many countries has been on ensuring that "no child is prevented access to education because of inability to pay school fees." The substantial increase in access resulting from fee abolition in the five countries reviewed (and in many others) clearly demonstrates that parents' cost is a serious constraint to access. Thus, to provide fee-free access is no trivial achievement if done in a sustainable manner. However, largely because of budget constraints and various institutional obstacles, the case studies raise questions about the sustainability of increased access in the medium term if quality is not maintained or improved. This aspect is most evident in Malawi, where deteriorating quality has threatened the long-term viability of the gains in access. The countries in which fee abolition is more recent have been stronger in implementing measures to address quality concerns. Indeed, the policies in Ghana and Mozambique were initially implemented as parts of projects that aimed at providing schools with some basic education inputs.

Four arguments are presented here in favor of dealing more explicitly with the quality dimension as an important and integral part of a fee abolition policy. First, access without adequate quality solves neither the equity problem nor the wider objective of reaching EFA. At the present stage of education development in Sub-Saharan Africa, the main emphasis in attaining EFA has shifted from increasing admission to ensuring access for vulnerable groups so far excluded from school, reducing dropout (which in many Sub-Saharan African countries means reducing repetition[22]), and improving acquisition of basic literacy and numeracy skills. Improvements in all three areas depend crucially on improving the quality of the learning process.

Second, as discussed above, apart from ensuring that governments pay all teachers, the priority for use of additional resources should be provision of essential nonsalary inputs such as textbooks, teacher manuals, better in-service training and support for teachers, and various basic operating costs for schools. Fees are used to pay for such services, and—in four of the five case study countries as well as in many other countries—school grants have proved effective in replacing fees. In all the five case study countries, the grants were provided as "capitation grants," that is, the level of the grant was fixed per pupil, and the total amount received per school was directly proportional to the number of pupils enrolled. Clearly, use of this instrument can be extended beyond replacement of money collected for "legally approved fees." Grants can provide schools with the nonsalary recurrent expenditures for an essential package of nonsalary education inputs to enhance education quality (see earlier reference to UNICEF's work to help countries develop and cost such a package). This is clearly the approach followed in Kenya, but it has also been used in the other case study countries as well as in many other countries where various types of school grants have been used to promote quality improvement at the school level.[23]

Third, as summarized above, the five case studies report that, apart from providing essential financing, use of school grants has many other positive impacts, such as promoting closer cooperation between, and empowerment of, schools and local communities; revitalizing school councils; and enhancing accountability of schools in use of money and learning outcomes. These positive results, in turn, are essential ingredients of a comprehensive strategy for quality improvement. School grants are an effective instrument for promoting quality improvement, as they increase resources made available to schools for quality inputs and they offer many advantages to schools and communities from managing these resources.

Finally, the salient question is how large the grant should be to provide the essential package of quality inputs. As stated in the next section (How Did the Five Countries Develop and Implement Their Fee Abolition Policies?), Kenya provided the largest grant by far, the equivalent of US$14 per pupil. However, this amount would not be enough to provide an essential learning package for all children. For example, 35 percent (360 of 1,020 Kenya shillings) was for textbooks and aimed at a textbook-pupil ratio of only 1:2 in the upper primary school and 1:3 in the lower primary school.

In addition to the work of UNICEF referred to above, other studies have attempted to estimate a reasonable per pupil allocation for an essential learning package. The Fast Track Initiative (FTI) Indicative Framework proposes that 33 percent of recurrent expenditures be spent on nonsalary inputs (see Bruns, Mingat, and Rakatomalala 2003). Van Uythem and Verspoor (2005, 293–321) provide an extensive analysis of the implications of this level of expenditure under different assumptions for recurrent expenditures per pupil. In particular, they quote a study (Rasera 2003) that proposes a list of basic inputs needed at the school level to obtain education of acceptable quality, estimating first a "minimum level of inputs" and second a "desirable level of inputs" The unit cost (as estimated by Rasera) for the former is in the order of US$16–19, and for the latter, US$33–37.

Van Uythem and Verspoor estimate that the US$16–19 range would be at the level of the 33 percent recurrent costs for nonsalary inputs suggested by the FTI Indicative Framework. They also review various ways part of this amount may be financed through more efficient use of existing resources. They conclude that while considerable scope for efficiency gains exists, the following is also true:

> There is an important timing issue, since the boost to non-teacher salary recurrent spending has to take place well before the quality improvements from it will take their full effect. The increased provision of quality enhancing material inputs with an estimated cost of US$16 per student (of which an estimated US$10–12 would be additional expenditures) is needed now to support immediate improvements in instructional practices, which can then bring about the efficiency gains (later in the period up to 2015) (2005, 300–01).

In summary, for the above and other reasons, a successful strategy to abolish school fees must examine the impact of fee abolition on quality as an integral and important part of that strategy.

HOW DID THE FIVE COUNTRIES DEVELOP AND IMPLEMENT THEIR FEE ABOLITION POLICIES?

The five country studies provide detailed information on the background of fee abolition, the implementation of the policy, lessons learned, and future challenges. The main features are summarized in annex table 1A.1. The purpose of this section is to present some highlights, while the next section summarizes the main practical lessons learned.

OBJECTIVE

The objective of the policy was to abolish all fees so that no child would be denied access to school because of an inability to pay. The fees that were abolished had covered most of the nonsalary financing (a small amount) available at the school level.

APPROACH

Three countries (Ethiopia, Kenya, and Malawi) followed a "big bang" approach whereby fee abolition was announced with little prior planning. However, in Malawi there was a four-month planning period, and in Ethiopia it took about a year before the policy announcement was transmitted proactively to schools for implementation. Ghana and Mozambique did some prior testing of provision of support to schools before scaling up fee abolition to all primary schools. In all cases, fee abolition formed part of wider reforms to promote other changes (decentralization of decision making, increased provision of training material, curriculum review, and more teacher support) though the content and scope of the reforms varied by country.

PRIOR PREPARATION AND COMMUNICATION

There was little or no time for prior planning and communication of the policy in the big bang countries, though all countries conducted information and awareness campaigns during implementation.

POLITICAL LEADERSHIP

The fee abolition policy was generally an electoral promise and had strong support at the highest political level in all countries.

MAGNITUDE OF FEE REVENUES AND METHOD USED TO REPLACE THEM

The share of total recurrent costs covered by fees is not available for all countries, but was as high as 11 percent in Malawi. As regards the method used to replace these revenues, four of the five countries provided grants to schools, while Malawi aimed to replace materials purchased by the fees (textbooks and school supplies) through central provision. Some of the case studies state that the replacement revenues (or materials supplied directly by government in the case of Malawi) were not sufficient to replace the materials financed through fees before the policy change.

SIZE OF GRANTS

Grant size per pupil varied considerably among the four countries. It was highest in Kenya at the equivalent of US$14.00 per student per year, designed to cover a well-defined set of training materials (two-thirds of the grant) and operating costs (one-third of the grant).[24] In Ghana, the grant was equivalent to US$2.70 for boys and US$3.88 for girls. However, in addition, preexisting policies stipulated supply of free textbooks for grades 1 to 6 and user fees not exceeding 10 percent of textbook costs for grades 7 to 9. In Ethiopia, guidelines issued in 2002 and 2003 fixed the annual grant at the equivalent of about US$1.20 per student for grades 1 to 4, US$1.76 for grades 5 to 8, and US$2.35 for grades 9 and 10. The Ethiopia case study notes that these grants were minimum levels, designed to match the preexisting annual school fees. However, the study also notes that in some areas, grants were below the recommended level because of a shortage of resources. Finally, Mozambique followed a phased implementation, and both the size and scope of the grant increased over time. The Mozambique case study does not specify the size of the per pupil grant. Based on the global data provided in the study, the grant appears to have been in the range of US$0.60 to US$0.90 per pupil in phases 1–3 and increased to the equivalent of about US$1.20 in phase 4. Initially, the grants were to cover learning materials for pupils and teachers, chosen according to a Ministry of Education list of eligible items. Later on, health-related items were included. Thus, in phase 4, about 71 percent of the grant was for school materials, and 29 percent for school health and HIV/AIDS-related activities.

SEQUENCING

The big bang countries did not phase in the reform over time or specify age or grade levels at which the removal of fees would apply. An illustration of the effect is that in Malawi, the highest enrollment increase (in relative terms) took place in the last grade of primary education, 81 percent for girls, 73 percent for boys, largely for children who wanted to retake the school-leaving examination.[25] Kenya also had a large enrollment increase in the last grade.

VOLUNTARY CONTRIBUTIONS

The case studies for four of the five countries underlined that parents and communities were encouraged to continue to provide voluntary contributions, as long as children whose parents could not contribute were not prevented from entering school.

ENROLLMENT IMPACT

The enrollment impact depends on many factors including (a) initial enrollment level, (b) extent to which fee abolition is phased in, and (c) magnitude of the fees. The increase in total primary school enrollment in the year following fee abolition ranged from 12 percent to 51 percent (the increase in grade 1 enrollment was even higher). Malawi had the highest increase, while the increase in the other four countries ranged from 12 percent to 23 percent. As regards initial enrollment levels, with the exception of Ethiopia, which had a very low GER (26 percent) at the time fees were abolished, the four other countries had quite similar GERs, ranging from 83 percent to 89 percent. Given this high initial GER, the enrollment increase is quite impressive. The two countries with the lowest increase—Ghana (14 percent) and Mozambique (12 percent)—both phased in the reform. This means that the impact was spread over several years; for Mozambique, the accumulated growth in primary enrollment over the three-year period 2003/04 to 2006/07 was an impressive 38 percent. Finally, while the data available in the country studies do not permit a detailed comparison of the relative level of the fees, it appears that the fees in Malawi were particularly high, probably contributing to the very high enrollment increase. In all cases, the enrollment increase clearly demonstrates that the fees represented a major barrier to enrollment.

IMPACT ON QUALITY

The impact on school quality in Malawi was clearly negative. While it is still early to assess the impact in Ghana, Kenya, and Mozambique, early indications are more positive.

IMPACT ON GENDER PARITY

Initially, the percentage increase in the enrollment of boys was larger than for girls in three of the five countries. However, after an initial negative effect on the parity index (though, of course, not on girls' enrollment), the index continued to improve.

IMPACT ON PUPIL-TEACHER RATIO

Three of the four countries for which data are available saw an increase in the PTR, suggesting that the most widely used mechanism to accommodate the enrollment surge was to increase this ratio through increased class size or use of multiple shifts. Interestingly, the country that experienced the largest enrollment surge (Malawi) also reported a decline in an already very high ratio, from 68:1 in 1993–94 to 63:1 in 1994–95. The lower ratio was achieved through a major recruitment of 20,000 new teachers, 90 percent of whom were untrained secondary school leavers who were deployed after a two-and-a-half-week orientation, with the intention of providing them with professional support while in school and continuing their training on the job. However, Malawi did not have the capacity to handle this massive undertaking, and the actual training only started in January 1997, more than two years after the enrollment surge. Further, uneven deployment resulted in increased variation in class size, with many classes exceeding 100 pupils.

OTHER BENEFITS OF FEE ABOLITION

All case studies report benefits related to decentralization of decision making, empowerment of schools and communities, and promotion of greater local-level accountability. It was felt that these benefits were closely related to the use of school grants.

ACCOMPANYING STRATEGIES

As mentioned above, countries complemented fee abolition with a range of measures to accommodate the enrollment surge: multishift teaching, increased class size and PTR, recruitment of various types of teachers (untrained, retired, volunteers), and use of temporary facilities to serve as classrooms. An immediate response often used to resolve quality issues was provision of textbooks and other training materials.

SUPPORT BY DONORS

All countries received donor support for fee abolition to varying degrees. This support was most closely related to the fee abolition in Ghana, Kenya, and Mozambique.

WHAT ARE THE PRACTICAL LESSONS LEARNED FROM THESE FIVE COUNTRIES?

The five case studies all draw lessons from the implementation of the fee abolition policies. The following lessons in particular deserve to be highlighted.

POLITICAL LEADERSHIP

When fee abolition is a major departure from current policies, strong political leadership at the highest level is a prerequisite for successful implementation. All five case studies emphasize this factor. Thus, the president or prime minister plays a leading role in advocating and explaining the policy, there is strong consensus at the level of the cabinet, and the ministry of education works closely with the appropriate administration officials in defining and implementing the policy. In particular, as underlined below, introduction of fee abolition must usually be part of a more comprehensive reform package. Implementation must also move quickly so that teachers, classrooms, and textbooks are available at the start of the school year. This may require urgent measures and difficult policy decisions to rapidly mobilize the necessary capacity and to unblock institutional bottlenecks.

CAREFUL PLANNING

Success requires careful planning, which involves prior analytical work to assess (a) the magnitude of existing fees to calculate the financing to replace them; (b) what the fees are used for, to determine the amount for replacement of those items (this is especially important if the materials and services financed are to be replaced directly by the government rather than procured directly by the schools through school grants); (c) existing mechanisms through which these materials and services or school grants can be channeled from the government to the schools; and (d) likely enrollment surge resulting from fee abolition and other measures associated with this policy.

Based on the analyses undertaken, assessments are needed of how to mobilize financial and other resources to replace the revenues collected through fees and how to cater to the enrollment surge. Two case studies (Ethiopia and Ghana) suggest that the capitation grants (or training materials and other resources provided directly to schools in Malawi) were not sufficient to cover the expenses that had previously been paid through school fees and were not available in a timely manner. The studies stress the importance of conducting rigorous assessments of the additional needs for teachers, classrooms, and training materials and of exploring what type of short- and longer-term measures can be implemented to meet these needs. In turn, this requires a solid database on key inputs such as location and utilization of existing classrooms (an up-to-date "school map"), the deployment and utilization of the existing teaching force, and availability of textbooks by subject and grade. Such information was not readily available in these five countries when the fee abolition policies were introduced.

Developing implementation and monitoring capacity is a very important element of the preparation process and is emphasized in various ways in all the case studies. In addition to stressing the importance of capacity building for effective implementation, the Kenya study also points out the important lesson that "there is a critical need for continuous reassurance and confidence building among stakeholders to prevent them from giving up under extreme pressure" (chapter 4, Lessons Learned).

COMMUNICATION AND BUILDING PARTNERSHIPS

Ideally, preparation of fee abolition should include comprehensive communication and consultation to explain the content, impact, and implementation process of the new policy to key stakeholders such as parents, teachers, local communities, political constituencies, and education administrators. It may also require consensus building with opposition politicians who may not have supported the new policy during the election campaign (as referred to in the Kenya case study), or with parts of the administration that may not be on board. However, in several of the five countries, the very short time between the decision to introduce the policy and the implementation itself meant that most of this information and consultation process needed to be conducted as part of the implementation process. The challenge faced by planners and implementers is described aptly in the following quote from the Kenya case study (chapter 4, Process of Planning and Implementation of Free Primary Education):

> Upon winning the December 2002 election, the NARC government implemented one of its preelection pledges to provide universal primary education. It declared that as of January 4, 2003, all Kenyan children were entitled to enroll in public primary schools. Following the initiation of free primary education, the new Minister for Education clarified that no child would be required to pay

fees or levies to any public primary school and that every child regardless of age should report to the nearest public primary school for admission. As schools were to open on January 6, 2003, the minister summoned senior officials from the Ministry of Education, Science and Technology (MoEST) to a crisis meeting on January 3, 2003, to strategize on the challenges in implementing FPE in Kenya. Of primary concern was the call for immediate implementation of FPE. Since the announcement for FPE was made in the middle of the financial year, there was no plan or budgetary allocation in place for its implementation.

Clearly, under such conditions, all the planning and preparation had to be done as part of the implementation of the policy.

PHASING IN THE REFORMS

Two of the five countries attempted to phase in the fee abolition policy, while three (Ethiopia, Kenya, and Malawi) did not, though Ethiopia only provided the instructions to schools one year after the decision was announced. Clearly, there may be difficult trade-offs between the big bang approach and various ways of phasing in fee abolition; for example, limiting new entrants to certain age groups or grades, or introducing fee abolition gradually, starting with grade 1. The big bang in principle allows all those who have so far not benefited from primary education to avail themselves of the opportunity to enroll.[26] The big bang approach avoids difficult choices such as who should benefit now and who should benefit later, which implies that some may not benefit at all because they have become overage by the time it is their turn. Apart from allowing a second chance for entry into grade 1 for youth who had not been able to enroll so far, the big bang approach in Kenya and Malawi also provided a second chance for children who had dropped out of primary school to reenter and sit for the Primary School Leaving Certificate (which was prominent in Kenya and Malawi). However, as the Malawi study points out, allowing reentry to the last grade of primary education also has a serious impact on the demand for secondary education.

On the other hand, in a case where abolition of fees may be expected to result in a major enrollment surge, to phase in the decision, such as was done in Ghana and especially Mozambique, has many advantages, permitting both to limit the "access shock," giving more time to mobilize the required teachers, classrooms, and training materials, test different procedures for channeling the fee-replacement funds to schools, put in place transparent mechanisms for managing these funds, and mobilize the financing.[27] There may also be pedagogical reasons for phasing in the decision to avoid a wide age range in each grade. To address this problem, some countries have established alternative learning systems for overage children. For example, the Malawi case study concludes that, with hindsight, it would have been better to restrict the age of entry and new enrollment to lower grades, possibly the first two grades only, and to develop alternative programs for overage children.[28]

FEE ABOLITION AS PART OF MORE COMPREHENSIVE REFORMS

The five case studies all emphasize that fee abolition should be a part of a wider policy package. For example, the Ethiopian study stresses that fee abolition by itself would not have been successful if it had not been a part of a wider policy reform. This reform included decentralization of decision making; curriculum reform; use of vernacular languages for instruction; and promotion of various innovative programs, such as alternative basic education, school feeding programs, and special programs for pastoral education and nonformal education. As indicated in the summary table (1A.1) at the end of this chapter, the other countries integrated fee abolition with other policy reform interventions. The importance of this broader approach is also underlined by Avenstrup (2004) in a review of the introduction of FPE in Kenya, Lesotho, Malawi, and Uganda. The reforms span the primary cycle (curriculum reform, revision of textbooks, and use of local languages as means of instruction), the period when the provision of basic education to underserved areas and population groups was widened and deepened (through provision of small schools within walking distance in sparsely populated areas, special measures to attract orphans, or alternative programs for overage children) to the integration of education development programs (of which school fee abolition is a part) into national poverty-reduction programs and medium-term expenditure frameworks.

MEASURES TO PROTECT QUALITY

The single most frequently expressed concern in the case studies is the need to avoid quality deterioration caused by the elimination of fee income at the school level. The Malawi study concludes the following:[29]

> Indeed, an important lesson to be learned from Malawi's experience is that the introduction of FPE, while achieving an increase

in access to education (quantity) adversely affected quality. The reason is that the financial resources were simply not enough to maintain the same quality of education. Already, just before the introduction of FPE, there had been growing public concern about the deterioration in the quality of education. (p. 191)

Similarly, the Ghana study states that to "safeguard quality of education" in a situation of rapid enrollment increase is the "overarching challenge" of the fee abolition policy (p. 118). The Kenya study emphasizes, "The challenges to quality should be dealt with before declaring an abolition of fees and levies so that the quality of schools is not compromised" (p. 157).

COMMUNITY INVOLVEMENT

The main lesson in this regard is to both present and implement school fee abolition so that it maintains the community's engagement in supporting its local school, while ensuring that the encouragement of the community for financial support does not prevent school entry for children. For example, the Ethiopian case study stresses that community support is encouraged and is substantial; and the Ghana study sees maintenance of community participation in a fee-free context as an emerging challenge. As pointed out, one effective way according to the Mozambique study is to closely involve the community in decision making for use of resources made available to schools through capitation grants. The study suggests that the empowerment of the community and school not only improves quality and administrative efficiency but also creates a stronger constituency for education.[30]

HIV/AIDS

The HIV/AIDS pandemic is cited as a challenge to SFAI in several case studies, especially with respect to teacher absenteeism and the special needs of the growing number of orphans. For example, the Malawi study emphasizes that HIV/AIDS poses a serious challenge to the attainment of universal primary education as more children drop out of school to attend to sick relatives or because of being orphaned, and more teachers are dying than can be replaced. The studies for Ethiopia and Kenya list a number of concrete actions under way or planned to address this type of problem.

SUPPORT FROM DEVELOPMENT PARTNERS

As shown in the summary table (1A.1) at the end of this chapter, all five countries received support from their development partners in preparing or implementing their fee abolition policies. This support was particularly important for the three countries where this policy was recently introduced (Ghana, Kenya, and Mozambique) and where the policy was introduced as part of donor-supported education sector programs. In the case of Malawi, the support was late in materializing. One could speculate that the deterioration in quality may have been avoided, at least in part, if Malawi's development partners had been more closely involved during the planning and preparation process as well as in providing emergency support to address the enrollment surge. At present, fee abolition forms an integral part of the sector-development program in all five countries. The same is the case for countries such as Cameroon, Lesotho, Madagascar, Tanzania, and Uganda.

USE OF SCHOOL GRANTS TO REPLACE FEE REVENUES

As already indicated in the third section of this chapter (How Did the Five Countries Develop and Implement Their Fee Abolition Policies?), four of the five case study countries used school grants to replace the revenues collected through fees. This approach has also been used in other countries (Madagascar, Tanzania, and Uganda). The case studies for the four countries that applied this method all conclude that this approach has several advantages, but also underline several preconditions for success and some further challenges.[31]

Advantages. The Ghana study in chapter 3 concludes that the use of capitation grants is a pro-poor strategy since "it is the poor, in particular, who have responded by enrolling their children in school. The strategy has also narrowed gender and geographical differences" (p. 117). The study also concludes that using capitation grants is a relatively simple and cost-effective strategy for achieving an immediate impact on access. The approach created a great deal of national momentum and additional support for education from, for example, faith-based organizations, the private sector, district assemblies, and local members of parliament. This added support helped the implementation by creating a multiplier effect. Interestingly, the Ghana case study also concludes that the higher grant for girls than for boys in the pilot did not have a significantly higher impact on narrowing the gender gap than the national implementation of the grant scheme in which the grant was not differentiated by gender.

On this aspect, the case study concludes that "changing cultural attitudes requires specifically targeted interventions that are better managed by a multisectoral approach" (p. 117).

The Kenya study emphasizes that school-level accounting in relation to the grant mechanism has ensured transparency and accountability of resources as it is mandatory for schools to publicly display on their boards all receipts of the grant funds and expenditures. Furthermore, availability of textbooks and other training materials has enhanced access and retention in primary schools. To enhance access in sparsely populated areas, the government has also used the grant scheme to support low-cost boarding primary schools and to increase the availability of training materials at nonformal schools.

Finally, the Mozambique study notes that the grants have promoted local-level accountability and local-level solutions. In turn, this local empowerment of the community and school has contributed to improving quality and administrative efficiency as well as to creating a stronger constituency for education. The monitoring of the implementation of the grant scheme has produced useful information that has both enhanced the scheme's impact and shown the importance of ensuring that the scheme is fully integrated in the overall sector program. More generally, this illustrates that, in addition to providing essential education inputs, the objectives of the grant scheme include promoting closer cooperation between schools and local communities, their empowerment, accountability of schools for use of money and learning outcomes, and revitalizing school councils. In turn, these factors are essential ingredients of a comprehensive strategy for quality improvement. For example, all the seven "pillars of quality improvement" identified in Verspoor (2005, 324–37) include interventions directly related to the type of benefits school grants stimulate.

Preconditions for the Sound Functioning of School Grants. The preconditions include the following:

- Simple implementation guidelines with training in their application for district education officers and head teachers
- A reliable school registry or school map with reliable enrollment data to ensure that all eligible schools receive their grants
- The existence of an effective financial system for transferring the resources from the central level to schools, bank accounts at the school level, and transparent management of the funds at the school level.

Further Challenges and Questions Regarding School Grants. Further challenges include the following:

- The financial sustainability of grants, as well as their timely availability to schools
- The effectiveness and transparency of grant mechanisms, including transparency in how much money is received and accountability about how the grants are used, cooperation and trust between school management and communities, and capacity in financial management at the school level
- The size of grants.

Regarding the size of grants, the Ghana study describes three findings. First, it suggests the use of two criteria for establishing the amount of money allocated to each school, the first providing an amount proportional to the number of pupils enrolled, and the second providing a fixed amount allocated for each school independent of the size of enrollment. This latter part of the grant will help small schools because there are many fixed costs largely independent of school size. Second, the size of the grant should be adjusted over time to account for inflation (also stressed in the Kenya study[32]). Third, "in most urban areas, the amount schools receive from the capitation grant is considerably less than the amount they received from the school levies" (p. 119).

The question about the size of the grant is important if grants are to be used as an instrument for financing quality-improvement inputs. As already discussed in the third section of this chapter (How Did the Five Countries Develop and Implement Their Fee Abolition Policies?), apart from Kenya, the grants in other countries were quite small (although in Ghana, textbooks were to be provided in addition to the grants). Further, as discussed in the second section on the Need to Protect Quality, even in the Kenya case, the grants may not be sufficient to finance a minimum package of essential quality inputs. In some cases, the grants were fixed at a level that would replace fee income. However, in general, the fee income sufficed to cover only some minimum training material and operating costs. Indeed, in the case of Ghana and Mozambique, the grants initially aimed to provide schools with some basic education inputs, not to replace fees.

In short, the potential utility of school grants surpasses their use as an effective mechanism for school fees replacement. Schools grants can be catalysts for developing capacity, accountability, and ownership at the school and community levels. Given these additional benefits and the shortage of school funds for nonsalary inputs to improve education quality, this underlines the importance of exploring the use of grants for nonsalary recurrent expenditures to improve education quality, an objective of SFAI.

INCLUSION OF PRIVATE SCHOOLS

Kenya and Malawi included private schools in their fee abolition policy (provided fees are not charged), implying that these schools would also benefit from capitation grants. The other three countries did not include private schools. This is raised as an "emerging issue" in the Ghana study, which notes that private schools "provide a service, but their enrollment may fall as a result of the capitation grant. Under the current scheme, private schools do not receive capitation grants" (p. 119). This is an important issue for Ghana, given the comparatively high share of primary enrollment in private schools (15 percent as compared to the median in Sub-Saharan Africa of about 8 percent). In the four other countries, the share of private schools is 4 percent or less (UNESCO 2007, 290). Perhaps a more important strategy in many countries is to ensure inclusion of various types of community schools, which are generally not included in statistics on private schools, but where the parents pay the teachers (see The Need for Targeted Programs above).

NEED FOR FURTHER RESEARCH TO IMPROVE THE KNOWLEDGE BASE

The importance of knowledge sharing and learning from other countries is stressed in all the case studies. The need for improving the knowledge base in this area is also underlined, especially in the studies for Ghana and Mozambique. Areas suggested for further research include the following:

- The degree to which education costs for poor families have been alleviated by fee abolition, and what other measures are required to attract children not yet enrolled
- How management of capitation grants has strengthened school management capacity and community participation, and how this benefits access and education quality
- Cost-effective strategies for protecting quality when fees are abolished
- How to respond effectively to the enrollment surge by, for example, developing more effective training methods for people with a good level of general education who want to become effective teachers, reducing both classroom costs and construction time; and rapidly

solving the perennial problem of shortage of low-cost, adequate-quality textbooks

- Effective programs to deal with overage children and to better adapt formal primary schools to a variety of local circumstances
- Methods of sustaining community participation in a fee-free environment.

Finally, many of the countries implementing school fee abolition are monitoring the process to learn how to better address challenges. SFAI should provide assistance in this area by facilitating exchange of experience between the national teams and by helping them systematize the lessons learned, thus further developing the knowledge base.

CONCLUSION

To achieve universal completion of primary education and acquisition of the knowledge and skills specified in national curricula will require concerted action to improve quality. In turn, this will require a comprehensive package of reforms as well as additional financing for nonsalary inputs at the school level. One of the key purposes of SFAI is to promote "bold actions" whereby school fee abolition becomes a catalyst for other basic reforms to reach the objective of equity in both access and quality learning opportunities. This suggests that SFAI give more importance to the quality improvement component of the actions needed to reach this objective.

Progress in literacy and learning, especially through universal primary education, has done more to advance human conditions than perhaps any other policy. Our generation has the chance of becoming the first generation ever to offer all children access to good-quality basic education. However, this will only happen if we have the political commitment—at the country as well as at the international level—to give priority to achieving this first in human history. It will also only happen if those who cannot afford to pay school fees can benefit from a complete cycle of good-quality primary education. Investment in good-quality fee-free primary education should be a cornerstone in any government's poverty-reduction strategy.

However, as concluded in the Malawi case study, the major lesson in implementing school fee abolition initiatives is that FPE is no quick fix; it requires planning, adequate financing, and resources. Implementation of FPE without sufficient resources and without thorough planning can undermine the quality of the education system and result in poor education outcomes.

ANNEX: FEE ABOLITION IN FIVE COUNTRY STUDIES

Table 1A.1 Summary Information on Fee Abolition in Five Country Studies

Issue	Ethiopia	Ghana	Kenya	Malawi	Mozambique
Approach and year of fee abolition	"Big Bang" in 1994. Instructions to schools provided one year after decision.	2005; scaling up of pilot started in 2003 for deprived districts. 1996 plan of free universal primary education by 2006 was not met.	"Big Bang" in January 2003 followed December 2002 election.	"Big Bang" in 1994 followed pledge during first multiparty election, although partial fee removal was introduced in 1991 and 1992.	Decision in 2003 became effective in 2004 after testing. Phased implementation of direct support to schools 2004–06.
Was fee abolition part of wider policy reform?	Yes, part of wide-ranging program: decentralization, curriculum reform, change in language of instruction, alternative basic education.	Yes, fee replacement spent on approved school improvement plan. Also part of wider education strategy and Growth and Poverty Reduction Strategy.	Yes, electoral promise to abolish fees comprised plans to undertake comprehensive review of education system. No "forced" repetition, encouragement to enroll children, free training material.	Yes, government to raise education budget to provide what had been financed through fees, promote girls' education, mother tongue instruction in grades 1–4, and more support for teachers.	Yes, major reform (e.g., direct support to schools beyond former fees, merger of two primary cycles, training materials, new curriculum, decentralization).
Driving force/ political leadership	Part of government's new education policy.	Success of pilot and civil society agitation led to scale-up after only one year of pilot.	Key election promise. Strong governmental leadership, including the president's.	Key election promise. Strong leadership by president and government.	Election promise. Leadership by minister of education; consultation with Ministry of Finance and donors.
Prior planning	Minimal	Pilot planned as part of World Bank–supported project. Staff training done. Decentralized structures were strengthened to manage funds.	None; school year began shortly after election. Intense preparation started just after election: stakeholder forum held, task force created. Ministry staff visited districts to assess needs. Used pretested system for money transfer to schools.	Four months between decision and start of implementation permitted some prior planning, but little analysis was done prior to reform, and there was little learning from previous partial fee removal experiences. Full-fledged investment plan only prepared in 2001.	Good. Phased, monitored implementation. Training of province, district, and school managers. Bank accounts opened with district directors.

Table 1A.1 (*continued*)

Issue	Ethiopia	Ghana	Kenya	Malawi	Mozambique
Communication of new policy	Little communication after directive issued. Gradual introduction over several years.	Campaign on fee abolition conducted in all public schools.	No time for prior consultations, but there was an extensive awareness campaign during implementation.	National Policy Symposium for stakeholder consultation, mass media campaign, and preregistration of pupils.	No negotiation with civil society, but wide range of communication took place.
Nature of fees abolished					
Which grades?	Grades 1–10	Grades 1–9	Grades 1–8	Grades 1–8	First, grades 1–5, then 1–7
Which types of fees?	All types	All types	All types	All types. Uniform not compulsory.	All types
Main use of fee income	For nonsalary costs at school level	Training materials, nonsalary operating costs	Most nonsalary expenditures and some salary expenditures	80% for textbooks and exercise books	Varied by school: for supplies, training materials, sport equipment.
Equal level of fees across schools?	No. Variation in amount and type and collection procedures.	No. Variations among schools.	No. Fee structures differed according to needs of individual schools.	No. Fees were lower in rural areas than in urban areas, lower for grades 1–5 than for grades 6–8.	Equal in principle since government set fees per grade.
Fees as share of recurrent expenditure	4%–6% of recurrent costs in public schools (1994)	Not available	Not available. However, fees were high, ranging from US$6.60 to US$132 per parent per year.	11% (1987). Until 2006, government had not fully replaced the fee income.	Not available. However, fees were quite high.
Was voluntary contribution permitted after fee abolition?	Yes, community support was encouraged and is substantial.	Yes, PTAs may raise money for school projects, provided no child is excluded because parents cannot pay.	Yes, parents reminded about obligation to provide construction funds and provide uniforms, but no child should be denied access if parents cannot pay.	Government to finance teachers, learning materials, and infrastructure. Government has been slow in developing and implementing strategy for community involvement.	Communities can raise funds but cannot exclude children whose parents cannot pay.

(Table continues on the next page.)

Table 1A.1 (*continued*)

Issue	Ethiopia	Ghana	Kenya	Malawi	Mozambique
Coverage of fee abolition					
Sequencing/ phasing by age, grade, over time?	No, but in practice, gradually introduced over a couple of years.	Priority in test year given to 40 of the most deprived districts.	No. Entry allowed in any grade at any age.	No. Entry allowed in any grade at any age, so that the highest increase was in grade 8 enrollment (76%).	Five phases 2003–06, gradually extending to grades 1–7, and increasing grant size and coverage.
Grant size and mechanism for transferring revenues to schools to replace fees	Block grants from districts to schools. In 2002 equivalent to US$1.20 per student for grades 1–4, US$1.76 for grades 5–8, and US$2.35 for grades 9–10.	Grant transferred to school bank account; equivalent to US$2.70 per boy and US$3.88 per girl per year. Plus free textbooks.	Grant of US$14 per pupil per year; 2/3 for training materials and supplies, 1/3 for operating expenses. Money transferred to school bank accounts through a system that was already pilot-tested. Plus school feeding in selected areas.	No grants. Government to provide all learning materials, teachers, classrooms, furniture, teachers' houses, sanitation facilities, and boreholes; also to finance "unassisted schools."	Equivalent of US$0.60 to US$0.90 per pupil in phases 1–3 and increased to US$1.20 in phase 4. Grant to finance supplies and training materials on approved list, support for OVC.
Includes private schools?	No, but private schools are 4% of enrollment.	No. This is important, given high private enrollment (15%).	Yes, provided fees are not charged (private schools 4% of enrollment).	Yes, provided fees are not charged (private schools only 1% of enrollment).	No. Private schools are only 2% of total enrollment.
Impact					
Increase in primary school enrollment	23% increase in total enrollment from 1994/95 to 1995/96; 29% growth in grade 1	14% increase in total enrollment from 2004/05 to 2005/06	18% increase in total enrollment from 2002/03 to 2003/04	51% increase in total primary enrollment from 1993/94 to 1994/95; 59% in grade 1; 76% in grade 8	12% increase in total primary enrollment from 2003/04 to 2004/05
Gross enrollment rate in primary education	1994/95: 26.2% 1995/96: 30.1% 2004/05: 79.8%	2004/05: 83.3% 2005/06: 92.7%	2002/03: 88% 2003/04: 103%	1993/94: 89% 1994/95: 134%	2003/04: 89.5% (grades 1–7) 2006/07: 113%
Gender parity index (girls/boys)	1994/95: 0.61 1995/96: 0.58 2004/05: 0.79	2004/05: 0.93 2005/06: 0.95	2002: 0.97 2003: 0.95 2004: 0.94	1993/94: 0.93 1994/95: 0.89 2005: 0.99	2003/04: 0.92 2004/05: 0.94
Pupil-teacher ratio	1994/95: 33:1 1995/96: 37:1 2004/05: 66:1	2004: 32:1	2002/03: 34:1 2003/04: 39:1	1993/94: 68:1 1994/95: 63:1	(Grades 1–5) 2003/04: 66:1 2005/06: 74:1

Table 1A.1 (*continued*)

Issue	Ethiopia	Ghana	Kenya	Malawi	Mozambique
Coping strategies to address enrollment surge and protect quality	Increased class size and increased pupil-teacher ratio.	Combination of measures: use of shifts in schools where needed; use of retired, volunteer, and pupil teachers; temporary classrooms; and extra training materials.	Rapid resource mobilization to finance school grants for training materials and operating costs. Teacher redeployment to address shortages. Special measures for disadvantaged areas.	Class size from 50 to 60; hired 20,000 secondary school leavers; use of temporary shelters; use of temporary classrooms; multiple shifts.	Several measures (e.g., multishifts, larger class size, restructuring teacher training to increase output, and lower construction costs to increase supply of classrooms).
Measures to address quality concerns	School grants to replace fee revenues to finance training material	Training of untrained teachers, more textbooks, and national standard test formulated	Main benefit: more training materials and supplies	Massive growth outstripped resources and further lowered quality (per pupil expenditure declined by 26% from 1993 to 1994).	Direct support to schools for training material and supplies
Early indications of impact on quality	Inconclusive	Marked improvement in scores on mathematics and English tests between 2003/04 and 2004/05	Reduction in repetition and dropout, and increased completion rates. Increased monitoring of quality	Inability to provide adequately for large enrollment surge led to serious decline in quality of learning environment.	Support to schools to replace fees was successful: early evidence of improved quality.
Other benefits of fee abolition	Decentralized decision making; community ownership of schools	Increased national momentum in favor of education	Stronger partnerships with stakeholders, strengthened decentralized management	Greater equity in enrollment by income group. However, inability to provide for large surge limited other benefits.	Local empowerment, revitalized school councils, and local-level accountability; support for orphans and vulnerable children.
Donor support	Initially financed by government, later by multi-donor sector program	Pilot and scaling up supported through World Bank project	DFID, UNICEF, World Bank, SIDA, WFP, OPEC, Oxfam, Action Aid	Initially, only UNICEF; then World Bank and DfID	World Bank, Dutch government, UNICEF

Source: Five country studies in this volume.

NOTES

1. The scarcity of data on the impact of private education costs on education demand makes a rigorous analysis of this role difficult. However, as demonstrated by the major surge in enrollment associated with fee abolition in the cases discussed in this chapter, the impact of sustainable fee abolition on the ability of countries to maintain the present growth momentum is likely to be considerable.

2. Botswana, Cape Verde, Mauritius, Namibia, the Seychelles, South Africa, and Swaziland.

3. Cameroon, the Republic of Congo, Ghana, Kenya, Madagascar, Nigeria, Tanzania, Zambia, and Zimbabwe. Of these countries, all but the Republic of Congo and Ghana had regained a GER of 99 percent or above in 2004.

4. The information for Ghana and Kenya is based on Williams (2006a and 2006b) and supplemented by enrollment rates from UNESCO (1999) and UNESCO-UIS (2005).

5. Enrollment figures for years up to 1982 are based on Fredriksen (1984a), and later figures on UNESCO (1984, 1999, and 2007). There may be slight discrepancies in data depending on the source, especially as population estimates used in calculating enrollment rates often differ.

6. Tanzania's GNP per capita increased annually at 2.0 percent during the period 1965–73, and it declined at an annual rate of 0.9 percent during the period 1973–80 and 1.7 percent during the period 1980–87 (see World Bank 1989, 221).

7. This refers to the increase between 1977 and 1978. The one-year growth of 23 percent in total enrollment and 43 percent in grade 1, quoted earlier in this chapter, refers to the increase from 2001 to 2002.

8. This decrease reflects Zambia's economic decline during the 1980s and 1990s and the resumed growth in recent years. Zambia's GDP per capita declined annually by 2.3 percent during the 1980s and 2.2 percent during the 1990s, and then it increased annually by 2.8 percent during the period 2000–04 (see World Bank 2006a, 27).

9. Example of a different type of external support is emerging for Cameroon, where support under the FTI (Fast Track Initiative) Catalytic Fund will help the government take over financing of "voluntary" teachers recruited to sustain the enrollment surge caused by fee abolition in 1999.

10. Calculated by the author on the basis of data from the World Bank (2000, 2006a) and UNESCO (2006).

11. UNESCO (2007) estimates that in 2005, Sub-Saharan Africa had about 45 percent of the world's out-of-school primary-school-age children, amounting to 32.8 million. This corresponds to about 29 percent of the region's population of primary-school-age children. Many of those out of school are likely to enroll as late entrants; UNESCO-UIS (2005) estimates that this is the case for about half of them. The enrollment surge in recent years has considerably reduced the number of out-of-school children in Sub-Saharan Africa (from 42.4 million in 1999 to 32.8 million in 2005) (UNESCO 2007, 49).

12. Cameroon had reached 102 percent GER in the mid-1980s, but saw a sharp decline in the 1990s to reach 81 percent in 1995, and then had a 59 percent increase in grade 1 enrollment between 1999/2000 and 2000/01 as a result of the

abolition of fees in 2000. The GER increased from 87.7 percent to 102.8 percent during the same one-year period (see World Bank/Pôle de Dakar 2003).

13. See UNESCO (2002) and a discussion of different studies in Van Uythem and Verspoor (2005). The case studies also refer to this factor; see fourth section of this chapter (What Are the Practical Lessons Learned from These Five Countries?).

14. For countries that are far from reaching universal access, good analyses of access problems are given in World Bank (2004) for Niger and World Bank (2005b) for Ethiopia.

15. The quality problem in education in Sub-Saharan Africa goes well beyond these five countries. For a comprehensive study, see Verspoor (2005).

16. In the late 1990s, OECD countries' annual average expenditure was US$3,851 per primary pupil (OECD 2000).

17. The level of teacher salaries varies widely in Sub-Saharan Africa. In some cases, salaries are too low for teachers to survive on teaching alone. When compared to other regions, teacher salaries in Sub-Saharan Africa have seen a severe long-term decline, reflecting a mix of decline in (a) GDP per capita and (b) average teacher salaries expressed in GDP per capita terms. As regards (a), excluding South Africa, Sub-Saharan Africa's GDP per capita (in 1987 U.S. dollars) declined from US$525 in 1970 to US$336 in 1997 (36 percent), as compared to increases from US$1,216 to US$1,890 (55 percent) in Latin America, from US$239 to US$449 (88 percent) in South Asia, and from US$157 to US$715 (355 percent) in East Asia (see World Bank 2000, 8). As regards (b), primary school teacher salaries in Sub-Saharan Africa decreased from 8.6 times GDP per capita in 1975 to 4.4 times in 2000. The drop was largely the result of a sharp decline in Francophone countries, from 11.5 times to 4.8 times per capita GDP (Mingat 2004).

18. In 2005, for the 39 countries in Sub-Saharan Africa for which data were available, the pupil-teacher ratio in primary education exceeded 50:1 in 11 countries, and 60:1 in 6 countries, including 3 of the 5 case study countries (Ethiopia, Malawi, and Mozambique) (see UNESCO 2006, 2007). In addition, the pupil-teacher ratio is often much higher in the early grades of primary schooling.

19. For Korea, Lee (2008, 170) says that "the implementation of the Low Cost Approach was an inevitable policy choice. The forced expansion of enrollment in elementary education resulted in large class size and double or triple shifts in classroom use. In the large cities . . . class size exceeded 90 in some schools. During the implementation periods of the Six-Year Compulsory Education Expansion Plan, some 40 percent of all classrooms practiced such double or triple shifts."

20. See, for example, information on UNICEF's Web site—www.unicef.org—under Essential Learning Package (ELP).

21. Few Sub-Saharan African countries have more than 750 hours in the school year, as compared to about 1,000 hours in the OECD countries.

22. In 2000, about 18.0 percent of primary school pupils in Sub-Saharan Africa were repeaters, compared to 7.1 percent in Arab states, 6.5 percent in South Asia, 5.9 percent in Latin America and the Caribbean, and 1.1 percent in Europe. In a thorough study of the impact of repetition, Bernard, Simon, and Vianou (2005) conclude that repetition is a very ineffective way of improving learning outcomes and, instead, often results in dropouts. In addition, based on data for

44 countries in Sub-Saharan Africa, they conclude that a 1 percent increase in repetition increases dropout by 1.3 percent.

23. There is considerable experience throughout the world in the use of competitive school grants to promote quality improvement through "school improvement projects." These grants typically provide financing for school development plans prepared by school staff, community management committees, or school boards. As pointed out by Van Uythem and Verspoor (2005, 317), the challenge with such grants is to ensure that poor communities with badly resourced schools can participate fairly. Robert-Schweitzer, Markov, and Tretyakov (2002) analyzed school development grant programs in 37 World Bank-supported projects.

24. For the period covered by the case studies, Kenya's grant size was of similar magnitude to Tanzania's: the equivalent of US$10 per pupil when introduced in 2002, with US$4 for textbooks and US$6 for other teaching and learning materials, school operations, administration, and teacher professional development. In Uganda, grants were introduced in 1997 as part of the free primary education policy and fixed at the equivalent of US$4 for grades 1–3 and US$6 for grades 4–7, with guidelines for how the funds were to be used. The grant size remained unchanged until 2007. However, in addition, the government has a separate budget line for instructional materials, and textbooks are provided free of charge.

25. The rate of new entry was higher for boys than for girls in all grades apart from grade 8, possibly as a result of the readmittance policy for pregnant girls.

26. This is well illustrated in Kenya, where an 82-year-old enrolled in grade 1. He was still enrolled in 2006 (at the time of the preparation of the case study), attending grade 4.

27. Countries such as Lesotho, Tanzania, and Uganda also phased in their fee abolition in different ways. The same was the case in Korea; for example, for middle schools, "The government implemented 'free of charge programs' covering the costs of textbooks, tuition, and school supporting fees, starting with remote and insular areas in 1985 and extending nationwide by 1997" (Lee 2008, 173).

28. The importance of providing "second chance education" is underlined in the 2007 World Development Report as one of three pillars to address issues faced by vulnerable youth (World Bank 2006b, 59–64). Examples of such programs are found in many countries. For example, parallel to school fee abolition, Tanzania initiated a complementary basic education program to cater to out-of-school children, ages 11–17, including child laborers. In Uganda, evening and mobile schools are part of the Complementary Opportunities for Primary Education (COPE) program, and a specific project has been designed for the urban poor, called Basic Education for Urban Poor (BEUP). Liberia is also providing "second chance education" through an Accelerated Learning Program, comprising a three-year program covering the sixth-grade primary education curriculum for ex-combatants and for those who missed out on primary schooling during the years of civil strife.

29. References are to the Malawi case study (chapter 5, Lessons Learned), the Ghana case study (chapter 3, Emerging Challenges), and the Kenya case study (chapter 4, Lessons Learned).

30. The references to the case studies are to Ethiopia (chapter 2, Lessons Learned); Ghana (chapter 3, Emerging Challenges); and Mozambique (chapter 6, Learning from Mozambique).

31. See Fredriksen (2007) for a more detailed review of the use of school grants to remove barriers on attaining EFA in Sub-Saharan Africa.

32. This aspect is also stressed in an earlier experience for Ghana, when one of the lessons learned from a cash-matching grant scheme under the Community Initiative Project was that "during periods of high inflation it is essential to make prompt payments to communities and to adjust grant levels (in the local currency) frequently" (see Bray 1995).

REFERENCES

Avenstrup, Roger. 2004. "Free Primary Education and Poverty Reduction: The Case of Kenya, Lesotho, Malawi and Uganda." Africa Region, Human Development Department, World Bank, Washington, DC.

Bernard, Jean-Marc, Odile Simon, and Katia Vianou. 2005. *Le redoublement: mirage de l'école Africaine?* Dakar: PASEC/CONFEMEN.

Bray, Mark. 1995. *Decentralization of Education: Community Financing. Washington*, DC: World Bank.

Bray, Mark, and Seng Bunly. 2005. *Balancing the Books: Household Financing of Basic Education in Cambodia.* The University of Hong Kong, Comparative Education Research Centre.

Bruns, Barbara, Alain Mingat, and Ramahatra Rakatomalala. 2003. *Achieving Universal Primary Education by 2015: A Chance for Every Child.* Washington, DC: World Bank.

Carceles, Gabriel, Birger Fredriksen, and Patrick Watt. 2001. "Can Sub-Saharan Africa Reach the International Targets for Human Development?" Africa Region, Africa Region Human Development Working Paper Series No. 9, World Bank, Washington, DC.

Fredriksen, Birger. 1981. "Progress Towards Regional Targets for Universal Primary Education: A Statistical Review." *International Journal of Education Development* 1 (April).

———. 1983. "The Arithmetic of Achieving Universal Primary Education." *International Review of Education* 29. Hamburg: UNESCO, Institute for Education.

———. 1984a. "Statistical Analysis of Demographic and Education Data in the United Republic of Tanzania." Document prepared for the National Training Seminar on Education Statistics in the United Republic of Tanzania, Arusha, February 20–March 2. Office of Statistics, UNESCO, Paris.

———. 1984b. "Statistical Analysis of Demographic and Education Data in Zambia." Document prepared for the National Training Seminar on Education Statistics in Zambia, Lusaka, September 17–28. Office of Statistics, UNESCO, Paris.

———. 2007. "School Grants: One Efficient Instrument to Address Key Barriers to Attaining Education for All." Paper prepared for Capacity Development Workshop on "Country Leadership and Implementation for Results in the EFA-FTI Partnership," Cape Town, July 16–19. Africa Region, Human Development Department, World Bank, Washington, DC.

Lee, Jae Chong. 2008. "Education in the Republic of Korea: Approaches, Achievements and Current Challenges." In *An African Exploration of the East Asian Education Experience,* eds. Birger Fredriksen and Tan Jee Peng. Washington, DC: World Bank.

Mingat, Alain. 2003a. "L'ampleur des disparités sociales dans l'enseignement primaire en Afrique: sexe, localisation, géographique et revenu familial dans contexte de l'EPT." Working Paper, Africa Region, Human Development Department, World Bank, Washington, DC.

———. 2003b. "Management of Education Systems in Sub-Saharan Africa: A Diagnostic and Ways toward Improvement in the Context of EFA." Paper presented at the joint UNICEF/World Bank "Regional Workshop on Investment Options in Education for All," Ouagadougou, Burkina Faso, June 25–27. Africa Region, Human Development Department, World Bank, Washington, DC.

———. 2004. "La rémunération des enseignants de l'enseignement primaire dans les pays francophones d'Afrique sub-saharienne." Africa Region, Human Development Department, World Bank, Washington, DC.

OECD (Organisation for Economic Co-operation and Development). 2000. *OECD Indicators*. Paris.

Rasera, J-B. 2003. "Le financement d'une education de qualité." Background paper prepared for "The Challenge of Learning: Improving the Quality of Education in Sub-Saharan Africa." Association for the Development of Education in Africa (ADEA), Paris.

Roberts-Schweitzer, E., A. Markov, and A. Tretyakov. 2002. "Achieving Education for All Goals: School Grant Schemes." World Bank, Washington, DC.

UNESCO-UIS (UNESCO Institute for Statistics). 2005. *Children Out of School: Measuring Exclusion from Primary Education*. Montreal: UIS.

———. 2006. *Global Education Digest 2006*. Montreal: UIS.

UNESCO. 1984. *Statistical Yearbook*. Paris: UNESCO.

———. 1999. *Statistical Yearbook*. Paris: UNESCO.

———. 2002. *EFA Global Monitoring Report 2002*. Paris: UNESCO.

———. 2004. *EFA Global Monitoring Report 2005*. Paris: UNESCO.

———. 2006. *EFA Global Monitoring Report 2007*. Paris: UNESCO.

———. 2007. *EFA Global Monitoring Report 2008*. Paris: UNESCO.

UNESCO/BREDA/Pôle de Dakar. 2005. *Education Pour Tous En Afrique: 2006; Rapport Dakar + 6*. Dakar: UNESCO.

Van Uythem, Bart, and Adriaan Verspoor. 2005. "Financing Quality Basic Education." In *The Challenge of Learning: Improving the Quality of Basic Education in Sub-Saharan Africa*, ed. Adriaan Verspoor. Paris: Association for the Development of Education in Africa (ADEA).

Verspoor, Adriaan, ed. 2005. *The Challenge of Learning: Improving the Quality of Basic Education in Sub-Saharan Africa*. Paris: Association for the Development of Education in Africa (ADEA).

Volan, Sissel. 2003. "Educational Reform and Change in the South: A Matter of Restructuring as Well as Reculturing-Experiences from Zambia." PhD diss., University of Southampton, King Alfred's College of Higher Education.

Williams, Peter. 2006a. "Kenya: Attainment and Maintenance of Universal Primary Education: Lessons from Past Quantitative and Qualitative Regression." Council for Education in the Commonwealth Secretariat, London.

———. 2006b. "Universal Primary Education—for the Second Time—in Anglophone Africa." Council for Education in the Commonwealth Secretariat, London.

———. 2006c. "UPE Mini Study: Tanzania." Initial draft for the *Study for the Commonwealth Secretariat on Sustainability of Universal Primary Education*. London: Council for Education in the Commonwealth Secretariat.

World Bank. 1989. *Sub-Saharan Africa from Crisis to Sustainable Growth*. Washington, DC: World Bank.

———. 2000. *Can Africa Claim the 21st Century?* Washington, DC: World Bank.

———. 2004. "La dynamique des scolarisations au Niger-evaluation pour un développement durable." Africa Region Human Development Working Paper Series No. 40, World Bank, Washington, DC.

———. 2005a. Le renouveau du système éducatif de la République Démocratique du Congo: Priorités et alternatives." Africa Region Human Development Working Paper Series No. 68, World Bank, Washington, DC.

———. 2005b. "Education in Ethiopia: Strengthening the Foundation for Sustainable Progress." Country Study, World Bank, Washington, DC.

———. 2006a. *African Development Indicators.* Washington, DC: World Bank.

———. 2006b. *World Development Report 2007: Development and the Next Generation.* Washington, DC: World Bank.

World Bank/Pôle de Dakar. 2003. "Rapport d'etat du système educatif national Camerounais: Eléments de diagnostic pour la politique dans le contexte de l'EPT et du DSRP." Report prepared by a team comprising Camerounian experts and staff from the World Bank and Coopération Française, Washington, DC.

Ethiopia

2

Financing Primary Education within a Decentralized System: The Case of Ethiopia

This chapter examines the abolition of school fees in Ethiopia in the context of financing primary education within a decentralized system. It assesses the school fee abolition policy as well as its strategies, measures, processes, outcomes, and impacts on the financial system of education and its related activities in the past 10 academic years. Moreover, the chapter reviews the challenges in implementing this policy and the lessons learned in coping with the challenges in waiving school fees, which were the bulk of the private cost of schooling for most parents. Special focus is given to the decentralization factor in enhancing or detracting from the bold initiative of free education.

This chapter uses the following four approaches:

1. Analysis of national and regional state policy and strategy documents, previous studies, and official statistical data of the Central Statistics Agency (CSA) and the Ministry of Education (MoE)
2. Focus group roundtable and consultative discussions with stakeholders—the officials of the MoE, Bureau of Education and Bureau of Finance and Economic Development (BoFED), as well as the MoE's Fee Abolition Team, which includes development partners
3. A short survey of case studies of a few schools that interviewed students and directors on the issues of school fees (the data on schools' financial profiles were used to complement facts from 1 and 2 above)
4. Country experiences from country papers and other documents presented in the Nairobi SFAI workshop and interactive discussions in the plenary sessions and group works at the workshop.

BACKGROUND

Ethiopia is a large country of more than 1 million square kilometers, with over 75 million inhabitants speaking over 80 languages. It is the second most populous country in Africa. It is physically, culturally, and linguistically extremely diverse. About 85 percent of the people are rural. In 2004/05, there were 14.3 million primary-school-age children; 11.4 million students were enrolled in the primary schools at that time (MoE 2005b). Despite an old and rich legacy of traditional education and a unique alphabet of its own, the illiteracy that marked its development is still prevalent.

ECONOMIC CHALLENGES

The Ethiopian economy is characterized by poverty. According to official documents, the per capita GNP in 2003/04 was only 1,189.40 birr (Br) (CSA 2006), which barely amounts to US$130. Government efforts to accelerate development include rapid changes in education, expanding infrastructure, devolving administration, reforming service delivery, and introducing change in the other sectoral and subsectoral domains of the society. Ethiopia's policies, strategies, and programs since 1992/93 have aimed at sustainable and equitable development and poverty reduction. The country believes in a holistic and integrated approach to its serious development problems. Thus, poverty reduction and sustainable development targets are based on four pillars (or building blocks). These are agricultural development–led industrialization (ADLI), justice system and civil service reform, decentralization and empowerment, and capacity building in the public and private sectors. It is within this context that other national sectoral programs such as the Education Sector Development Program (ESDP) must be examined. The Sustainable Development and Poverty Reduction Program (SDPRP) was the Poverty Reduction Strategy Paper (PRSP) of the country, which makes sustainable development and poverty reduction the centerpiece of transformation. All other sectoral programs act in a concerted manner and maintain the same focus; they also recognize the vital role of education and training in fulfilling this economic development mandate. Thus, SDPRP has now completed its three-year span (2002/03–2004/05) and has been replaced by SDPRP II (its new title is "A Plan for Accelerated and Sustainable Development to End Poverty" [PASDEP]) (2005/06–2009/10).

POLITICAL WILL

In the twentieth century, Ethiopia experienced three entirely different political systems: monarchy, communism, and federalism. In 1991, the third type of political order (federalism) came into existence when a new charter, which involved different political organizations, nationalities, civic societies, religious leaders, and others was set as a guide to the transitional government. The charter was then replaced by a constitution, which gives supreme power to the nations and nationalities. The legislative system is bicameral and consists of the House of Representatives and the House of Federation. The House of Federation, which is composed of representatives from each nation, nationality, and people, among others, "determine[s] the division of the subsidies that the federal government may provide to the state" (see Constitution, Articles 61 and 62). In keeping with the Constitution, national regions or regional states, if they like, could choose to secede and declare independence. It is these states' will to unity that has created the Federation of Ethiopia. This decentralized system of governance is new to the nation, and the basis for the way in which the Federal Democratic Republic of Ethiopia (FDRE) is organized.

SCHOOL FEES VERSUS FREE EDUCATION: SOME THEORETICAL CONSIDERATIONS

People pay for their basic needs such as food and clothing. Should they also be responsible for their education or should that be free? This question is not as simple as it may seem. The issue may be argued from different viewpoints: the interplay of human rights, politics, and finance create dilemmas for decision makers. Thus, after writing lengthy books, some writers fail to reach a concrete and plausible conclusion or offer concrete recommendations. The United Nations Universal Declaration of Human Rights states:

> Everyone has the right to education. Education shall be
> free, at least in the elementary and fundamental stages.

Other international documents followed suit and declared that education, especially at the primary level, should be not only free but also compulsory. Those who do not support free education often base their argument on the differential rate of return in education at each level and so recommend loans or fees for higher education. According to this argument, per student cost is much lower at the primary level, whereas the social return is high. Additionally, primary fee-free provision supports governments' pro-poor claims and is therefore less debatable than higher levels of education (Bray 1996, 1998, 1999).

Similarly, the World Bank (1995) policy preference was "free public basic education" together with "selective charging of fees" for upper senior secondary education, and "fees for all public higher education." As shown later in this chapter, Ethiopia has more or less adopted such a trend. As to the issue of who benefits from education and who should pay, Peano's (1998) conclusion is that "education is [a] public good when its effects are consumed collectively by the society and at the same time a private good when it directly benefits an individual." He thus concurs that governments should cover the cost of basic education, which offers more social benefits, and devise other arrangements for the higher levels.

There is no single solution for this debate as it encompasses multiple interests. However, it is important to remember the purpose of public subsidy of education—the aim must not and cannot be to provide free education for all, including those who have the resources to pay. Bray (1996) argues that the poor are more sensitive to direct cost charges and opportunity costs and need the support; whereas for higher levels of education, a partnership with other nonpublic sources must be considered. In the case of Ethiopia, this approach is supported by many organizations and researchers (CSAE 1997; World Bank 2004a).

The Centre for the Study of African Economies (1997) believes that diversification of financial sources and institutionalization of cost recovery wherever possible help sustain fee-free education at the primary level. Thus, the issue is not whether fee-free education should be provided—but to provide fee-free education to those who deserve it and accompany that provision with measures to compensate for lost fees.

Finally, it is important to note that almost all countries have signed and ratified the following:

- The Universal Declaration of Human Rights (1948)
- The UNESCO Convention against Discrimination in Education (1960)
- The Convention on the Elimination of All Forms of Discrimination against Women (1979)
- The Convention on the Rights of the Child (1989)
- The World Declaration on Education for All (1990)
- The Millennium Development Goals (2000).

Therefore, the legal basis for quality fee-free primary education cannot be doubted. Ethiopia also supports all the above international conventions because it has signed and ratified them; Article 9:4 of the federal Constitution guarantees that "all international agreements ratified by Ethiopia are an integral part of the law of the land" (FDRE 1995). Hence the correct question for universal primary education (UPE) is not *why* but *how*.

FINANCING EDUCATION IN DIFFERENT GOVERNMENT SYSTEMS (PRE–FEE ABOLITION)

Prior to the twentieth century, the curriculum and financing of education in Ethiopia was not the task of the government. It was a nongovernmental affair. The traditional school was the purview of the Church and the Mosque. Literature shows that in traditional schools, most people paid for their education in kind (grains), in labor, and sometimes in cash. The state's financial responsibility for education started at the beginning of the twentieth century when the Western system of education was introduced in the country. At that time, the government took on the entire cost, and there were no fees until five decades later.

Thus, until the 1950s, education was almost free of any direct costs to households. In fact, in some government boarding schools, every basic need and facility was provided free of charge. In some cases, students were also supported with bursary arrangements. Moreover, in other schools, students were provided free learning materials, including books, exercise books, and stationery and learning tools. However, this arrangement did not last long; by the 1960s, as enrollment increased, resources became acutely limited. Nevertheless the government continued to bear the main responsibility of education, although gradually community contributions covered 20 to 30 percent of the financing (TGE 1993).

The household contribution was at the kindergarten, primary, and secondary levels. Higher education was free and almost completely publicly financed. In those days, an average of 12 percent of the national budget (about 4 percent of the GDP) was spent on education (TGE 1993). However, the overall limited financial resources of the country, combined with certain other factors, prevented the qualitative and quantitative development of services.

As shown in table 2.1, education expenditure has been greater since 1995, when the new Education and Training Policy was implemented and fees abolished (see section on Prioritization below for further details on this policy change). There were grave disparities in opportunities among the disparate tiers of schooling. In the 1970/71 academic year, 46.0 percent of the primary schools and 45.3 percent of the secondary schools (which enrolled a smaller proportion of students due to their sizes) were nongovernment schools. In 1975 when the military government placed all private schools under the public administration of the communities, the problem was aggravated. When private initiative was abolished as part of the command economy, nongovernmental participation was highly frustrated.

Table 2.1   Education Expenditure Trends in Different Government Systems, 1970–2005

Year	Education expenditure (million birr)	Total government expenditure (percent)	Government system
1970	65.5	10.4	Monarchy
1975	129.9	14.1	
1980	203.6	8.6	Communism
1985	328.3	8.2	
1990	491.9	7.5	
1995	1,337.0	13.8	Federalism
2000	2,485.1	13.6	
2005	4,638.9	16.7	

Source: MoE "Education Statistics Annual Abstracts."

ABOLITION OF SCHOOL FEES

During the later years of the monarchy and throughout the Dergue administration, that is, the Communist military junta that ruled Ethiopia from 1974 to 1991, students were a supplemental financial source for schools, which spontaneously introduced registration, facility, or maintenance fees; book rents; sports dues; payment for certificates; or for occasional pretexts such as construction or extension. The capitation fees gradually spread systemwide because of the need in schools.

Nonsalary cash sources were used for buying stationery and for minor day-to-day school maintenance. In fact there was virtually no petty cash allotted for government schools other than these fees. Schools covered their operational expenses from such fees and from internal revenues.

The Policy and Human Resource Development (PHRD) survey of 1996 (PHRD 1996) pointed out that although about 93 percent of the schools surveyed had introduced registration fees, there was no regulation on the amount. The fee varied from school to school and was decided by each individual school usually on an ad hoc basis (table 2.2 and annex table 2A.2). This could be related to the origin of these fees from the free education era to the "fee-paying free education" era as mentioned in the section Financing Education in Different Government Systems (Pre–Fee Abolition). These fees spontaneously evolved in every school to cover the essential cost of operations.

There were variations not only in the amount to be paid but also in the procedures of payment. According to the CSAE (1997), some schools collected fees at the beginning of the year. Some allowed poor students to pay the part that was forwarded to the *woreda* education office (WEO)[1] for

Table 2.2   Annual Fees Paid by Students Just before
Fee Abolition
(birr)

Grade	Government schools	Public schools[a]
1	9.8	126.00
2	9.3	130.30
3	10.2	118.10
4	10.9	144.20
5	11.0	144.30
6	13.0	157.40
7	15.3	237.60
8	14.3	243.60

Source: Computed from data in annex table 2A.1.
a. Public schools in Ethiopia are schools administered by communities.

its own operations and pay the rest (the school's share) when they were able to afford it, some time within the year. Some did not charge registration fees to poor and disabled students. Both the PHRD survey and CSAE study mentioned above concurred that annual school registration fees increased in each successive grade (see annex table 2A.1).

After fees for registration, textbook rental was the next sizable capitation fee in education. Rental payment affected all students except those in grade 1; those fees were the only ones officially approved by the Ministry of Education. The annual rent ranged from 10 Ethiopian cents to Br 2 per student per year in the government schools and from 10 cents to Br 100 in the nongovernment (community or public) schools. A proportion of the book rental money was forwarded to the woreda education offices.

The 1996 survey showed that, in general, the largest supplement to government expenditure at the school level was this capitation fee. It accounted for 1.1 percent and 25 percent of the expenditure of government schools and nongovernment schools, respectively.

Some schools generated sizable internal revenue, but many were not able to progress to that stage. When they were able to (in many parts of the country), the revenue was considered a part of the national revenue and deposited into the treasury, leaving the school unrewarded. This was a disincentive for the active schools.

A review of Ethiopia's history of education reveals that there were no regulated tuition fees in the government schools and in higher education institutions; however, there were payments in various forms in these educational institutions. These payments (registration fees, cleanliness fees, rental book fees, and sport fees) were significant for most parents sending their children to school. According to the PHRD study, on average, a government school was levying about Br 10 to Br 15 per year per student. For a family with four children in school, the fees amounted to Br 40 to Br 60 per household. Although the amount was not large, it had three important effects on the education system. The first is that the fees functioned as a gatekeeper: the fees precluded many students from joining the schools. The fees may seem diminutive by the standards of some countries, but they were a burden for most of Ethiopia's rural population. Second, the fees played a vital role in the teaching-learning process in the classroom, as they were the major source of reliable cash for school management. Third, with millions of students, the cumulative total of the payments was sizable; to waive the fee would require another regular financial source. This means that one could expect an additional budget of at least Br 143 million to Br 215 million for the primary enrollment of 2004/05. The supplement may be as high as Br 1,697 million to Br 3,475 million if the public school rate is applied.

THE PROCESS OF SCHOOL FEE ABOLITION AND SOME IMMEDIATE EFFECTS

After policies such as the Education and Training Policy were issued, it took one year for instructions on fee abolition to be forwarded to the regions and to the schools. As the progress and magnitude of decentralization differed among states and local authorities, the arrangements in the abolition process also varied.

The experts in the bureaus of education and school directors mention two problems in the school fee abolition process when they assess it retrospectively. First, public relations were not adequately conducted to inform the public about the introduction of the fee-free and cost-sharing policy. Second, this fee-free schooling policy was not introduced after the completion of the woreda decentralization, but simultaneously with it. The unfinished and parallel decentralization process affected the efficient implementation of the fee abolition directive.

However, the first constraint, the lack of adequate popularization of the policy, had some default benefits as well. The silent implementation averted political opposition to fee abolition, which was a problem in many African countries. Moreover, less publicity about fee-free education may have minimized misunderstanding about the "free" education concept and kept community participation and contribution on board. Although some localities took their time in implementing the school fee abolition policy, the majority of schools stopped the registration fees by 1996.

It has been over a decade since the school fee abolition policy started to be enforced. Although the directives were issued from the federal Ministry of Education, they were not readily implemented. There were two reasons for this. First, the fees were generally introduced by individual schools, and the practice had become an established tradition at each school. Second, because of some delays in woreda governance decentralization and staffing preconditions, the supplemental money to meet direct needs at the school level was not readily budgeted. The gradual process of decentralization, which first reached as far as the regional states (not the zones, woredas, *kebeles*,[2] and schools), was a democratic process—consensus building among the regional states was necessary.

During the earlier period of the abolition, funds for nonsalary operational costs did not pass immediately from the regions to the zones, then to the woredas, and finally to the schools. Delays and time gaps forced grassroots school administrators to exploit community involvement to bridge this temporary rift. This also helped many of the directors to act creatively and boost their internal revenue, although some complained that their attention was diverted from their major task of curricular and academic affairs to financial matters.

At present, government schools cannot request any levy per student in grades 1 to 10. This "free" schooling does not mean, however, that there are no "residual" school fees or that the community cannot contribute in the form of labor, materials, technical assistance, or cash at those levels; in fact, by policy and in practice, communities are encouraged to make such contributions for establishment, expansion, and maintenance of schools and for teaching material expenses. "Residual" school fees imply that some directors request capitation charges from students and parents on certain pretexts (see table 2.3) because of the scarcity in the schools' operational budgets.

Despite these bottlenecks in implementation, the fee waiver has been an important factor in the rapid growth in general education enrollment.

ACHIEVEMENTS: ACCESS AND EQUITY

Generally, access, equity, and budget target indicators set for the ESDP at country level have performed satisfactorily. By attracting and retaining students who may have dropped out for lack of cash, school fee abolition is believed to have influenced considerably the rather fast growth of enrollment in general education. During the four-year period from

Table 2.3 Some "Residual" Fees Paid by Students, 2006

Serial number	Purpose of payment	Paying students		Average payment (birr)
		Number	Percentage	
1	Registration	4	6.3	30.00
2	Sports	20	31.7	1.08
3	Sanitation	10	15.8	1.00
4	Construction	37	58.7	38.00
5	Stationery	10	15.8	0.70
6	Certificates	15	23.8	0.33
7	ID cards	7	11.1	1.00
8	Others	18	28.6	1.72
Average including construction				25.50
Average without construction				3.20

Source: Survey by the consultant.
Note: Number of schools surveyed was 63.

Table 2.4 Primary School Gross Enrollment Rate by Gender and Region, 1994/95 and 2004/05

(percent)

Region	1994/95 (1987 EC)			2004/05 (1997 EC)		
	Male	Female	Total	Male	Female	Total
Addis Ababa	84.4	85.3	84.9	141.1	159.0	150.2
Afar	10.0	6.8	8.4	24.0	17.0	20.9
Amhara	19.9	16.8	17.9	79.0	72.6	75.9
Benishangul Gumuz	49.3	20.2	35.4	125.1	88.8	107.4
Dire Dawa	42.8	39.1	41.0	90.8	76.6	83.9
Gambella	67.8	38.2	53.9	150.0	103.3	127.4
Harare	55.3	51.4	53.4	102.5	81.8	92.4
Oromia	27.2	14.9	21.2	100.5	74.3	87.5
SNNPR	39.5	17.4	28.8	91.7	66.0	78.9
Somali	16.2	6.6	11.6	27.6	18.3	23.3
Tigray	49.0	38.0	43.7	90.8	91.1	91.0
All Ethiopia	31.7	20.4	26.2	88.0	71.5	79.8

Source: MoE 2005b.
Note: Primary school includes grades 1–8. EC = Ethiopian calendar; SNNPR = Southern Nations, Nationalities, and Peoples Region.

2000/01 to 2004/05, the average annual growth of enrollment at the primary level was 12.7 percent. The average was higher in the case of the disadvantaged regions (and groups). The pastoral regions of Afar and Somali grew by 17.3 percent and 22.4 percent, respectively. This is a positive trend toward equitable distribution of the service (see table 2.4).

The participation in primary education in 2004/05, with a GER of 79.8 percent, has exceeded the nationally planned figure of ESDP II[3] by 14.8 percentage points (see annex table 2B.1), compared to the previous year when the increase was 12.4 percentage points for girls and 10.6 percentage points for boys. Even though much remains to be done, this is an encouraging step toward gender parity.

Another important indicator of the impact of the fee waiver is the admission for grade 1 students. The new intake in the decade before the introduction of the policy was either declining or stagnating because of internal warfare, instability, and droughts (see annex table 2A.3). The actual surge came with the introduction of the policy in 1995/96. However, there was also an apparent surge in 1993/94, when relative stability and peace reversed the decline and 840,061 new students were enrolled. Actually, that was less than the number of new students in 1986/87, when grade 1 intake was 905,188. Table 2.5 shows that there was a high increase of new enrollment in grade 1 in the total government and nongovernment schools during the three academic years from 1994/95 to 1996/97, when the policy of fee abolition was issued and implemented (annex table 2A.3). This was the time of the first big surge in enrollment. However, the intake rate of girls was consistently higher than that of boys throughout the decade for grade 1 students in the rural areas (table 2.6). Although such factors as peace and stability have also contributed to the fast growth in enrollment in the past decade, many experts (for instance,

Table 2.5 Enrollments for Grade 1 in Government and Nongovernment Primary Schools, 1994/95–2004/05

Year (EC year in parentheses)	Boys		Girls		Total	
	Number	Growth (percent)	Number	Growth (percent)	Number	Growth (percent)
1994/95 (1987)	714,492	Base year	393,259	Base year	1,107,751	Base year
1995/96 (1988)	919,473	28.69	505,281	28.49	1,424,754	28.62
1996/97 (1989)	1,031,122	12.14	580,806	14.95	1,611,928	13.14
1997/98 (1990)	1,086,801	5.4	664,799	14.46	1,751,600	8.66
1998/99 (1991)	1,091,065	0.39	749,120	12.68	1,840,185	5.06
1999/2000 (1992)	1,124,386	3.05	830,649	10.88	1,955,035	6.24
2000/01 (1993)	1,163,731	3.5	903,000	8.71	2,066,731	5.71
2001/02 (1994)	1,159,879	−0.33	911,553	0.95	2,071,432	0.23
2002/03 (1995)	1,174,839	1.29	937,571	2.85	2,112,410	1.98
2003/04 (1996)	1,321,818	12.51	1,132,505	20.79	2,454,323	16.19
2004/05 (1997)	1,758,167	33.01	1,572,134	38.82	3,330,301	35.69

Source: MoE "Education Statistics Annual Abstracts."
Note: EC = Ethiopian calendar.

Table 2.6   Grade 1 Enrollment in Rural Areas, 1994/95–2004/05

Year (EC year in parentheses)	Boys and girls	Percentage increase	Girls	Percentage increase
1994/95 (1987)	820,539	Base year	260,345	Base year
1995/96 (1988)	1,097,216	33.7	355,604	36.6
1996/97 (1989)	1,251,611	14.1	418,099	17.5
1997/98 (1990)	1,364,288	9.0	488,279	16.8
1998/99 (1991)	1,453,325	6.5	568,875	16.5
1999/2000 (1992)	1,566,967	7.8	647,688	13.9
2000/01 (1993)	1,644,912	5.0	701,157	8.3
2001/02 (1994)	1,627,842	−1.0	697,381	−0.5
2002/03 (1995)	1,655,049	1.7	715,588	2.6
2003/04 (1996)	1,983,395	19.8	900,235	25.8
2004/05 (1997)	2,851,359	43.8	1,336,355	48.4

Source: Computed from MoE "Education Statistics Annual Abstracts."
Note: EC = Ethiopian calendar.

from the bureaus of education) with intimate experience of the system believe that the breakthrough is attributed to the abolition of school fees.

An additional positive result has been to lessen disparity. The trend in data in table 2.6 shows that the increase in female enrollment had a better momentum. As we can see from the data, the policy has helped all students at the primary level; it has helped rural students more; and rural female students much more. It is definitely a policy favoring the disadvantaged.

Similarly, the disadvantaged regions have benefited more from the fee abolition policy. A review of the regional annual enrollment growth rate between the years 2001 and 2005 shows the highest growth rates were 22.4 percent and 17.3 percent, respectively, for Somali and Afar, the most disadvantaged regions. The lowest growth rates of −0.9 percent, 3 percent, and 5.9 percent were for Harare, Addis Ababa, and Dire Dawa, respectively, the most advantaged regions in the provision of education. The other regions were not far from the average national enrollment growth of 11.5 percent during that period.

The year 2004/05 had another surge of admission and enrollment of new students (annex table 2A.3) when over 3.24 million new (grade 1) students began their education. It is a great leap compared to the previous year with only 2.35 million new students. That was an increase of 38 percent.

This second surge, unlike the first of 1995/96 (due to fee abolition), cannot be attributed mainly to the fee waiver. In addition to fee-free education, this second surge seems to have been caused by the special intensive work of the PTAs, kebele education and training boards, woreda education and training boards, and woreda education offices. These grass-roots organizations spent two years in advocacy, school construction, and encouraging parents to send their children (and particularly girls) to schools. They were deeply involved in innovative programs such as alternative basic education (ABE) and a pastoral education package of satellite schools. In ABEs, which are community-based paraformal schools, 741,758 students were enrolled in 3,686 centers handled by 8,392 facilitators. These groups were also actively involved with the Woreda Food Program (WFP), a school feeding program.

POST–FEE ABOLITION CONSTRAINTS

On the other hand, certain crucial constraints related to the fast enrollment growth have also evolved, such as the following: high pupil-teacher ratio (PTR) and low qualifications of some teachers; high pupil-section ratio (PSR); lower proportion of recurrent budget to nonsalary component, and related problems; management problems resulting from large size of schools; high dropout and repetition rates; and learning performances below expected national standards.

Pupil-Teacher Ratio and Pupil-Section Ratio. The PTR and PSR are very important general indicators of demand and supply in the provision of education. In the past 10 years, the PTR has changed from 33:1 in 1994/95 to 66:1 in 2004/05 (see table 2.7). This 100 percent increase in the number of students per teacher is one undesirable consequence of the fast

Table 2.7   Primary Education Growth Indicators, 1994/95–2004/05

Year (EC year in parentheses)	Gross enrollment rate (percent)	Pupil-section ratio	Pupil-teacher ratio	Female (percent)
1994/95 (1987)	26.2	48:1	33:1	37.9
1995/96 (1988)	30.1	53:1	37:1	36.8
1996/97 (1989)	34.7	57:1	42:1	36.4
1997/98 (1990)	41.8	60:1	47:1	36.7
1998/99 (1991)	48.8	63:1	51:1	37.8
1999/2000 (1992)	51.0	66:1	56:1	39.2
2000/01 (1993)	67.9	70:1	60:1	40.3
2001/02 (1994)	61.6	73:1	63:1	40.9
2002/03 (1995)	64.4	73:1	64:1	41.2
2003/04 (1996)	68.4	74:1	65:1	42.6
2004/05 (1997)	79.8	69:1	66:1	44.2

Source: Computed from MoE "Education Statistics Annual Abstracts."
Note: EC = Ethiopian calendar.

growth in enrollment. Classrooms are also becoming extremely crowded. The pupil-section ratio in 1994/95 was 48:1 and grew to 69:1 in 2004/05 (see table 2.7). This student-space relation, which is a national average, could be more than 120 students per section in extreme cases.

The rapid rise in enrollment makes it extremely difficult to manage some school populations or to ensure the desirable level of discipline and order, both at the classroom and at the campus level. In the observed schools, students themselves complained about the disciplinary disorder in the school and in their respective sections.

Qualifications of Teachers. Teachers' qualifications for the second cycle of the primary level have failed to reach the planned 80 percent figure. In 2006, nearly half the teachers at that level were underqualified, which means they did not have the professional diploma qualification for teaching. Woredas were forced to employ less qualified or assistant teachers and to use intern teachers to cope with the expansion in enrollment. In-service training programs and capacity-building courses are desirable (Joint Review Mission [JRM] 2004).

Low Proportion of Recurrent Budget. The growth in enrollment is challenging the government in terms of recurrent budget allocation. Table 2.8 shows that the allocation per student at the national level has a decreasing trend. In 1994/95, just before the fee abolition, the government allocated Br 239.30 per student; by 2004/05 that had decreased gradually to Br 199.07.

Table 2.8 Enrollment Trend and Recurrent Cost of Primary- and Secondary-Level Education, 1994/95–2004/05

Year (EC year in parentheses)	Recurrent budget (million birr)	Enrollment in government schools	Annual expenditure per student (birr)
1994/95 (1987)	756.13	3,159,700	239.30
1995/96 (1988)	834.15	3,870,840	215.50
1996/97 (1989)	880.53	4,563,609	192.95
1997/98 (1990)	961.80	5,233,445	183.78
1998/99 (1991)	1,120.35	5,912,411	189.45
1999/2000 (1992)	1,101.10	6,706,945	164.17
2000/01 (1993)	1,294.99	7,803,176	165.96
2001/02 (1994)	1,437.00	8,318,870	172.73
2002/03 (1995)	1,847.30	8,834,746	209.09
2003/04 (1996)	2,031.70	9,707,260	209.30
2004/05 (1997)	2,332.21	11,715,717	199.07

Source: Collated from MoE "Education Statistics Annual Abstracts."
Note: EC = Ethiopian calendar.

The decrease is, of course, crucial to the overall supply of primary education. However, more worrying is the fact that the rapid growth in enrollment has caused the allotted recurrent budget to be consumed increasingly by wages and salaries, leaving a negligible amount for the nonsalary operational expenditure, which, in the past, had been supplemented by fees.

The nonpersonnel expenditure data of the schools in table 2.8 show the following:

- There is considerable variation in the per capita cost per student among the schools; and the number of students does not seem to have been considered in allocation.
- The share of the nonsalary operational budget has decreased in 2004/05 compared to the previous year. This, again, is not a positive trend in terms of the quality of education.

The most striking feature of the educational budget is the high proportion allotted to the recurrent budget, which is spent on personnel services (salaries and allowances). Among the nine schools covered in the field survey, the share of the budget for personnel service in the primary system of education ranged from 89 percent to 98 percent, although the government has made a concerted effort to augment the percentage it spends on education. This problem persists, and it has some relation to school fees (see table 2.9 and annex table 2A.4).

Table 2.9 Some Indicators of Recurrent Cost at Primary Schools, 1997 and 1998

School	Recurrent expenditure per student (birr)		Nonpersonnel per capita expenditure (birr)		Nonpersonnel expenditure of total (percent)	
	1997 EC	1998 EC	1997 EC	1998 EC	1997 EC	1998 EC
Adi Haki	218.22	253.36	22.21	27.97	10.2	11.0
Dima	129.26	190.69	6.37	4.14	4.9	2.2
Lekatit 23	207.48	256.84	16.84	17.26	8.1	6.7
Meskerem	293.75	460.65	42.56	49.23	14.5	10.7
Minilik	414.78	328.00	20.38	6.07	4.9	1.9
Romanat	154.01	224.41	13.64	17.98	8.8	8.0
Sertse Dingil	314.74	312.76	32.52	24.41	10.3	7.3
Yewket Fana	204.94	221.91	26.50	6.45	12.9	2.9
Zenzelima	137.16	211.65	5.09	9.22	3.7	4.4
Average	252.65	275.71	21.57	16.41	8.5	5.9

Source: Computed from field survey.
Note: EC = Ethiopian calendar.

The nonsalary component of the recurrent budget is shrinking with time and creating operational deficiencies in the schools. Textbook-pupil ratio of 1:1 was the target for primary education for 2004/05. Because of the unavailability of data, the ratio was never assessed. However, the problem still lingers. The Joint Review Mission report of 2004 has observed several problems from production to provision of textbooks. The present survey in relation to this chapter lists textbook provision deficiencies in schools in Addis Ababa as well as schools in the regions. For example, among the schools visited, of the 60 students who responded on the provision of textbooks in three subject areas, 70.2 percent said there was one book for each of them for every subject, whereas 19.7 percent were sharing, and 10.1 percent had no books; again, these deficiencies need serious intervention.

Internal Efficiency. A joint study by USAID and MoE observed high rates of dropout and repetition. The magnitude of these internal deficiencies is serious and, unless arrested in a timely fashion, could affect the EFA and MDG target of achieving universal primary education by 2015. The primary-level repetition rate was reduced by 50 percent but is still as high as 3.7 percent (AED/BESO 2005).

Dropouts are more serious at the first year of schooling. At the national level, 22.4 percent of the students enrolled in grade 1 in 2004/05 did not proceed to grade 2 in 2005/06. This is a critical problem of wastage. According to the study by the Academy for Educational Development (AED) and MoE, "Dropout and repetition are both the cause and the result of the poor quality of primary education" (AED/BESO and MoE 2005). Classroom conditions and the treatment of beginners in schools need to improve.

Quality. Quality is a very important aspect of system evaluation. The target was to check the sample test results for grade 4 to see whether students have achieved the minimum desirable points of 50 percent performance. The activity was not performed as planned and was not assessed. However, it is important to recall that the National Organization of Examination (NOE) conducted two previous learning assessments of grades 4 and 8. The first learning assessment was the Ethiopian National Baseline Assessment in 1999 (NOE 2000, 2001). The second one was the Ethiopian Second National Learning Assessment in 2004 (NOE 2004a, 2004b). Both involved grades 4 and 8, the final years of the first cycle and second cycle of primary level, respectively. Results in both assessments in both levels in almost all subject areas were below the nationally set minimum achievement standard of 50 percent (annex table 2A.9). Such assessments must continue because they are instrumental not only in evaluating outcomes but also in examining the efficacy of inputs, including finance.

THE PRESENT FINANCIAL SYSTEM OF EDUCATION

The new Education and Training Policy of 1994 based school finance on the principles of efficiency and equity. On the one hand, it is understandable that scarce financial resources are allocated with strict prioritization for activities that offer maximum output from minimum inputs. On the other hand, it is evident that a federal country of over 80 ethnic groups with numerous faiths and traditions and modes of livelihood needs an equitable system to fund education. In the process of developing the Education and Training Policy document, the necessity of state involvement in financing education was justified for the following reasons:

- Most of the people who deserve the service not only could not afford it but also had low consciousness about the utility of education.
- The value of education is essential not only for the private individual but also for the whole society. It is a public good when its outcome benefits people collectively; it is also a private good when its benefits accrue directly to the individual.
- Education must create cultural and social cohesion among the diverse people of the country, and its financing strategy ought to be instrumental to that end.
- The education sector must be coordinated centrally and administered locally. Accordingly, central policies of educational finance should be implemented and monitored by local authorities (FDRE 1995, Article 90:1).

Educational finance since fee abolition may be characterized in the following seven ways:

1. Developmental function
2. Democratization function
3. Prioritization
4. Diversification of sources
5. Cost sharing
6. Community participation and private investment
7. Decentralized financial management and resource flow.

DEVELOPMENTAL FUNCTION

The central role of financing education in Ethiopia is to speed up socio-economic development and to enhance the building of a democratic nation. According to the prevailing Ethiopian ethos, it is desirable and expected that all citizens must be involved and make constructive and effective contributions. To allow citizens to realize this mandate, access to primary education is imperative. The Ethiopian Constitution states that "to the extent the country's resources permit, policies shall aim to provide all Ethiopians access to public education" (Article 90:1). To create learned citizens who play an active role in the economic, sociocultural, and political process of nation building, fundamental problems such as education finance must be resolved through thoughtful policy guides and strategies.

Besides its obligation to meet the social demand of education, Ethiopia believes that much of its underdevelopment syndrome could be resolved by alleviating the dire limitations in implementation capacity. As Ethiopia believes capacity building is a major tool of development (MoFED 2002), it is the rationale for issuing the Capacity Building Strategy and Programs in 2002, along with the establishment of a Ministry of Capacity Building to ensure its implementation. Education and training are therefore mandated to realize this economic dimension of development. This is also the basic reason for prioritizing education and training in the budgetary allocations.

Therefore, in a situation where the system of education had numerous formidable problems—such as limited access, inequitable distribution of schooling, internal and external inefficiencies, lack of quality and relevance, undemocratic content, and manpower deficiencies—sound policy and concerted direction is required. Such complex problems require a sound financial system. For this reason, financing is considered an important aspect of the policy of overall reform for education and training.

DEMOCRATIZATION (EQUITY) FUNCTION

The focus of the financial system with regard to Ethiopian education is that educational services should be accessible to all. Accordingly, the government has the responsibility "to provide free education for all that are willing to learn" at the primary tier of education (GFDRE 2002). People are not obliged to pay for their primary and general secondary education, that is, grades 1 to 10.

As pointed out earlier, "free" education attempts to change a system that allows access to schooling to those who can afford it and denies the opportunity to the poor. Hence, according to the capacity-building policy, it is the government's duty to provide the means to make primary education accessible to all.

PRIORITIZATION

Prioritization of financial allocation is another guiding principle of policy implementation. Under this principle, the government's priority is primary education. Accordingly, the bulk of the budget is devolved to the grassroots level to be managed by the woredas.

The Education and Training Policy of 1994 states that "the priority for government financial support will be up to the completion of general secondary education and related training (grade 10) with increased cost sharing at higher levels of education and training" (TGE 1994b, Article 3.9.1).

Both the Constitution and the Education and Training Policy, together with the Education Sector Strategy, have focused on resource limitation and thus emphasized the need to prioritize the allocation of resources in education. This is all that is stated about free education in these documents; one may need to study other strategy and program documents to derive more specificity.

Another guide to policy is the Capacity Building Strategy and Programs, issued in February 2002. The document clearly highlights that general education (grades 1–10) should be free in government schools and that "the government has the obligation to facilitate conditions and provide free education for all that are willing to learn" (GFDRE 2002, 31).

DIVERSIFICATION OF SOURCES

As the government alone cannot shoulder the immense educational expenditure of the country, the private sector and the community are expected to play a vital role in supporting the educational system financially and administratively. Private educational institutions were strongly encouraged by incentives such as free land to investors.

The CSAE study (1997) asserts that "although the government (GFDRE) has committed a large share of its budget for education in general and primary education in particular, the sector will remain underfinanced as long as it is almost exclusively dependent on the public sector." Thus, it needs to diversify the sources of finance and institutionalize cost-recovery schemes wherever possible" (184).

The Capacity Building Strategy and Programs elaborates the four main sources of finance as the following: the government allocation (consolidated budget from treasury, external loan, and grant), community contribution, internal revenue generation, and private education.

COST SHARING

Although the government is committed to giving priority to education spending, it believes that the share of the other three sources should gradually grow and account for a considerable segment of the expenditure together with what accrues from the cost-sharing mechanism for all students above grade 10.

The new Education and Training Policy has also encouraged schools and institutions of higher education to generate income through production and service activities. Besides these, community support in cash, materials, or labor was combined with revenue from cost sharing in higher education and upper secondary levels to supplement the main source of finance—that is, the combined funds from the government, private sources, and the internal income of the school itself. School fees were abolished in principle as of the 1995/96 academic year, but other contributions were encouraged by the decentralized management to serve this mandate. According to the CSAE study, "User fees in education should exist in Ethiopia given the underfinancing of education, but preferably not at the primary school level in rural areas" (1997).

Cost sharing is part of the strategy of financing education. It has already been launched in all regions. From grade 11 onwards, cost sharing is being introduced to the schools and colleges with three basic considerations. First, the cost-sharing policy should be introduced gradually. This means that the payment may progress step by step with time and each successive level of schooling based on society's capacity to pay. Second, the cost sharing should be introduced by each woreda after thorough assessment of the capability of the parents. Third, no student should be excluded from school because parents cannot pay the prescribed contribution. Table 2.10 illustrates the level of cost sharing above grade 10 in four regions.

Table 2.10 Cost-Sharing Payment
(birr per student)

Level	Oromia	Amhara	Addis Ababa	Tigray
Grade 11	40–50	60.0	150	37–50
Grade 12	40–50	60.0	150	37–50
10 + 1	40–50	175.3	250	50
10 + 2	40–50	175.3	250	50
10 + 3	40–50	—	350	—
University	100% boarding and lodging, 15% tuition			

Source: Bureaus of Education (Oromia, Amhara, Addis Ababa, and Tigray).

In 2006 the payment recommended by MoE was not followed strictly by the regions. All students above grade 11 were involved in this scheme of partial cost recovery of education. Although secondary and tertiary education are not within the scope of this study, it is important to think, in clear and concrete terms, how the money generated in one subsector could benefit another subsector. The revenues from cost sharing at the second level of education were being utilized by the secondary schools. This is an important mechanism of resource allocation at a higher level of planning of resources for the sector. The Council of Ministers issued Higher Education Cost Sharing Regulation Number 91/2003 in September 2003, which stipulates the following:

- All higher education students shall share full cost related to boarding and lodging and a minimum of 15 percent of tuition-related costs.
- They will sign contracts when they start their studies.
- They shall start paying back the amount within six months after graduation if earning income, or after a year in a form of graduate tax.

COMMUNITY PARTICIPATION AND PRIVATE INVESTMENT

The Education and Training Policy and the Education Sector Strategy, together with the Capacity Building Strategy and Programs, maintain that community participation should play an important role in education financing. Accordingly, the system of education, and in particular, primary education, is presently supported by the community. Some examples of community-generated support in 1997 EC (2004/05) in some regions are given below (see table 2.11). Community contribution is quite significant compared to the overall budget (capital and recurrent) and even more meaningful when compared only to the recurrent budget, although much of the contribution is usually for the capital budget, which is related mainly to construction.

Table 2.11   Community Contribution in Some Regions, 2004/05

Region	Community contribution (birr)	Percentage of total	Percentage of recurrent
Addis Ababa	33,500,000	1.8	4.9
SNNPR	63,000,000	4.7	5.7
Oromia	95,000,000	4.1	5.1
Amhara	117,400,000	7.6	9.2

Source: Computed from data obtained from each Bureau of Education.
Note: SNNPR = Southern Nations, Nationalities, and Peoples Region.

The findings of the 2006 Joint Review Mission draft report prepared on community participation in primary education include the following:

- PTAs have been a driving force in enhancing community participation.
- The contributions are aggregated into specific purposes.
- Total cost of primary education is being covered in the rural areas, although there are concerns about the quality (standards).
- Some communities also hire teachers, but at a much lower salary (ranging from one-quarter to one-half of the government scale).
- There are variations in payment among different places, but only parent households are required to pay. (Information is based on the schools visited).
- Contributions may be per student or per parent.
- Payment in the Southern Nations, Nationalities, and Peoples Region (SNNPR) "seems [like] registration fees" because it is done at the beginning of the year and is levied per capita while in other cases, payment is done after harvest.

The involvement of private investors is an important aspect of reducing the government's financial burden and allowing it to extend free education to the poorest areas and groups. The number of private schools increased considerably because, on the one hand, the demand was pressing and, on the other hand, concrete incentives were taken, such as giving free land to build schools and importing teaching materials free of duty. For instance, enrollment increased in the nongovernment primary schools up to 494,029 (that is, about 4.8 percent of the total) in 2004/05. This implies that the contribution of private investors in the financing of primary education was about 4.8 percent. Similarly, according to the Educational Management Information System (EMIS) in 2005, about 3 percent of the enrollment in general secondary schools is in private schools.

DECENTRALIZED FINANCIAL MANAGEMENT AND RESOURCE FLOW

As discussed below, decentralization affects financial management and resource flow at the different administrative levels, from the central level down to the school level.

General Issues. In principle, the financial system of education in Ethiopia is an offspring of the overall system of governance. Federalism implies decentralization. The Capacity Building Strategy and Programs document states:

> A decentralized financial administration system is said to be desirable not only because it is the best option from the point of view of financial management, but also because it has been established that it is possible to build a democratic system in our country based on popular participation only when power is adequately shared with the lower hierarchies of the administration (GFDRE 2002, 34).

Accordingly, the government believes that "it is just impossible to maximize the participation of the people at the grassroots level under a centralized financial administration system" (GFDRE 2002).

It is in recognition of these principles that Ethiopia is trying to follow a highly decentralized system of management in general and devolved financial administration in particular. The first steps to implement decentralization are to share resources (the consolidated budget) fairly. As mentioned earlier, there is a formula of distribution of resources among the regions. Every region gets its share of the supplemental budget from the federal government by a formula issued by the House of Federation and implemented by MoFED. The formula has three basic criteria: population, development indexes, and the efforts of the region to increase their revenue.

Given Ethiopia's long tradition of highly centralized power, there was uproar when devolution to the regional states was effected in the early 1990s. Many technocrats did not believe that the regions would be able to manage their affairs. There is no longer any concern about decentralization to the regional states or zones, but rather to the lower strata of woredas and service centers, such as schools.

Legislative provisions and operational manuals and directives have been issued and distributed for implementation. One notable document is the *Directive for Educational Management, Organization, Public Participation, and Finance.* This document, which was prepared by the MoE in 2002, serves as a road map for the region to implement devolved management and decentralized finance (MoE 2002a).

It has been a few years since the phenomenon of block grants to woredas was introduced. To facilitate this decentralization process, budgetary and accounting systems are changing. All the regions have given block grants to woredas, following criteria that were generally similar but modified by each region according to its own context (details given below).

Decentralization at the Woreda Level. The administration of education paralleled the devolution of power to the regions, and thereby to zones, woredas, and kebeles.[3] Hence, all schools and training institutions, except the higher education institutions, were bound by law to operate under the woredas, with the WEO as a facilitating office.

Currently, the zone is neither a legislative nor a financial administrative stratum of the government. Its role is to coordinate with the regional administration in technical and political affairs. The zonal education office (ZEO) is responsible for supporting the woreda when specifically assigned by the region and for coordinating the distribution of material resources, such as textbooks, which are produced at the central level but purchased at the regional level.

The real nexus of decentralization in Ethiopian administration is at the woreda level. The WEO, in particular, is responsible for the following:

- Planning education of the woreda
- Ensuring standards and accreditation of institutions
- Implementing and evaluating projects
- Administrating primary and secondary schools
- Monitoring and supervising programs
- Enhancing community participation by establishing administrative boards, PTAS, and other committees
- Integrating and coordinating programs between schools
- Allocating budget to schools
- Capacity building of educational personnel in the woreda.

The WEO, which is administratively subordinate to the woreda council, is also professionally and technically answerable to the regional bureau of education. It is axiomatic that relations have to be fine-tuned whenever double subordination such as this exists. However, it is obvious that decentralization cannot be complete without either of the two aspects. Besides the structured line of responsibility, it is important to recall that one important aspect of decentralization is the principle of professionalization of the management by encouraging teachers to participate and to share responsibility (TGE 1994b, Articles 3.8.3 and 3.8.4).

The region gives block grants to woredas, and woredas give them to schools. In other words, the schools expect to receive block grants from the woredas to run their day-to-day activities, with the assistance of the kebele education and training board and PTAs. This is one of the most critical unfinished agendas in the process of decentralization (see the problems below).

Decentralization Up to the School Level. To function as cost centers, schools are required to prepare their annual plans and have them approved by the kebele education and training boards and forwarded to the woreda council (MoE 2002a).

Schools are organized into clusters with about five members. These clusters are instrumental in capacity building, supervision, experience sharing, resource supply and utilization improvement, curriculum enrichment, plan monitoring and evaluation, continuous professional upgrading, and teacher motivation. Schools can further decentralize and establish satellite schools of one or two beginning grades. In cases when young boys and girls are unable to join school because of distance, the schools send teachers to the students. In regions like Amhara, the community provides for the facilities and salaries of the teachers of alternative basic education (ABE). When the girls and boys mature, they can join the mother school if the satellite itself has not grown and been established on its own merits as a full-fledged school.

The government has decided to give block grants to schools to replace the money from fee collection. The regional governments give woredas their total annual budget in lump sums using three basic criteria with varying weights, namely, the population of the woreda, the socioeconomic indexes of the woreda, and the efforts of the woreda to generate revenue.

However, the MoE in its "Directive for Educational Management, Organization, Public Participation, and Finance" (2002a) and its strategy on "Financing Technical and Vocational Education and Training [TVET] in Ethiopia" (2003b) proposed block grants from woredas to each school with a recommended rate of allocation as follows:

- Br 10 for grades 1–4 (per year per student)
- Br 15 for grades 5–8 (per year per student)
- Br 20 for grades 9–10 (per year per student)
- Br 50 for grades 11–12 (per year per student)
- Br 62 for grades 10+1 (per month per student)
- Br 84 for grades 10+2 (per month per student).

These recommended minimum figures match the preexisting annual school fees, as presented in the section on Abolition of School Fees. Thus, in principle, this match makes the policy realistic from many angles (see table 2.2).

According to the MoE, the government budget allocation to schools serves three major functions:

1. Ensures that schools possess the minimum financial requirement to conduct the teaching and learning process
2. Ensures that the block grant credited to a school is equitably apportioned

3. Ensures that with the help of the grant the community sense of ownership is further enhanced with its participation in monetary and nonmonetary terms.

The "Directive for Educational Management, Organization, Public Participation, and Finance" (MoE 2002a) set out the responsibility between the WEO and the school: capital and salary components would be managed by WEOs, and nonsalary recurrent expenditures would be managed by the schools. In principle the woreda council, which gives the budget to the WEOs and the schools, adheres to this directive except that it does not strictly follow the recommended rates presumably because of resource limitations. In Amhara, for example, the woreda provides an itemized grant of Br 5 per student for both levels of the primary schools, whereas Tigray forwards Br 10 for both levels. Addis Ababa claims to allocate Br 10 and Br 15 for grades 1 to 4 and 5 to 8, respectively. Education officials observe that woreda councils tend to hold on to schools' budgets and process procurements on behalf of the schools with the rationale that the latter do not have the capacity—the struggle is ongoing, but the woreda councils seem to be giving in gradually.

CONSTRAINTS AND CHALLENGES

Regional bureau heads of education believe that decentralization, together with fee abolition, have revolutionized access to and community ownership of education. They say that PTAs can creatively calculate incurred cost; at times they prefer younger teachers to senior ones as they are paid the least possible for a comparable level of service. However, the JRM and other studies point out that the decentralized system of finance has critical problems. These occur at the federal, regional, woreda, and school levels. Some of the challenges are listed below.

SOME CHALLENGES AT THE FEDERAL AND REGIONAL LEVELS

- Given the growing importance of inclusion in preschool education and of the pressing problem of orphans and vulnerable children in and out of school, a policy guide is needed to deal with the scope of free education and EFA.
- The enrollment surge in access to primary education will, in the foreseeable future, result in rapid growth of the second level of education.
- The problem of opportunity costs as an impediment to universal primary education needs further and continuous research.

- Decentralization is instrumental to democratic management, but if responsibilities such as education finance are left completely to sub-national governments, decentralization may produce inequities, as observed in Mexico and Nigeria. Therefore, rigorous and continuous resource flow and utilization analysis is required.

CHALLENGES AT THE WOREDA LEVEL

- Currently many posts at woredas, especially remote ones, are not filled with the requisite number of qualified personnel. Both the JRMs of 2003 and 2004 have concluded that many woredas are understaffed; and among woredas with adequate staffing, a number of the personnel are underqualified. As a result of this problem, Amhara is trying to reduce staffing of WEOs by half. In 2004, even the woredas in Addis had less than 50 percent of the required staff in place.
- A problem related to staffing is the delay in responses to or from the woreda. Directors complain about delays in financial and other resource flows to the schools.
- Some woredas are draining staff from schools by recruiting them to the offices.
- Although the woreda pool system is sound, the poor flow of information from the "all-sector-serving" offices in the woreda council to the education sectors makes communication difficult. This was, for example, experienced during the preparation of this chapter. Regional education bureau heads should readily receive financial information from the WEOs.
- Block grants are not given to the schools yet—and, as a result, the woredas are overtasked.
- Woreda allocations of nonsalary budget vary among schools, indicating that a standard unit cost is lacking at present.

SOME CHALLENGES AT THE SCHOOL LEVEL

- Schools are overpopulated and often have insufficient space and resources required to meet standards.
- School leaders say that the fee-free education policy has relieved them from the fee-collection routine, but as the resources they receive from woredas are insufficient, they have been engaged in the tedious job of project preparations and other fundraising activities to supplement operational costs.

- There are many orphans and vulnerable children (OVC) whom the school leadership and the PTAs must handle. Sertse Dingil School in Bahir Dar has 438 orphans, 18 percent of the student population. Similarly the rural-based Zenzelima School has 138 or 6.7 percent orphans.
- Delay of supplies and finance from the woredas is another serious problem.

LESSONS LEARNED

According to the Ethiopian experience, changes in the financial policies of education are implemented without political problems when they are applied holistically, as part of the larger socioeconomic context. School fee abolition is only a small element in a system of interrelated national policies of poverty reduction and sustainable development that strives for democracy and good governance. Consequently, programs do not succeed unless they are supported by diverse, integrated, and innovative methods of implementation. A case in point is that fee abolition alone could not have been as successful in expanding access without the following: (a) the policy of decentralization; (b) curricular reform and vernacular language application; and (c) innovative programs such as the alternative basic education satellite school system, school feeding program, pastoral education package, and nonformal education.

In a decentralized system, policy implementation is a slow process, but it is a certain way to reach targets. This is because continuous consultations are required with stakeholders for consensus.

The rapid rise in enrollment as a result of school fee abolition and other factors, like school construction and community involvement, has raised other serious challenges. These include crowded classes and overworked teachers, and hence, quality and school discipline problems.

The alleviation of the small but direct costs of schooling for children from poor families in the form of fee abolition has greatly affected enrollment. Administrators must be careful in differentiating between community contributions and capitation payments. The residual fees in some schools may serve as warnings in this regard.

Size of enrollments should be the major criterion for resource allocation. Local authorities, such as the WEOs, must strictly monitor by setting standard units of allocation.

In a decentralized system, an effective mechanism of communication of financial information to the higher levels of management in education (regional bureaus of education and the Ministry of Education) is imperative to guarantee the necessary results.

The more communities contribute to education, the more the non-salary component of recurrent expenditure tends to decrease when fees are abolished. This requires close attention in instances of free government schooling.

Fee abolition may cause stress, such as overcrowded schools that require external sources of assistance.

THE WAY FORWARD WITH SCHOOL FEE ABOLITION

Fee-free primary and general secondary education in Ethiopia has sparked rapid growth in enrollment and created serious challenges in efficiency, quality, and financing. The problems with school fee abolition and their solutions should be viewed as one segment of the comprehensive education plan. These cannot be approached in a piecemeal manner. The abolition of school fees has created certain situations and trends that should be treated in the context of the Education Sector Development Program III (ESDP III) 2005/06–2009/10. This five-year plan encompasses all the elements that determine the way forward with school fee abolition.

Nevertheless, it is important to identify specific activities pertinent to school fee abolition and treat them explicitly. Accordingly, a number of activities and targets that are relevant to school fee abolition are envisaged.

ACCESS MODALITIES SHOULD BE MORE INCLUSIVE

To meet the grade 1 target net intake rate of 96 percent in 2011 (the end of ESDP III), the following enrollment activities will have to be undertaken.

Enhance the Alternative Basic Education Programs. ABE programs are critical as emergency short-term measures to accommodate the school fee abolition–triggered enrollment surge to achieve universal primary education by 2015, and to increase school access for the hard-to-reach, remote rural and dispersed communities, pastoralists, and semiagriculturalist societies.

To make school fee abolition effective through the ABE, there will be (a) condensed curriculum in the first cycle of primary education; (b) clearly defined student learning objectives; (c) continuous training of facilitators to plan, implement, and monitor; (d) encouragement by facilitators to communities, NGOs, and other local organizations to provide ABE; (e) modular approach in developing student textbooks and facilitator guides; (f) outreach to community leaders and local artisans to share their indigenous knowledge and skills with learners in the classroom; and (g) flexible implementation of ABE programs.

Use Multigrade Classes. Multigrade classes will be used to mitigate the shortage of teachers in fee-free schooling. Toward this end, the following will occur: (a) multigrade classes will be introduced to improve and maintain access to and internal efficiency of first-cycle primary schools in hard-to-reach areas; (b) appropriate training courses and materials will be developed to train multigrade teachers; (c) teachers will also be trained in pedagogy and management of multigrades and different-age students; and (d) textbooks will be modified so that many self-learning approaches and exercises are incorporated to meet the needs of multigrade class students—these will be distributed free of charge.

Make Pastoralists and Semiagriculturalists Better Beneficiaries of School Fee Abolition. This goal can be reached using the following methods: (a) curriculum will be localized to incorporate desirable social values, indigenous knowledge, and local issues (HIV/AIDS, gender, harmful traditional practices); (b) mobile as well as permanent village schools will be established, and community-based boarding schools and hostels will be constructed; (c) special attention will be given to increasing girls' participation, and the involvement of women in the management of such schools will be increased; (d) beneficiary communities will be involved in the selection of facilitators of these schools; and (e) teacher-training institutions will be organized to train paraprofessionals, and they will be required to improve their admission criteria for trainees from these communities.

Arrange Special Program for Overage Children. School fee abolition has attracted a large number of overage children (81 percent of grade 1 students in 1995/96 were overage). In addition to the appropriate age of seven for children in grade 1, there are 4 million out-of-school children whose ages range from 8 to 14. Thus, the government has modified the curriculum and made it flexible to maintain its relevance to the target group and reduce the time required (eight years in the standard process) to complete primary education. Accordingly, a national guideline will be issued to address the GER target of over 100 percent.

Promote Adult and Nonformal Education. In the course of the five-year plan, 5.2 million adults will be reached through the functional adult literacy program.

Enhance the Special-Needs Component of Education. The special-needs education strategy developed by the MoE defines the following priorities: (a) prepare special-needs education (SNE) plans; (b) develop guidelines for support systems; (c) prepare professional support for the SNE teacher-education program; (d) improve curriculum; (e) establish support system in the regions; and (f) identify and share good practices among the woredas and schools.

HIV/AIDS AND EDUCATION OF ORPHANS AND VULNERABLE CHILDREN

The needs of orphans and vulnerable children (OVC) are both varied and huge. School fee abolition alone cannot address these needs. The provision of special, targeted support that complements fee abolition is required. For example:

- In collaboration with development partners, the provision of school feeding programs in food-insecure areas needs to be scaled up. (The program has so far increased enrollment, reduced dropouts, and increased efficiency.)
- Responsible government agencies and development partners will develop strategies and programs that embrace orphaned students and out-of-school children.
- Situation analysis of OVC in each region and at all levels of the education system will be conducted to ensure access to schooling.
- Organize OVC coordinating bodies at all levels of educational management.
- Launch series of nationwide advocacy campaigns and sensitization activities on care, support, and education of OVC.
- Strengthen the technical capacity of community-based supporters and implementers of OVC (training, coaching, and supervision).
- Establish a matching grant–community-support fund for OVC (may be administered by selected and already active NGOs).
- Obtain minimum quality standards for care and support of OVC (in collaboration with relevant authorities such as the Ministry of Health, Ministry of Labor and Social Affairs, and the Ethiopian Commission for Human Rights).
- Facilitate the development of culturally sensitive and appropriate information education and communication (IEC) and behavioral change communication materials on care and support of OVC.
- Facilitate the establishment of educational support groups for orphans.
- Revitalize existing, culturally valued, community-based orphan fostering and educating mechanisms through support of voluntary caregivers.
- Solicit volunteers to care for orphans.
- Organize volunteer neighborhood committees of pensioners to care for orphans (experience in Dire Dawa).
- Provide school materials and uniforms for orphans (UNICEF).
- Give financial support to caregiving families (UNICEF's program in Dire Dawa).

- Provide school-based counseling for orphans through trained teachers (North Gonder).

The following concrete arrangements are planned to address the concerns mentioned above:

- Workplace policy and implementation guidelines will be in place.
- HIV/AIDS will be integrated into all aspects of educational planning and management, including projection of teachers' demands for all levels. Training and recruitment of teachers shall take into account teachers' sensitivity and attention to HIV/AIDS issues.
- Key persons will be designated, and coordinating committees will be established at the federal, regional, woreda, and school or institution level for effective management and coordination of HIV/AIDS activity in the education sector.
- Existing curriculum will be strengthened by offering life skills–based HIV/AIDS prevention.
- All teacher-education programs will incorporate HIV/AIDS messages and preventive measures.
- Systematic data collection will be in place to understand the scope and effect of HIV/AIDS on students, teachers, and administrative staff.
- Anti-HIV/AIDS clubs will be strengthened to promote peer education and minimize fear and discrimination.
- More attention will be given to children ages 5–14 (window of hope), young girls, and orphaned students.

ENHANCE COMMUNITY PARTICIPATION

School fee abolition has greatly boosted enrollment; to cope with the challenges of resource limitations, the community must:

- Participate in the construction and management of schools and ABE centers.
- Contribute labor, local materials, and cash based on own capacity and initiative for the construction of schools and ABE centers.
- Raise money to cover part of nonsalary expenditure of schools as required and as capacity allows.
- Be involved (through PTAs) in the day-to-day management of schools, which includes monitoring student attendance and performance discipline to reduce dropouts and make schools child-friendly, especially for girls.

PROMOTE THE CONSTRUCTION OF LOW-COST SCHOOLS AND CLASSROOMS

The low-cost construction of 194,748 furnished and equipped additional classrooms for increased enrollment must make substantial use of local materials and labor. Communities' direct involvement in school construction will lead to effective participation in maintenance and management of the schools. Revised alternative models will be provided to the communities.

IMPROVE QUALITY AND EFFICIENCY OF EDUCATION

The most critical challenge for SFAI was the effect on the quality of education. To improve quality:

- Curriculum will be revised for today and for the citizen of the future.
- Students' achievements will be monitored by national educational assessments.
- School improvement program with a focus on school leadership and management, parent and community partnership, student-centered learning, professional development and collaboration, and quality instruction will be implemented. A guide to this program will be developed.
- Educational inspection will be strengthened.
- Public examinations will give feedback to improve quality.
- Diverse measures will be taken to ensure the availability of qualified and committed teachers. In the first and second primary cycles, the share of qualified teachers will be 99.8 percent and 99.3 percent, respectively. A total of 294,760 additional teachers (168,847 first cycle and 125,913 second cycle) will be recruited to take care of the additional enrollment and reduce pupil-teacher ratios.
- Textbook-pupil ratio will be 1:1. There will be a liberal provision of textbooks: 146.9 million copies will be printed and distributed to schools.
- Schools will be provided with an adequate nonsalary recurrent budget so that they can purchase and use the necessary instructional materials. The nonsalary recurrent budget will constitute 39.5 percent of the recurrent budget.
- Pupil-section ratio in both primary cycles will be reduced to 1:50.
- Similarly, one teacher will be provided for 45–50 students.
- Improving quality indicators will improve efficiency by reducing dropouts and repetition.

- Continuous assessment will be strictly conducted.
- To increase students' time-on-task, the shift system will gradually be decreased through additional construction.

GENDER EQUITY

School fee abolition and other policies are expected to meet the year 2011 target of 49.3 percent of girls in total net enrollment in the primary school (grades 1–8). To achieve this goal, the following targets are set:

- Develop reference materials that present women role models
- Expand adult literacy programs to enhance parents' awareness for girls' education
- Set up a system so that management is accountable for addressing the harassment of girls in schools
- Celebrate "Girls' Day" in schools
- Allow any girl who leaves school (after completing grade 10) to be entitled for training (TVET)
- Strengthen counseling services for girls
- Provide tutorial services and special support for female students
- Incorporate gender training as part of the preservice teacher-training program
- Organize female education forums.

FINANCING EDUCATION

The following conditions must be realized for the provision of fee-free education (see also annex 2C):

- During the planning period, education will be treated as the priority sector.
- The education share of GDP in 2003/04, 3.1 percent, will grow to over 7 percent in 2009/10, and allocation will grow from Br 5 billion to Br 10.9 billion in 2009/10. Additionally, community contribution is expected to reach Br 1.13 billion by the final year of the plan. However, both these sources add up to only 85 percent of the required total cost.
- The remainder, 15 percent of the cost (about Br 2.1 billion in 2009/10), is expected from bilateral and multilateral partners.
- Within the sector, primary education is the priority subsector and should receive a share of 55 percent.

ANNEX 2A: BACKGROUND STATISTICS

Table 2A.1   Types of Fees (Mean) Reportedly Charged per Year by Government and Nongovernment Schools

Type of school	Grade	Types of fees by grade and amount (birr)							
		Tuition fee	Annual registration	Construction	Instructional materials	Text books	Uniforms	Sports	Other fees
Government	1	1.00	6.10	1.00	0.00	0.00	0.00	0.90	0.80
	2	1.00	5.80	1.00	0.00	0.10	0.00	0.60	0.80
	3	1.00	6.20	1.00	0.00	0.70	0.00	0.50	0.80
	4	1.00	6.30	1.00	0.00	0.90	0.00	0.70	1.00
	5	1.00	6.60	1.00	0.00	0.90	0.00	0.50	1.00
	6	2.00	6.80	1.00	1.00	0.90	0.00	0.50	0.80
	7	0.00	10.00	1.00	1.00	2.00	0.00	0.50	0.80
	8	0.00	10.00	0.00	1.00	2.00	0.00	0.50	0.80
	9	0.00	14.00	1.00	1.00	2.00	3.00	0.60	1.70
	10	0.00	14.00	1.00	1.00	2.00	3.00	0.60	1.70
	11	0.00	15.00	1.00	1.00	2.00	4.00	0.60	1.80
	12	0.00	15.00	1.00	1.00	2.00	5.00	0.60	1.80
Nongovernment	1	80.00	15.10	2.00	1.00	0.00	14.00	0.70	13.20
	2	81.00	15.10	2.00	1.00	0.70	14.00	0.70	15.80
	3	82.00	15.10	2.00	1.00	0.70	14.00	0.70	3.20
	4	94.00	15.50	2.00	1.00	0.90	14.00	0.70	16.10
	5	94.00	15.60	2.00	0.00	0.90	14.00	0.70	16.10
	6	91.00	16.40	2.00	0.00	26.80	6.00	0.70	14.50
	7	135.00	22.00	2.00	0.00	47.00	8.00	0.60	23.00
	8	138.00	22.00	2.00	0.00	50.00	8.00	0.60	23.00
	9	481.00	74.00	0.00	8.00	383.00	22.00	0.80	54.50
	10	483.00	74.00	0.00	8.00	563.00	0.00	0.80	54.50
	11	486.00	74.00	0.00	8.00	693.00	0.00	0.80	54.50
	12	489.00	69.00	0.00	8.00	700.00	0.00	0.50	54.50

Source: Survey of Educational Facilities (Policy and Human Resource Development [PHRD], Project Office 1996).
Note: "0" indicates that no fee was charged. The mean fee collected from students for maintenance was "0," and it is excluded from this table.

Table 2A.2   Types of Schools by Ownership and Management, 2006

Governance	Type of school	Ownership
Government	Government schools	Local, regional, or federal government
Nongovernment	Public schools	Organized local community
	Private schools	Private profit making
	Religious and NGO schools	Charitable organizations
	International community schools	Diplomatic corps schools

Source: Ministry of Education.

**Table 2A.3   Grade 1 Intake of Government Schools,
1985/86–2004/05**

Year (EC)	Student intake	Annual increase (percent)
1985/86 (1978)	749,373	Base year
1986/87 (1979)	905,188	20.79
1987/88 (1980)	917,701	1.38
1988/89 (1981)	829,849	−9.57
1989/90 (1982)	719,660	−13.28
1990/91 (1983)	606,139	−15.77
1991/92 (1984)	530,570	12.47
1992/93 (1985)	572,998	8.00
1993/94 (1986)	840,061	46.61
1994/95 (1987)	1,033,956	23.08
1995/96 (1988)	1,349,527	30.52
1996/97 (1989)	1,534,643	13.72
1997/98 (1990)	1,679,350	9.43
1998/99 (1991)	1,775,413	5.72
1999/2000 (1992)	1,884,949	6.17
2000/01 (1993)	1,979,718	5.03
2001/02 (1994)	1,975,182	−0.23
2002/03 (1995)	2,009,131	1.72
2003/04 (1996)	2,346,060	16.77
2004/05 (1997)	3,236,814	37.97

Source: MoE "Education Statistics Annual Abstracts."
Note: EC = Ethiopian calendar.

Table 2A.4   Regional Recurrent Expenditure and Budget of Education, 1997 and 1998

	Addis Ababa				Tigray			
	1997 EC (expenditure)		1998 EC (budget)		1997 EC (expenditure)		1998 EC (budget)	
Item	Birr	Percent	Birr	Percent	Birr	Percent	Birr	Percent
Total education (recurrent)	143,106,622	100	180,660,034	100	189,690,000	100	233,630,000	100.0
Total primary (recurrent)	68,241,454	48	87,728,963	49	129,640,000	68	141,730,000	60.7
Primary salary (recurrent)	62,096,765	91	79,000,062	90	120,340,000	93	133,880,000	94.5
Primary nonsalary (recurrent)	6,144,689	9	8,728,901	10	9,300,000	7	7,800,000	5.5

Source: Bureaus of Education (Addis Ababa and Tigray).
Note: EC = Ethiopian calendar.

Table 2A.5   Secondary Education Growth Indicators, 1994/95–2004/05

Year (EC)	Gross enrollment rate (percent)	Pupil-section ratio	Pupil-teacher ratio	Female (percent)
1994/95 (1987)	6.6	63:1	33:1	44.3
1995/96 (1988)	8.1	63:1	33:1	43.2
1996/97 (1989)	8.4	65:1	35:1	41.5
1997/98 (1990)	8.9	68:1	38:1	40.9
1998/99 (1991)	9.7	71:1	40:1	40.6
1999/2000 (1992)	10.3	75:1	43:1	40.8
2000/01 (1993)	12.9	78:1	46:1	41.5
2001/02 (1994)	17.1	80:1	49:1	39.3
2002/03 (1995)	19.3	77:1	45:1	36.6
2003/04 (1996)	22.1	79:1	48:1	(35.3)
2004/05 (1997)	27.3	78:1	51:1	(35.7)

Source: MoE "Education Statistics Annual Abstracts."
Note: The data for 2003/04 and 2004/05 for females are for grades 9–10. EC = Ethiopian calendar.

Table 2A.6   Capital and Recurrent Expenditure of Education in Ethiopia, 1994/95–2004/05

Year (EC)	Total expenditure of general education and TVET (birr)	General education and TVET enrollment	Expenditure per student (birr)
1994/95 (1987)	876.37	3,159.700	277.33
1995/96 (1988)	974.15	3,870,840	251.72
1996/97 (1989)	1,120.40	4,563,609	245.70
1997/98 (1990)	1,146.27	5,233,445	219.17
1998/99 (1991)	1,599.81	5,912,411	270.70
1999/2000 (1992)	1,501.64	6,706,945	223.79
2000/01 (1993)	1,834.13	7,803,176	239.42
2001/02 (1994)	1,867.47	8,318,870	224.46
2002/03 (1995)	2,024.10	8,834,746	228.97
2003/04 (1996)	2,236.50	9,707,260	230.33
2004/05 (1997)	2,597.08	11,715,717	221.78

Source: MoE "Education Statistics Annual Abstracts."
(Federal Ministry of Education budget not included.)
Note: EC = Ethiopian calendar; TVET = technical and vocational education and training.

Table 2A.7 Recurrent Expenditure of Some Schools, 1997

Name of school	Region	No. of classrooms	No. of students	No. of teachers	Total expenditure (birr)	Wage and salary (birr)	Operational expense (birr)	Location
Meskerem	Addis Ababa	25	1,673	45	491,446	420,236	71,210	Capital city
Minilik Primary	Addis Ababa	35	3,570	116	1,480,781.54	1,407,989.76	72,791.78	Capital city
Sertse Dingil	Amhara	24	2,437	52	767,024	687,756	79,268	Regional city
Yewket Fana	Amhara	32	2,793	59	572,409	498,384	74,025	Regional city
Zenzelima	Amhara	27	1,900	25	260,607	250,932	9,675	Rural
Adi Haki	Tigray	17	2,065	35	450,636.02	404,772	45,864.02	Regional city
Lekatit 23	Tigray	20	1,218	20	252,711	232,192	20,519	Regional city
Romanat	Tigray	9	910	24	140,155.25	127,740	12,415.25	Rural
Dima	Oromia	12	1,867	28	241,346	229,452	11,894.5	Small town
Total		201	18,433	404	4,657,115.81	4,259,453.76	397,662.55	

Source: Field survey.

Table 2A.8 Recurrent Budget of Some Schools, 1998

Name of school	Region	No. of classrooms	No. of students	No. of teachers	Total budget (birr)	Wage and salary (birr)	Operational expense (birr)	Location
Meskerem	Addis Ababa	25	1,673	46	754,100	673,400	80,600	Capital city
Minilik Primary	Addis Ababa	35	3,478	114	1,140,804.88	1,119,680.14	21,124.74	Capital city
Sertse Dingil	Amhara	24	2,420	53	756,889	697,800	59,089	Regional city
Yewket Fana	Amhara	32	3,081	54	683,716	663,818	19,898	Regional city
Zenzelima	Amhara	27	2,059	31	435,798	416,796	19,002	Rural
Adi Haki	Tigray	17	2,101	34	532,311.83	473,544	58,767.83	Regional city
Lekatit 23	Tigray	20	1,485	27	381,416	355,776	25,640	Regional city
Romanat	Tigray	9	1,330	33	298,465.57	274,548	23,917.57	Rural
Dima	Oromia	12	1,568	30	299,012	292,512	6,500	Small town
Total		201	19,195	422	5,282,513.28	4,967,874.14	314,539.14	

Source: Field survey.

Table 2A.9 Primary Education Learning Assessment Results, 1999 and 2004
(percent)

Grade	Subject							Composite
	Reading	English	Math	Env. Sci	Biology	Chemistry	Physics	
Ethiopian National Baseline Learning Assessment, 1999								
Grade 4	64.3	40.5	39.3	48.4	n.a.	n.a.	n.a.	n.a.
Grade 8	n.a.	38.7	n.a.	n.a.	47.2	40.3	n.a.	n.a.
Ethiopian Second National Learning Assessment, 2004								
Grade 4	64.9	38.7	39.7	51.7	n.a.	n.a.	n.a.	48.5
Grade 8	n.a.	41.1	n.a.	n.a.	41.3	40.1	35.3	39.7

Source: NOE 2000, 2001, 2004a, 2004b.
Note: n.a. = not applicable.

ANNEX 2B: THE EDUCATION SECTOR DEVELOPMENT PROGRAM

The second Education Sector Development Program (ESDP II) spans the three years from 2002/03 to 2004/05 and gives priority to the quality of education. The targets set for 2004/05 and the achievements (status) for the same year are presented in table 2B.1.

ANNEX 2C: THE PRESENT SYSTEM OF EDUCATION AND ITS IMPLICATIONS FOR FINANCING

The following are some systemic characteristics of the education sector that have direct or indirect bearing on the financing of the system in general and school fees in particular.

STRUCTURE AND CURRICULUM

The 1994 policy replaced the old structure of general education from 6-2-4 to 8-2-2 by making the following changes:

- Kindergarten for children, ages 4–6 years
- Primary education (ages 7–14 years) of grades 1 to 8 subdivided into two cycles: the first cycle of basic education from grade 1 to grade 4 and the second cycle of basic education from grade 5 to grade 8
- General secondary education for grades 9 and 10
- Preparatory senior secondary education for grades 11 and 12 and parallel certificate program of 10 + 1 and 10 + 2 TVET system
- Higher education diploma program of 10 + 3 (or equivalent) and first degree program of 3 to 5 years after grade 12
- Postgraduate studies toward master's and doctoral degrees.

In addition to the formal system, integrated and parallel subsystems of nonformal programs of education and training, special education, and different delivery mechanisms such as distance education complement the entire structure of the system.

The curriculum at all levels should incorporate the general knowledge of basic and transferable cognition as well as specialized skills to fit the manpower requirement of the country and promote the right mix of values to build a harmonious democratic "nation of nations" (Nahum 1997).

The design of the curriculum is aimed at the following:

- Preparing productive and problem-solving citizens who stand for equality, justice, and democracy

Table 2B.1   Performance Indicators of the Ethiopian System of Education

Number	Suggested indicators	Base year 2000/01	Status of 2004/05	Target set for 2004/05
1	*Budget and expenditure*			
	Education's share of the total budget (current FY) (percent)	13.8	16.7[a]	19.0
2	*Access*			
	Gross enrollment rate at primary (1–8) level (percent)	57.4	79.8	65.0
	Girls (percent)	47.0	71.5	57.0
	Boys (percent)	67.3	88.0	72.8
	Total number of primary schools	11,780	16,513	13,201
	Gross enrollment rate at secondary (9–10) level (percent)	14.1	27.3	16.0
	Girls (percent)	12.1	19.8	14.4
	Boys (percent)	16.1	34.6	17.0
	Number admitted to technical and vocational education and training	25,000	51,845	55,000
	Number admitted to undergraduate program (degree)	13,000	31,997	30,000
	Number admitted to graduate program (MSc, MA, PhD & Spec.)	900	4,836	6,000
	Share of female students in higher education enrollment	21.4	24.4	30.0
3	*Quality*			
	Share of lower primary (1–4) teachers who are qualified (percent)	96.6	97.1	99.0
	Share of upper primary (5–8) teachers who are qualified (percent)	23.9	54.8	80.0
	Share of secondary (9–12) teachers who are qualified (percent)	36.5	40.6	73.2
	Primary school student-textbook ratio	2.5	—	1.0
	Secondary school student-textbook ratio	1.5	—	1.0
	Grade 4 sample assessment of learning achievement	47.0	—	50.0
4	*Efficiency*			
	Primary school student-section ratio	70	69	60
	Secondary (9–12) school student-section ratio	78	78	60
	Grade 1 dropout rate (percent)	27.9	22.4[b]	14.2
	Total primary school dropout rate (percent)	17.8	14.4[b]	8.9
	Average primary school dropout rate for girls (percent)	16.9	13.6[b]	8.5
	Average grade 4 to 8 repetition rate (percent)	10.3	5.3[b]	6.4
	Average grade 4 to 8 repetition rate for girls (percent)	13.4	6.2[b]	8.1
	Coefficient of primary school efficiency (percent)	31.8	49.2	50.0
5	*Equity*			
	Gross primary enrollment rate in the two most underserved regions (percent):			
	Afar	11.5	20.9	20.0
	Somali	10.6	23.3	20.0
	Share of girls in primary school enrollment (1–8) (percent)	40.3	44.2	43.3

Source: MoE 2005b.
— Not available.
a. Provisional expenditure of 2004/05.
b. Data from 2003/04.

- Harmonizing theory and practice (praxis)
- Integrating national and regional realities (that is, federal and state conditions)
- Maintaining international education standards
- Promoting the principles of nations, nationalities, and gender

One fundamental emphasis that bears directly on finance is that the curriculum should be practical and student-centered in approach so that it cultivates inquisitiveness and creativity in young girls and boys.

The other novelty in the curriculum is the shared responsibility between the federal and the regional state governments. The federal Ministry of Education prepared the draft syllabus and flow chart. It was then discussed and developed by professionals from the regions. Consequently, teachers' handbooks and the textbooks for grades 1 to 8 were produced by regions in the languages of their choice, while those for grade 9 and above were produced by the federal Ministry of Education with English as the medium of instruction. Therefore, over 23 vernacular languages are currently in use as media of instruction in the primary subsector of education.

ORGANIZATION AND MANAGEMENT

Under the auspices of federal administration, it was imperative to reorganize the management of education to make it democratic, decentralized, professional, and coordinated (GFDRE 2002). The power that was once centered in Addis Ababa was devolved to the lower echelons of administration, and responsibilities divided between the federal Ministry of Education and the regional bureaus of education as legally defined in Proclamation Number 260 and Number 471/2005. Knowledge of the division of major tasks between these management tiers may rationalize resource flow and administration. Generally, the MoE is responsible for the following:

- Setting education and training standards, and to ensure their implementation
- Formulating a general framework of curricula for education
- Setting minimum educational qualification requirements for primary and secondary school teachers
- Setting standards for vocational and technical training and certification
- Setting minimum standards for higher education institutions
- Establishing, expanding, and accrediting higher education institutions; and ensuring that they offer quality and relevant education
- Undertaking national programs to popularize education and training.

The regional bureau of education has the following responsibilities:

- Administering and directing education from kindergarten to the junior college level in line with the education policy of the country
- Strengthening and expanding education in the region
- Providing basic education for all
- Designing curriculum for primary education and kindergarten that is relevant to each region's specific needs and culture
- Building, rehabilitating, maintaining, and repairing educational establishments in the region
- Training, employing, managing, and firing teachers and other educational staff
- Supplying educational materials and equipment and issuing certificates
- Licensing the establishment of private institutions of education
- Initiating and enhancing the participation of the community at all levels

Figure 2C.1 The Governance Structure of Ethiopia

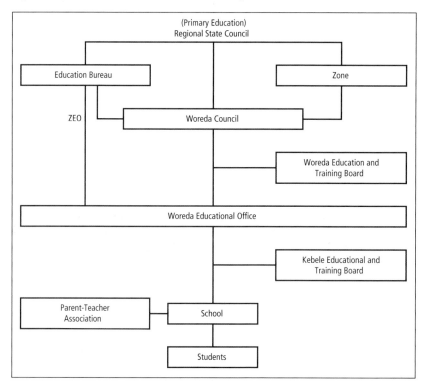

Source: Compiled by authors.

Table 2C.1 General Structure of the Regular System of Education, on the Basis of Education and Training Policy

Level	Age	Description	Curriculum	Medium	Direct supervision	Financial responsibility
Kindergarten	4–6	3 years of preschool education	Local	Vernacular	Regions	Household
Primary	7–14	1st cycle of basic education (1–4) and 2nd cycle of general primary education	Regional	Regional	Regions	Government
General secondary	15–16	2 years of general secondary education	Central	English	Regions	Government
Senior secondary	17–18	2 years of preparatory or preuniversity	Central	English	Regions	Cost sharing (parents)
TVET (certificate)	17/ 17–18	1, 2, or 3 years of training (i.e., 10 + 1 or 10 + 2)	Central	English	Regions	Cost sharing (parents)
TVET (diploma)	17–19	3 years of vocational technical training	Central	English	Regions	Cost sharing (graduate)
Higher education, 1st degree	19+	3–5 years of first degree education	Institutional	English	Federal	Cost sharing (graduate)
Higher education, postgraduate	22+	2 years of master's and 3 years of PhD programs	Institutional	English	Federal	Cost sharing (graduate)

Source: MoE 1996.
Note: TVET = technical and vocational education and training.

The zonal education office (ZEO), which is under the regional bureau of education, is further subdivided into woreda education offices. The proclamations do not clearly delineate the responsibilities of the ZEO, whereas those of the woredas are clearly set (see organization structure).

NOTES

1. *Woreda* is a small administrative unit in Ethiopia, equivalent to a district.
2. A *kebele* is the smallest administrative unit of Ethiopia, similar to a ward.
3. The Second Education Sector Development Program (ESDP II) covered the three-year period 2002/03–2004/05.

REFERENCES AND OTHER SOURCES

AED/BESO (Academy for Educational Development/Basic Education Strategic Objective) II Project and MoE (Ministry of Education). 2005. *Dropout and Repetition in the Primary Schools of Ethiopia.* Addis Ababa.

Berhanu, Befekadu, and T. Getahun. 2000/01. *Second Annual Report on the Ethiopian Economy.* Vol. 2. Addis Ababa: Ethiopian Economic Association.

Bray, Mark. 1996. *Counting the Full Cost: Parental and Community Financing of Education in East Asia.* Washington, DC: World Bank.

——. 1998. "Privatization of Secondary Education." In *Education for the Twenty-first Century,* corporate author, UNESCO. Paris: UNESCO.

——. 1999. *The Private Costs of Public Schooling.* Paris: UNESCO.

CSA (Central Statistical Agency). 2006. *Ethiopia: Statistical Abstract—2005.* Addis Ababa.

CSAE (Centre for the Study of African Economies), University of Oxford. 1997. *Federal Democratic Republic of Ethiopia: Social Sector Review/Public Expenditure Review (PER) III.* Vols. 1–3.

DTC (East African Development and Training Consultants). 1998. "Strategy to Encourage Private Investment in Education and Training." Policy of Human Resource Development (PHRD), Berhanena Selam, Addis Ababa.

ETER (Ethiopian Education Consultants). 1998. "Options for Sustainable Provision of Textbooks and Instructional Materials." Policy of Human Resource Development (PHRD), Berhanena Selam, Addis Ababa.

FDRE (Federal Democratic Republic of Ethiopia). 1995. *The Constitution of the Federal Democratic Republic of Ethiopia.* Addis Ababa.

GFDRE (Government of the Federal Democratic Republic of Ethiopia). 2002. "Capacity Building Strategy and Programs." Ministry of Information, Press and Audio-Visual Department (unofficial translation). Addis Ababa.

JRM (Joint Review Mission). 2003. *Ethiopia: Education Sector Development Report.*

——. 2004. *Ethiopia: Education Sector Development Program (ESDP) II Final Report.*

Kuawab Audit Services and Business Consultants. 1996a. "Cost and Financing of Education." Policy of Human Resource Development (PHRD), Educational Material Production and Distribution Agency (EMPDA), Addis Ababa.

——. 1996b. "Household Demand for Schooling." Policy of Human Resource Development (PHRD), Educational Material Production and Distribution Agency (EMPDA), Addis Ababa.

MoE (Ministry of Education), FDRE. 1996. "Education Statistics Annual Abstract 1987 EC (1994–95)." Addis Ababa.

——. 1997. "Education Statistics Annual Abstract 1988 EC (1995–96)." Addis Ababa.

——. 1998. "Education Statistics Annual Abstract 1989 EC (1996–97)." Addis Ababa.

——. 1999a. *Education Sector Development Program (ESDP I): Program Action Plan.* Addis Ababa: Central Printing Press.

——. 1999b. "Education Statistics Annual Abstract 1990 EC (1997–98)." Addis Ababa.

——. 1999c. "Education Statistics Annual Abstract 1991 EC (1998–99)." Addis Ababa.

——. 2000. "Education Statistics Annual Abstract 1992 EC (1999–2000)." Addis Ababa.

——. 2001. "Education Statistics Annual Abstract 1993 EC (2000–2001)." Addis Ababa.

——. 2002a. "Directive for Educational Management, Organization, Public Participation, and Finance." Addis Ababa.

——. 2002b. *Education Sector Development Program II (ESDP II) 2002/03–2004/05: Program Action Plan.* Addis Ababa: United Printers.

———. 2002c. "Education Statistics Annual Abstract 1994 EC (2001–02)." Addis Ababa.

———. 2002d. "The Education and Training Policy and Its Implementation." Addis Ababa.

———. 2003a. "Education Statistics Annual Abstract 1995 EC (2002–03)." Addis Ababa.

———. 2003b. "Financing Technical and Vocational Education and Training in Ethiopia: National Strategy to Raise Resources." Addis Ababa.

———. 2004. "Education Statistics Annual Abstract 1996 EC (2003–04)." Addis Ababa.

———. 2005a. "Education Sector Development Program III (ESDP III)." Addis Ababa.

———. 2005b. "Education Statistics Annual Abstract 1997 EC (2004–05)." Addis Ababa.

MoFED (Ministry of Finance and Economic Development), FDRE. 2002. "Ethiopia: Sustainable Development and Poverty Reduction Program." Addis Ababa.

Nahum, Fasil. 1997. *Constitution for a Nation of Nations: The Ethiopian Prospect.* Lawrenceville, N.J.: Red Sea Press.

NOE (National Organization for Examination). 2000. "Ethiopian National Baseline Assessment on Grade Four Pupils' Achievement." Addis Ababa.

———. 2001. "Ethiopian National Baseline Assessment on Grade Eight Students' Achievements." Addis Ababa.

———. 2004a. "Ethiopian Second National Learning Assessment of Grade Eight Students." Addis Ababa.

———. 2004b. "Ethiopian Second National Learning Assessment of Grade Four Students." Addis Ababa.

Peano, Serge. 1998. "The Financing of Education Systems." In *Education for the Twenty-first Century,* corporate author, UNESCO. Paris: UNESCO.

PHRD (Policy of Human Resource Development). 1996. *Education Sector Review: Synthesis and Summary.* Addis Ababa: Commercial Printing Enterprise.

TGE (Transitional Government of Ethiopia). 1993. "Atekalay Yetimhrtina Siltena Rekik Policy Mabrariya." Prime Minister's Office, Addis Ababa.

———. 1994a. "Education Sector Strategy." Addis Ababa.

———. 1994b. "Education and Training Policy." Educational Material Production and Distribution Agency (EMPDA), Addis Ababa.

Wolday, Amha. 1990. "Private and Social Return to Schooling." Policy of Human Resource Development (PHRD), Educational Material Production and Distribution Agency (EMPDA). Addis Ababa.

World Bank. 1995. *Priorities and Strategies for Education: A World Bank Review.* Washington, DC: World Bank.

———. 2004a. *Education in Ethiopia: Strengthening the Foundation for Sustainable Progress.* Washington, DC: World Bank.

———. 2004b. *Ethiopia, Public Expenditure Review, Volume III—Medium-Term Trends and Recent Developments in Public Spending.* Washington, DC: World Bank.

Ghana

CHAPTER 3

From Pilot to National Scale: Ghana's Experience with the Abolition of School Fees

The Free Compulsory Universal Basic Education (fCUBE) initiative in Ghana was launched in 1996 and enhanced through a Capitation Grant Scheme strategy in 2004/05, which was first piloted in deprived districts in Ghana, and then scaled at a national level in 2005/06. This study examines the design, planning, and implementation of the strategy, at the pilot and national levels, and concludes with lessons learned.

BACKGROUND TO EDUCATION PROGRAMMING AND SECTOR DEVELOPMENT

The Education Strategic Plan (ESP) (2003–15), which was developed in 2003, guides education sector development. As a long-term plan, it is consistent with and in support of the Growth and Poverty Reduction Strategy (GPRS). The ESP serves as the framework through which Ghana meets its commitment to achieve the Millennium Development Goals (MDGs)—namely, gender parity in primary schooling by 2005 and universal primary completion by 2015—and other international development goals on education. To facilitate the achievement of these targets, primary education has been designated a sector priority within the ESP.

The Growth and Poverty Reduction Strategy II, developed in 2005, updates Ghana's development agenda with a new emphasis on growth and wealth creation as a means of reducing poverty over the period 2006 to 2009. The following are the prioritized policy objectives for the education sector under the GPRS II:

- Increase access to and participation in education and training.
- Bridge gender gap in access to education.

- Improve quality of teaching and learning.
- Improve quality and efficiency in delivery of education service.
- Promote and extend the provision of science, mathematics, technology, and information and communication technology (ICT) education and training.
- Enhance and strengthen the linkages between academic research and all sectors of the economy.
- Mainstream issues of population, gender, health, HIV/AIDS/sexually transmitted infections (STIs), fire and road safety, and environment in the curricula of schools and institutions of higher learning.

These policy objectives are carefully selected to inform the thematic areas of the Education Strategic Plan—namely, access and participation, quality, management for efficiency, and science and technology (see table 3.1).

The Ministry of Education, Science and Sports (MoESS) has the overall responsibility for policy formulation, including the planning, setting, and enforcing of educational standards and the provision of educational services. Education service delivery has been delegated by the MoESS to its various agencies, regions, and districts. The Ghana Education Service (GES) is the agency that implements the basic and senior secondary education components, including technical and vocational institutes and the teacher

Table 3.1 Links between the Policy Goals of the Growth and Poverty Reduction Strategy II and the Education Strategic Plan Focus Areas

Education Strategic Plan—area of focus	Policy goals of the GPRS II
Access and participation	Increase access to and participation in education and training
	Promote and extend preschool education
	Provide girls with equal opportunities to access the full cycle of education
Quality	Improve quality of teaching and learning for enhanced student achievement
	Promote good health and environmental sanitation in schools and institutions of higher learning
	Improve the quality of academic and research programs
	Identify and promote programs that assist in the prevention of HIV/AIDS
Educational management	Strengthen and improve educational planning and management
Science, technology, and TVET	Extend and improve TVET
	Promote and extend the provision of science and technology education and training

Source: Adapted from the GPRS II.
Note: GPRS II = Growth and Poverty Reduction Strategy II (developed in 2005); TVET = technical and vocational education and training.

education division. As GES is responsible for these subsectors, it controls about four-fifths of the annual public sector expenditure on education.

Other major agencies engaged in education include the National Council for Tertiary Education (NCTE); the National Council for Vocational Education and Training (NACVET), which also includes technical education; and the Nonformal Education Division (NFED), which also includes lifelong learning. The broad responsibilities of other prominent stakeholders (the Ministry of Local Government and Rural Development, the district assemblies, religious bodies, development partners, and service providers) include provision of financial resources to support the sector's programs, participation in the policy and planning processes of the sector, and delivery of educational services.

THE EDUCATION SYSTEM

After the launch of the education reforms in September 2007, the education system in Ghana operates in the following manner. Basic education includes two years of kindergarten in addition to the existing six years of primary and three years of junior high school. The entire basic cycle is free and compulsory. The overarching target is 100 percent completion rates for male and female students at all basic levels by 2015. Moreover, to significantly improve quality and relevance, the basic school syllabus is being streamlined to focus on the core areas of literacy, numeracy, and life skills; ICT courses will also be introduced in all 6,300 public junior high schools.

Second cycle education has been expanded from three to four years and serves as a terminal point of entry into work or tertiary education and will be universal by 2020. The major initiatives and sector policies proposed in the reforms include second cycle, which will consist of an apprenticeship program, including work-based and academic training; and senior high school, which will consist of general, vocational, technical, and agricultural streams, with an emphasis on vocational, technical, and agricultural education as a credible alternative to the general grammar education.

It is expected that graduates from the senior high school system will qualify for entry into tertiary education programs, depending on the courses studied. The tertiary system consists of polytechnics and universities. Polytechnics provide subdegree (certificate, diploma) qualifications for most of their programs, while universities provide primary and postgraduate degree programs.

DECENTRALIZATION

The decentralization of education in Ghana necessitates that the MoESS and GES redirect their efforts from the executive management of a country-wide network of schools, staff, supplies, and finances toward the establishment and enforcement of educational standards, the development of books and other educational materials, and the promotion of quality education.

The district education offices will become a department under the district administration, which will have the following responsibilities:

- Build, equip, and maintain public basic schools in the district.
- Establish public schools that the district director of education (DDE) and the district chief executive consider necessary in the district.
- Appoint a district education oversight committee to oversee the following: the conditions of school buildings and any other infrastructural requirements of the schools; the provision of teachers and the regular and punctual attendance of teachers and pupils in schools; the adequate performance of duties by the staff at the schools; the moral and professional behavior of the staff and pupils, and matters relating to general discipline; the complaints about teachers and from teachers, and about nonteaching staff; the environmental cleanliness of the schools, lands, and other facilities; and the supply of textbooks and other teaching and learning materials.

BASIC EDUCATION INDICATORS

There are two basic indicators: access to education and quality of education. Access to education includes availability by both gender and geography to kindergarten, primary, and junior secondary levels. Quality of education focuses on teacher training, textbook availability, and student testing and assessment.

Access to Education. Overall, there have been very positive trends in student enrollment, retention, and transition between the school years 2003/04 and 2006/07. A number of key indicators for basic education are highlighted in table 3.2 and show good progress in access to basic education at all three levels: kindergarten, primary, and junior secondary education.

There are, however, considerable geographical and gender differences in access to education as shown in the two maps (3.1 and 3.2) on primary net enrollment rates by district and gender parity in gross enrollment rates (GERs). Net enrollment rates in the southern part of Ghana are considerably higher than in the northern part, while very few districts report a

Table 3.2 Enrollment and Access Trends at Kindergarten, Primary, and Junior Secondary Education Levels, 2003/04–2006/07

Education level	2003/04	2004/05	2005/06	2006/07
Kindergarten				
Enrollment (number)				
Girls	316,176	362,312	500,295	551,784
Boys	320,939	369,019	498,524	552,995
Total	637,115	731,331	998,819	1,104,779
Net enrollment rate (percent)				
Girls	34.4	38.5	49.9	55.6
Boys	34.3	38.4	50.2	56.1
Total	34.4	38.5	50.0	55.8
Primary				
Enrollment (number)				
Girls	1,282,220	1,403,988	1,516,725	1,633,600
Boys	1,403,913	1,525,548	1,606,178	1,732,162
Total	2,686,133	2,929,536	3,122,903	3,365,762
Net enrollment rate (percent)				
Girls	54.7	58.3	68.1	77.3
Boys	56.5	60.0	69.6	79.8
Total	55.6	59.1	68.8	78.6
Junior secondary				
Enrollment (number)				
Girls	420,548	462,090	483,741	527,232
Boys	498,786	548,156	557,261	605,086
Total	919,334	1,010,246	1,041,002	1,132,318
Net enrollment rate (percent)				
Girls	29.7	31.8	41.7	49.7
Boys	29.3	31.3	41.5	51.7
Total	29.5	31.6	41.6	50.7

Source: Education Management Information System.

gender parity index for GER between 0.95 and 1.05. In 2004/05, in 62 out of the 110 districts, the gender parity index (GPI) for GER was lower than 0.95, demonstrating that there are far fewer girls than boys in school in these districts. It should be noted, however, that the differences based on geographical area and sex have been narrowing over the past few years.

Quality of Education. Key issues and areas of progress include the following:

• Teachers are being trained through distance education—the first intake was 5,000 teachers in March 2005; a further 8,000 enrolled in

Map 3.1 Primary Net Enrollment by District, 2004/05

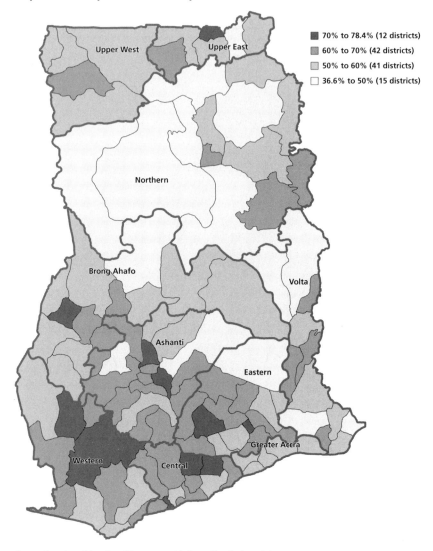

- 70% to 78.4% (12 districts)
- 60% to 70% (42 districts)
- 50% to 60% (41 districts)
- 36.6% to 50% (15 districts)

Source: Based on Education Management Information System data.

September 2005. The training seeks to reduce the level of untrained teachers from 21.2 percent at the primary level and 12.8 percent at the junior secondary level to not more than 5 percent throughout basic education by 2015 across the country.

- Basic-level textbooks were delivered to public basic schools in the first term of the 2005/06 academic year. Approximately 90 percent were delivered by the end of the year, so that each student has a textbook for all the subjects studied.

Map 3.2   Gender Parity Index of Primary Gross Enrollment, 2004/05

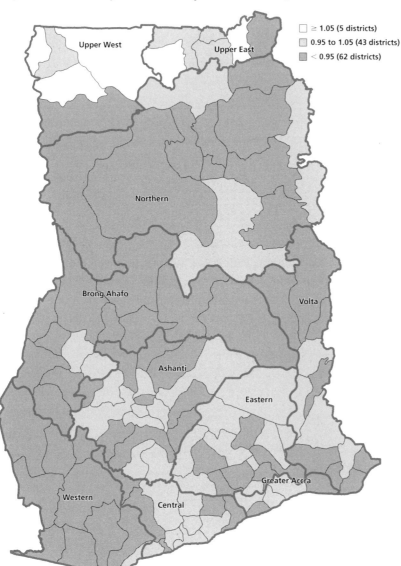

Source: Based on Education Management Information System data.

- To develop a reliable pupil testing and assessment system, a minimum national standard test was chosen, with the first sample of students (25 percent) tested for competency in 2005.

Even though there has been progress in implementing interventions to improve the quality of education, and as shown in table 3.3, on

Table 3.3 Basic Education Certificate Examination Results for Mathematics and English, 2002/03–2004/05
(percent)

Subject	2002/03	2003/04	2004/05
Mathematics			
Boys	60.7	62.7	76.8
Girls	54.1	56.0	72.4
Total	57.7	59.0	74.8
English			
Boys	60.6	58.7	77.2
Girls	59.9	57.8	75.5
Total	60.3	58.3	76.5

Source: Ministry of Education, Science and Sports.

examination results in English and mathematics, there is scope for further improvement. It should be noted that there are substantial regional differences. Especially in the remote and rural districts in the northern part of Ghana, examination results are considerably lower than the national average. It is especially in these areas that quality of education will come under pressure because of the above-average national increase in enrollment.

FREE COMPULSORY BASIC EDUCATION

The Mission of the MoESS is "to ensure that all Ghanaian children of school-going age are provided with quality formal education and training through effective and efficient resource management that will facilitate the making of education delivery relevant to the manpower and social needs of the nation." The Constitution of the Fourth Republic of Ghana, Article 38 (2) states, "The Government of Ghana shall, within two years after Parliament first meets after coming into force of this Constitution, draw up a program for implementation within the following ten years, for the provision of free, compulsory and universal basic education." It is against this background that the Free Compulsory Universal Basic Education (fCUBE) initiative was launched in 1996, at which time approximately 30 percent of Ghanaian children of school-going age were still not in school.

Although the fCUBE initiative was a laudable intervention, and education officials made great efforts through enrollment drives and sensitization of communities to induce children to school, the initiative did not have the expected impact two years before the expiry of the implementation period. (For the 2003/04 academic year, primary GER at the national level was 86.3 percent and for deprived districts, 76.1 percent).

The cost-sharing or recovery schemes under the fCUBE program addressed the main issues of cost as follows:

- Tuition: tuition shall be free in all basic schools in the public system.
- Textbooks: textbooks shall be supplied free to basic schools, grades 1–6 in the public system and in the private sector. Pupils in basic schools, grades 7–9 will, however, pay textbook-user fees, which should not be more than 10 percent of the average total cost of textbooks supplied to one pupil in basic schools, grades 7–9.
- Stationery: stationery cost will be borne to a large extent by parents of pupils in grades 1–9 in the public and private basic schools. Exercise books with unused pages shall be carried over to the next stage and will be replaced only when all the pages are used.
- Equipment and tools: equipment shall be supplied free to all basic schools in the public system.
- Meals and transportation: it will be the responsibility of parents to provide adequate meals for their children as well as money to cover their transportation to and from school.
- Fees and levies: subject to approval from the district assemblies, communities and parent-teacher associations (PTAs) may impose special levies or fees on their members for the purpose of raising funds for school projects, provided that no student shall be asked to leave school if his or her parents cannot pay.

Despite the policy of fee-free tuition in basic schools, as part of the cost-sharing program under the fCUBE, three main partners were given responsibility for education financing—the government (state), the district assembly, and parents and communities.

The mandate given to the district assemblies stated, "Subject to approval from the district assemblies, communities and PTAs shall impose special levies or fees on their members for the purpose of raising funds for school projects provided that no child shall be sent out of school for failure of his/her parents to pay such levies/fees." In other words, fees could be charged to parents but should not serve as a barrier to entry to school for any student.

Unfortunately, experiences ran counter to the policy according to the results of a survey conducted in 4 out of 10 regions in 2004. It identified about 76 different types of levies ranging from 3,000 cedis (¢) (US$0.33) to ₵120,000 (US$13.33). The level of fees or levies was highest in the urban areas. The effect of the fees and levies was that

- 11 percent of children worked while in school,
- 9 percent had irregular attendance in public basic schools, and
- 3 percent dropped out in public basic schools.

Therefore, despite the instruction that nonpayment of fees should not reduce a child's chance to receive an education, the fees had a negative impact on attendance at basic schools.

As a response to this situation, the MoESS decided to implement additional strategies to increase access to education. One of the key strategies has been the design and piloting of the Capitation Grant Scheme.

CAPITATION GRANT: PILOTING IN 40 DISTRICTS

In the 2004/05 academic year, the MoESS and the Ghana Education Service (GES) introduced fee-free education at the basic level, which was initiated on a pilot basis through a Capitation Grant Scheme in the 40, and later 53, most deprived districts in Ghana. The implementation of the Capitation Grant Scheme began as a strategy formulated under the Pilot Programmatic Scheme of the World Bank Education Sector Project to address the low enrollment figures in the most deprived districts in Ghana.

This strategy put plans in place to abolish basic school fees and levies by the 2004/05 academic year and replace these with a per capita allocation to every basic school. These allocations would be accounted for and spent in accordance with the School Performance Improvement Plan. This first-year implementation of the pilot coincided with agitations from civil society groups that the country was unable to fulfill its pledge under the fCUBE—to provide free, compulsory, and universal basic education for every Ghanaian child by the year 2006.

Under this scheme, all forms of fee paying at the basic level in public schools were to cease and, in their place, the schools were to be given capitation grants (₵25,000 [US$2.70] per boy and ₵35,000 [US$3.88] per girl) to replace the lost revenue from the total abolition of school fees. These amounts were chosen based on an analysis of the average fees charged nationwide at the basic level.

Arrangements made for the successful introduction of the scheme included the following:

- Interministerial collaboration. A joint committee of senior officials of MoESS and the Ministry of Local Government and Rural Development was set up to iron out all institutional impediments to the implementation of fee-free education.

- Scaling-up mechanism from pilot to national. The original plan was to scale up the program from the pilot in 40 districts to the national level over a three-year period. This phased approach would help to guide the process and to respond to emerging challenges more effectively.
- Development of simple but comprehensive guidelines. Experiences from the pilot phase were used to update the guidelines for use of and reporting on the grant for the nationwide program. A full set of the guidelines is available.
- Training programs to build the capacity of staff.
- Campaigning for the abolition of fees in all public schools.
- Strengthening decentralized structures to ensure a proper flow of funds.
- Monitoring systems to facilitate accountability of the scheme.

SELECTION OF DISTRICTS

The 40 districts under the pilot phase (see map 3.3) were selected based on a nationwide assessment exercise to identify the most deprived districts for additional funding to bring them up to the standards of the endowed districts over a period of time. The inputs used for the assessment were as follows:

- *Input criteria:* seating places per pupil, core textbooks per pupil, percentage of qualified primary teachers, per student budget at primary level, and pupil-teacher ratio at primary level
- *Access criteria:* GER and percentage of girls enrolled
- *Achievement criteria:* pass rate in the Basic Education Certification Examination for English and mathematics.

FINANCIAL ALLOCATIONS AND FLOW OF FUNDS

The government has shown a great deal of commitment in releasing funds for the program to abolish fees in public schools. The funds for the pilot program, totaling ¢28.5 billion (US$3,275,900), were provided as counterpart funds to the Pilot Programmatic Scheme of the World Bank Education Sector Project within the 2004/05 academic year, with the first release to the schools in November 2004.

The GES has a main account, where the central government deposits funds for the payment of the capitation grant. Individual checks are issued to each of the districts (on the basis of enrollment in each district) to be deposited in specially designated bank accounts for capitation grants. To ensure smooth implementation of the school programs, separate bank accounts are opened for each school, and funds are transferred from the

Map 3.3   School Fee Abolition and Introduction of Capitation Grant, 2004

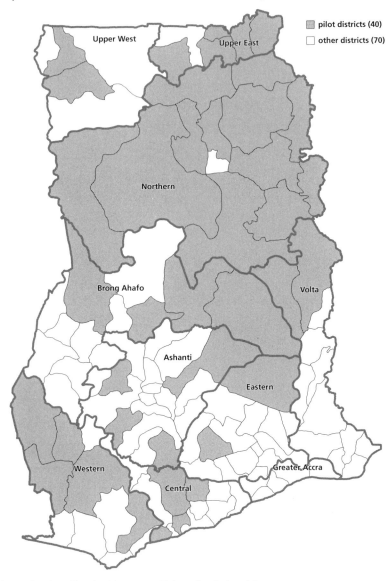

Source: Based on Education Management Information System data.

district account to the school account. (In most districts, school accounts are kept in the same bank as that of the district office.)

OPERATIONAL GUIDELINES

Selection of Schools. All registered public schools with the GES in the selected districts should have a code with the Education Management Information System (EMIS) as well as the Integrated Personnel and

Payroll System Database to facilitate monitoring and assessment of the impact of the program.

The Number of Pupils. The actual enrollment at the end of the third term for the previous year is used as the base and is then projected upward, using expected enrollment growth to calculate the estimated number of pupils. This figure is then used for budget purposes. Enrollment numbers for actual disbursement, however, should be based on actual figures.

Eligible Expenditures. The capitation grants are to be used to support the implementation of the School Performance Improvement Plan (SPIP).

Management of the Grant. The key players in the management of the capitation grant are the following: district director of education (DDE), assistant director—supervision, circuit supervisors, district accountant, school management committee (SMC), and head teacher.

Preparation of a School Performance Improvement Plan. The SPIP is to be designed to cover the following areas: components and targets, actions to be taken, who is responsible, resources needed, time frame, and who monitors. Some of the key activities to be undertaken are the following: enrollment drives, provision of teaching and learning materials, school management (including stationery), community and school relationship, support to needy pupils, school and cluster-based in-service training, minor repairs, and payment of sports and culture levies (to be approved nationally). The SPIP is to be prepared by the head teacher or staff with the approval of the SMC. It is to cover the entire academic year but should be broken down into terms. The SMC is to oversee the implementation of the SPIP. The SPIP is then forwarded to the DDE for review and approval. The review will ensure that the activities undertaken are in line with the Education Strategic Plan and other priority areas of education.

Special Bank Account. The district education office should open a special account to lodge funds for the capitation grants. The signatories to this account are the DDE and the district accountant. To ensure smooth implementation of the school programs, separate bank accounts should also be opened by the district for each school. The signatories to the school account are the head teacher and the assistant.

Release of Funds. A projected estimate of enrollment levels in each school is made at the beginning of each academic year (based on the GER for the district). This estimate is the basis for the transfer of 50 percent of funds to the school at the beginning of the first term. Subsequent transfers for the first term are dependent on the submission of adequate returns on the actual enrollment for the school in the course of the term. For the second and third terms, based on the enrollment levels as established in the first term, funds are transferred to schools at the beginning of term. Efforts should, however, be made to confirm that these enrollment figures have not changed because of attrition.

Disbursement Process. The executor of an activity within the SPIP applies to the head teacher for funds with a Request Form. Cash equivalent to that activity is withdrawn from the bank, an Advance Form is completed, and cash is given to the executor to be used for the purpose indicated on the request form. After the completion of the activity, the executor submits the relevant documentation (receipts, honor certificates, and activity report) to the head teacher and completes an Accounting for Advances Form to end the process.

Management Control. At the school level, requests for funds are to be endorsed by both the SMC chairman and the head teacher. These persons are jointly responsible for the use of funds to attain targets set out in the SPIP.

Record Keeping. The school is to maintain financial records, which document all capitation grants disbursed and received, along with all appropriate receipts and documentation. These records are to be made available for the review of the SMC, the district education office, and the internal audit office.

Reports. Monthly and quarterly reports describing activities completed and under way during the period, together with a statement of expenditures for these activities, are to be sent to the district education office by the head teacher and the SMC chairman. The district education office is also to report on a quarterly basis to the director general on capitation grant operations.

Monitoring Mechanisms. The circuit supervisor is to visit each school twice per term and will report to the district education office on the following: abolition of all levies in the school, implementation status of the SPIP, and submission of all reports on a timely basis. The DDE as well as the district teacher support team and district head teacher adviser are to pay regular visits to each school to review progress on implementation of activities. Progress reports are to be submitted by the head teacher through the SMC to the DDE. The regional monitoring teams are to monitor and report on the disbursement and use of funds at the districts and schools on a term-by-term basis.

Audit. The GES internal auditors will monitor the school accounts and will conduct at least one audit of the use of the capitation grants, half yearly. They will submit copies of their report to the SMC, the DDE, and the regional director of education.

Implementation Problems. Implementation of the guidelines has been quite smooth, except that head teachers have complained of too much additional work in the preparation of SPIPs and the documentation of disbursements.

IMPACT ON ENROLLMENT

After one year of implementation, total enrollment in public schools in these 40 districts rose to 1,160,922 from 1,013,287. This was an increase of 147,635 in absolute figures, or 14.6 percent over the 2003/04 academic year (see table 3.4 and figure 3.1 for increase in enrollment by level and table 3.5 and figure 3.2 for increase in enrollment disaggregated by gender).

Compared to the national average (including the pilot districts), the pilot districts performed better than the national average. Between the

Table 3.4 Increase in Enrollment by Education Level in 40 Pilot Districts, 2003/04 and 2004/05

Education level	Enrollment in 2003/04	Enrollment in 2004/05	Increase in enrollment	Percentage increase in enrollment (2003/04–2004/05)
Preschool	138,175	184,706	46,531	33.7
Primary	700,006	779,786	79,780	11.4
Junior secondary	175,106	196,430	21,324	12.2
Total	1,013,287	1,160,922	147,635	14.6

Source: Education Management Information System.

Figure 3.1 Increase in Enrollment by Education Level in 40 Pilot Districts, 2003/04 and 2004/05

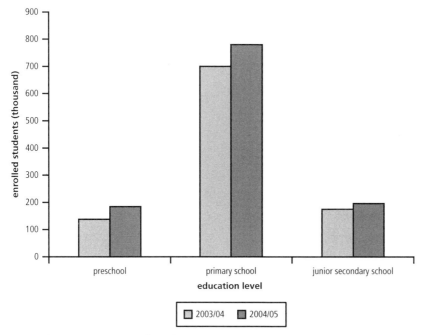

Source: Education Management Information System.

Table 3.5 Increase in Enrollment by Gender in 40 Pilot Districts, 2003/04 and 2004/05

Gender	Enrollment in 2003/04	Enrollment in 2004/05	Increase in enrollment	Percentage increase in enrollment (2003/04–2004/05)
Boys	551,462	624,559	73,097	13.2
Girls	461,825	536,363	74,538	16.1
Total	1,013,287	1,160,922	147,635	14.6

Source: Education Management Information System.

Figure 3.2 Increase in Enrollment by Gender in 40 Pilot Districts, 2003/04 and 2004/05

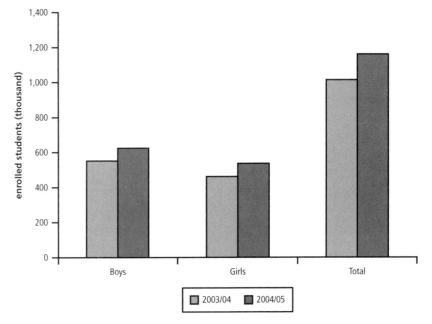

Source: Education Management Information System.

period 2003/04 and 2004/05, the deprived districts had a substantial increase of 5.0 percentage points in GER, compared to a decrease of 0.2 percentage points in other districts and a fairly small increase of 1.2 percentage points at the national level (see table 3.6, figure 3.3, and map 3.4).

ISSUES WITH THE PILOT PROGRAM

The following issues came to the fore after the introduction of the scheme:

- It was felt that inadequate publicity had led to less stakeholder involvement. Most of the arrangement for the rollout of the program was

Table 3.6 Enrollment Growth in Deprived Districts, 2001/02–2004/05

Location	Total GER 2001/02 (percent)	Total GER 2003/04 (percent)	Total GER 2004/05 (percent)	Percentage point change in total GER (2003/04–2004/05)
Deprived districts	70.2	76.1	80.1	5.0
Other districts	90.4	91.1	90.9	−0.2
National	83.8	86.3	87.5	1.2

Source: Education Management Information System.

Figure 3.3 Analysis of Gross Enrollment Rate by Pilot and National Education Levels, 2002/03–2004/05

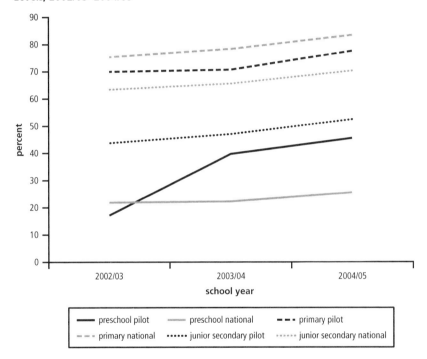

Source: Education Management Information System.

limited to education authorities; there was also a lack of preparedness to deal with the immediate challenges of implementation.

- The scheme led to an above-average increase in enrollment with narrowing geographical and gender disparities.
- With the momentum that was created in the pilot districts, several other assemblies of nonpilot districts implemented similar by-laws without the necessary preparation; this posed additional difficulties for educational authorities.

Map 3.4   Relative Increase in Primary Enrollment, 2004/05

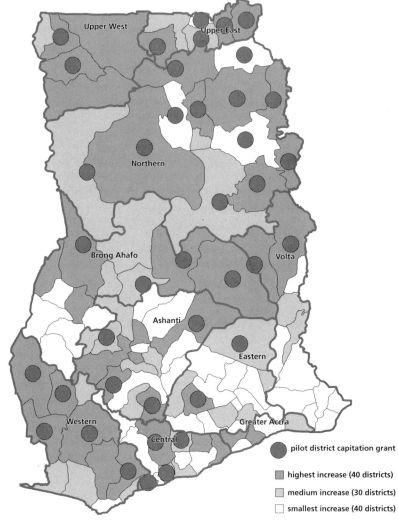

Source: Based on Education Management Information System data.
Note: The map includes the 40 capitation grant pilot districts.

- There is anecdotal information that in some cases, children from adjoining districts crossed over to enroll in schools across the border of a pilot district.
- In some cases, parents in nonpilot districts protested and demanded introduction of capitation grants in their district.
- Inconsistency in the flow of information between politicians and education officials led to confusion among communities on the scope of the pilot. Originally the pilot was meant only for primary schools,

BOX 3.1 SUCCESS STORIES IN SOME REMOTE AREAS

In Nkwanta District in the Volta region, the capitation grant led to a 100 percent increase in school enrollment in the town of Kpassa (from 48 percent to 96 percent). A mother who had sent her child to serve as domestic help to earn money to learn a trade rushed to retrieve the 10-year-old girl to send her to school because she no longer had to pay any fees.

The junior secondary schools around the light industrial area in Kumasi noted that auto mechanical engineering (for the repair of all kinds of vehicles), which employs a large number of apprentices between the ages of 11 and 20, is now overenrolled. With the abolition of fees, these apprentices can go to school in the morning and learn their trade in the afternoon.

Source: Ministry of Education, Science and Sports.

but during implementation, preschools and junior secondary schools (JSS) were included as well (see box 3.1).

Since many districts implemented similar interventions on their own initiative, increasing public pressure on the MoESS to scale up faster than originally planned, the MoESS decided to scale up to cover all basic schools in Ghana with effect from the 2005/06 academic year.

FROM PILOT TO NATIONAL SCALE

Since the 2005/06 academic year, the Capitation Grant Scheme has been extended to all schools in Ghana. Every basic school receives ₵30,000 (US$3.31) per pupil enrolled. The capitation grant should remove the financial barrier created by levies, and more than compensate the schools for any loss of revenue. Both boys and girls receive the same amount of capitation grant to ensure smooth implementation of the scheme at the national level.

THE PLANNING PROCESS

The success stories from the pilot phase (see box 3.1) and the public pressure to expand the scheme nationwide as soon as possible led to a major cabinet decision to roll out the program after just one year instead of a phased three-year period as originally intended.

Major concerns raised by the public immediately after the announcement of the scheme were the following:

- Whether the district education officers and the school head teachers had been given adequate training to handle the scheme at the local level
- The possibility of the scheme stifling community initiative and involvement in education
- Funding and sustainability of the scheme
- The necessity of control measures to ensure that funds for schools are secured.

These concerns guided review of the process. Arrangements made for the successful introduction of the scheme included the following:

- Interministerial collaboration. A joint committee of senior officials of MoESS and the Ministry of Local Government and Rural Development was established to remove institutional impediments to the implementation of fee-free education.
- Training programs were conducted countrywide to build staff capacity. This was done as part of a program of District Education Financial and Operational Capacity Strengthening, which was supported by the European Commission. The extension of capacity building to the school level by the district education offices, however, has had many problems as some school heads did not show interest or did not want the program to succeed.
- The campaign for the abolition of fees in all public schools countrywide was announced by the minister for Education, Science and Sports at a press conference in early 2005, followed by directives to district chief executives to pass by-laws eliminating all forms of fees or levies in their districts.
- Various techniques for information dissemination including radio discussions and announcements on political platforms and at churches, mosques, and community gatherings.
- Further strengthening of decentralized structures to ensure a proper flow of funds.
- Monitoring systems to facilitate accountability of the scheme.

FUNDING

The Government of Ghana proposed to fund the scheme from the Heavily Indebted Poor Countries (HIPC) Initiative and the Social Impact Mitigation Levy Funds. A total amount of ₵129 billion (US$14.72 million) has been released by the government for the program in its first year of implementation from the following sources: HIPC Fund, ₵47.5 billion or US$5.40 million, and the Social Impact Mitigation Levy Fund, ₵82.0 billion or US$9.32 million. Subsequent financing for the 2006/07 academic year was included in the national budget for the year.

EXPERIENCE SO FAR WITH NATIONWIDE IMPLEMENTATION

The scheme has led to substantial increases in enrollment across public schools in the country. Whereas the increase in GER over the past few years has been an average of 1.7 percentage points, preliminary figures received from districts have recorded increases of 5.3 percentage points at the preschool level, 9.4 percentage points at the primary level, and 5.9 percentage points at the junior secondary level (see table 3.7 and figure 3.4). This

Table 3.7 Gross Enrollment Rate Increases by Education Level, 2004/05 and 2005/06

Education level	2004/05 (percent)	2005/06 (percent)	Percentage point increase in total GER (2004/05–2005/06)
Preschool	25.5	30.8	5.3
Primary	83.3	92.7	9.4
Junior secondary	70.2	76.1	5.9

Source: Education Management Information System.

Figure 3.4 Gross Enrollment Rate Increases by Education Level, 2003/04 and 2004/05

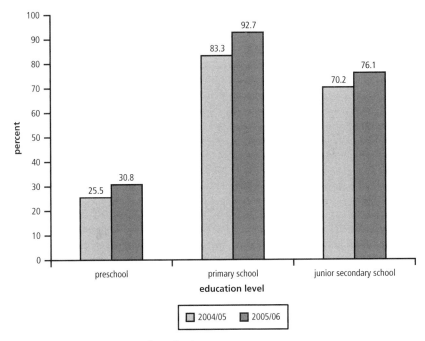

Source: Education Management Information System.

Figure 3.5 Gross Enrollment Rate Increases by Education Level and Region, 2004/05 and 2005/06

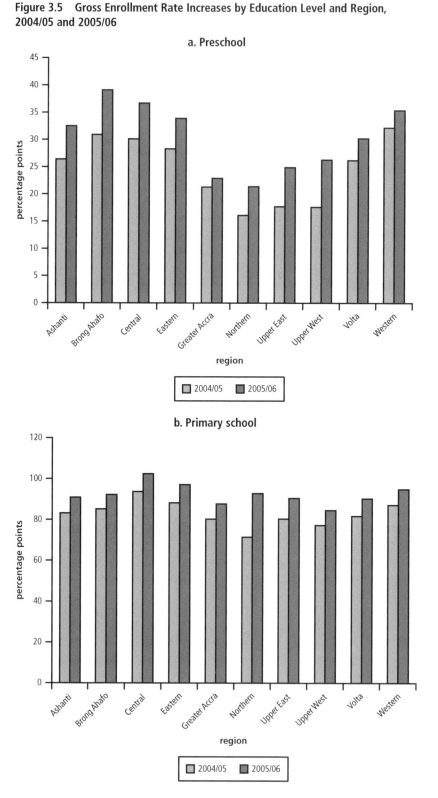

Figure 3.5 (*continued*)

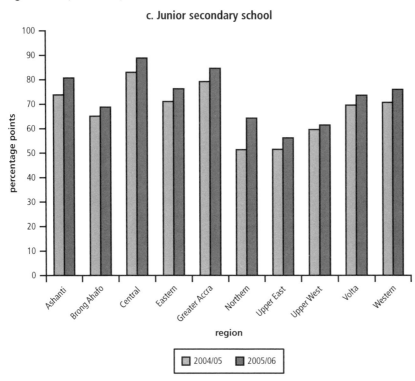

c. Junior secondary school

Source: Education Management Information System.

trend is consistent when disaggregated by region (see figure 3.5). In terms of the gender parity index, the comparative national figures for the two years, 2004/05 and 2005/06 show an increase at all three education levels (see table 3.8).

Figures collected from the districts on public schools for the implementation of the Capitation Grant Scheme demonstrate that the scheme has contributed to a tremendous rise in enrollment (see table 3.9). In terms of absolute figures, an additional 616,439 pupils (295,114 boys and 321,325 girls in table 3.10) above the 2004/05 enrollment figures were in school at the end of 2006. This represents a general increase of 16.7 percent. Specifically, preschool has seen an increase of 36.6 percent; primary, 14.2 percent; and JSS, 10.3 percent. These increases in raw enrollment

Table 3.8   Gender Parity Index by Education Level, 2004/05 and 2005/06

Education level	2004/05	2005/06	Change
Preschool	0.97	0.98	0.01
Primary	0.93	0.95	0.02
Junior secondary	0.88	0.90	0.02

Source: Education Management Information System.

Table 3.9   Increase in Enrollment Following National Implementation of Capitation Grant Scheme, by Education Level, 2004/05 and 2005/06

Education level	2004/05	2005/06	Increase	Percentage increase
Preschool	547,950	748,411	200,461	36.6
Primary	2,328,373	2,659,506	331,133	14.2
Junior secondary	822,125	906,970	84,845	10.3
Total	3,698,448	4,314,887	616,439	16.7

Source: Ministry of Education, Science and Sports.

Table 3.10   Increase in Enrollment Following National Implementation of Capitation Grant Scheme, by Gender, 2004/05 and 2005/06

Gender	2004/05	2005/06	Increase	Percentage increase
Boys	1,943,909	2,239,023	295,114	15.2
Girls	1,754,539	2,075,864	321,325	18.3
Total	3,698,448	4,314,887	616,439	16.7

Source: Ministry of Education, Science and Sports.

figures are reflected in the GER as tabulated in table 3.7. Significantly more girls than boys appear to have been drawn into school by the capitation scheme. This is mirrored by the general rise in GPI in all programs.

CONCLUSIONS AND LESSONS LEARNED

The increase in enrollment appears less dramatic than in countries such as Kenya and Malawi, which have also abolished school fees. Although no research has been undertaken, Ghana's comparatively smaller increase may result from the following conditions:

- Initial enrollment levels in Ghana may have been higher.
- The pilot achieved a more balanced growth over two years.
- The fees and charges were lower in Ghana than elsewhere as much of the cost of education was borne by the government (fCUBE).
- The cost of education is a smaller portion of total household expenditure in Ghana.
- Remote and rural areas in Ghana have fewer schools (a barrier to increased access that cannot be addressed by the capitation grant).
- Private sector involvement lowers costs; for example, local banks have agreed to waive all bank charges for accounts related to the capitation grant.

LESSONS LEARNED FROM THE PILOT AND FROM THE NATIONWIDE IMPLEMENTATION OF THE CAPITATION GRANT

- The capitation grant is a pro-poor strategy. It is the poor, in particular, who have responded by enrolling their children in school. The strategy has also narrowed gender and geographical differences.
- The abolition of school fees and introduction of capitation grants constitute a relatively simple strategy that has an immediate and considerable impact on access to education; in comparison to other strategies (school feeding, for example), it is more cost effective.
- The capitation grant creates national momentum. In Ghana, the capitation grant has created a great deal of momentum and generated additional support from faith-based organizations, the private sector, district assemblies, and local members of parliament, thus facilitating implementation. Such support creates a multiplier effect and adds value to the government's investment.
- Implementation guidelines must be simple and straightforward but should cover all necessary components, including the training of district officers and head teachers.
- An effective financial system for the transfer of funds from the central to the school level has been the key to successful implementation. In most cases, schools already had their own bank accounts.
- An information campaign is essential for disseminating details on the scope and details of a scheme such as the capitation grant. Before launching an information campaign, there should be consensus on the scope and details of the scheme to avoid miscommunication and conflicting statements and expectations.
- The abolition of school fees and introduction of the capitation grant will not suffice in themselves to overcome certain challenges, such as enrolling all children in school, particularly children with special needs. Additional interventions will be required to achieve full enrollment.
- In the pilot, the higher capitation grant for girls did not lead to a significantly greater narrowing of the gender gap compared to the national implementation where the grant was the same for boys and girls. This raises the question whether capitation grants should be differentiated to promote girls' education. It also confirms that the abolition of school fees and introduction of capitation grants are insufficient for achieving gender parity and for ensuring universal enrollment in school. The low enrollment of girls may be caused by factors that are not within the domain of the MoESS. Changing cultural attitudes requires specifically targeted interventions that are better managed by a multisectoral approach.

- A more systematic inventory of school sites as well as an identification of new sites (through school mapping, for example) are required. Capitation grants are only provided to existing schools.

EMERGING CHALLENGES

The overarching challenge in a situation of rapid enrollment increase is to safeguard quality of education. The additional demand that is created in the sector in terms of teachers, school infrastructure, and textbook requirements poses a real threat to the quality of education and is directly related to learning outcomes of students.

A number of challenges and risks have been identified that require a policy response. Strategic policy options must be reviewed against their possible impact on access and quality, financial requirements, and sustainability.

The following challenges must be confronted with great urgency:

- Additional classrooms are required. Preexisting gaps and the inability to estimate infrastructural requirements before introduction of the scheme have created conditions of inadequate facilities across the country. As enrollment has increased, class sizes have expanded significantly.
- An additional 17,612 teachers are needed to meet the shortages.
- Additional textbooks and other teaching and learning materials are required.
- Methods to sustain community participation in a fee-free context are needed.
- Consensus is required on the definition of "free education." In addition to well-known opportunity costs such as loss of income, the costs of education that remain the responsibility of parents and communities must be clarified. This relates directly to cost-sharing principles of the fCUBE.
- Amounts and proportions of capitation grants allocated to kindergarten, primary, and JSS and to boys and girls should be examined. The introduction of a flat fee at each school to support small schools in rural areas has also been proposed.
- Funds should be released according to guidelines. Even though actual release of funds has been smooth and effective, the timely release of funds to districts and schools remains problematic and must be implemented according to guidelines.
- Transparency at the school level should be promoted. Schools should be transparent about the amount of funding they receive and about the

allocation of the funds. Relations between schools and the community should be open to enhance accountability and good governance.

- Overage children entering or reentering the education system must be assimilated. The capitation grants have allowed a number of overage children to reenter the schools, creating specific challenges that require attention.
- The School Performance Improvement Plan should be prepared and used effectively.
- The effects on private schools must be considered. Private schools provide a service, but their enrollment may fall as a result of the capitation grant. Under the current scheme, private schools do not receive capitation grants.
- It is important to maintain general financial management, capacity, record keeping, accountability, and transparency at district and school levels.
- Effective monitoring is required. The monitoring team consists of the district internal auditor, accountant, and circuit supervisors. Circuit supervisors play a key role in auditing.
- The issue of payment for examinations should be considered.
- In most urban areas, the amount schools receive from the capitation grant is considerably less than the amount they received from the school levies.
- Plans are needed to satisfy the increased demand for secondary education as students transition from primary to lower secondary education and beyond.

COPING STRATEGIES AND THE WAY FORWARD

The MoESS reviewed strategic options to cope with the challenges and instructed district directors of education on the following:

- The introduction of the shift system in schools where it has become absolutely necessary and practicable
- The use of church buildings, market stalls, or other suitable public meeting places for use as temporary classrooms
- The reengagement of retired but hardworking teachers
- The engagement of pupil teachers and other volunteer teachers
- The procurement of additional copies of pupils' textbooks and other teaching and learning materials to cater to the extra demand
- The pursuit of any other measures considered appropriate in addressing the situation.

It will be of key importance that comprehensive reviews and research take place, as many of the above options may have negative impacts in terms of education financing and education quality in the medium and long term.

It has to be emphasized that the abolition of school fees is a major strategic intervention under the framework of the Education Strategic Plan (ESP) and is in line with its longer-term objectives and strategic vision. The vision outlined in the ESP will continue to guide strategies and interventions in the education sector. A review of the ESP in 2006 ensured that new realities were incorporated in its design, including alignment with the new GPRS.

The MoESS and the Ghana Education Service have planned a number of initiatives for implementation now and in the near future: first, to address emerging challenges to sustain and enforce the momentum created through the abolition of school fees; and second, to continue on the path already outlined in the Education Strategic Plan.

The Annual Education Sector Review, held in June 2006, identified a number of existing challenges and provided key recommendations. The success of the capitation grant in increasing access is undisputed as demonstrated by a 10-percentage-point jump in net and gross primary enrollment rates in one academic year.

Major challenges that have been identified are increases in demand for teachers, school infrastructure, and textbooks. Addressing these challenges requires a mixture of interventions that are briefly explained below. A cross-cutting, underlying challenge is the quality of information on education and current capacities for education planning and management and coordinated service delivery, particularly at the district level. In previous years districts have made progress in strengthening their capacities as demonstrated by the existence of district school mapping reports, district education plans, and district performance reports. However, in the context of ongoing decentralization, demands on the districts and capacities of district education officers will continue to increase.

SUSTAINING THE MOMENTUM: ADDRESSING EMERGING CHALLENGES

As an immediate response to the challenges, the ministry has identified a number of actions related to the abolition of school fees. As part of Education for All (EFA) Fast Track Initiative (FTI), Ghana has received an additional grant of US$11 million. These funds will be used for the procurement of 13,100 sets of school furniture, the procurement of textbooks, construction and rehabilitation of classrooms and teacher accommodations, recruitment and training of untrained teachers, and transport for 53 deprived districts. The main focus will be on the most deprived districts. Because of the increase in demand for teachers, it is increasingly difficult to find trained teachers for schools in deprived areas. The ministry has also decided to allow communities to hire local untrained teachers. In-service training programs are foreseen to upgrade their skills. Introduction of multishift education is also anticipated. In addition, manuals for multigrade teaching have been developed and will be disseminated. This is especially relevant for small schools with too few teachers in rural areas where distances to schools are a barrier. As a result of an investment of US$46 million in 2005 for the procurement of text-books, the textbook-pupil ratio in primary school is good; still, additional textbooks will be procured with EFA/FTI funds.

The increase in enrollment has been considerably higher in kinder-garten compared to primary and lower secondary schools. The MoESS acknowledges the importance of kindergarten education as a strategy to improve internal efficiency of the education system through reduced rep-etition and dropout rates and to ensure children enter grade 1 at the age of six years. However, the lack of a coordinated curriculum and the high proportion of untrained kindergarten teachers compromise the quality of teaching and learning. This was reinforced by the success of the abolish-ment of school fees. The MoESS has responded by developing a national kindergarten curriculum and teaching manual, printing and disseminat-ing 30,000 copies, and training all 20,000 kindergarten teachers with support from development partners.

IMPROVING SCHOOL HEALTH AND NUTRITION

Getting children in school is one thing, but keeping them in school and making sure that they learn is another. School health and nutritional status of children are key in this respect and are seen as interventions rein-forcing the initial success of the abolition of school fees. Several major interventions are taking place.

Ghana initiated the Ghana School Feeding Program as a pilot at the end of 2005. To date the program has been introduced to nearly 1,000 schools, covering approximately 450,000 pupils. Expansion to all public primary schools is foreseen by the end of 2010. The Ghana School Feed-ing Program is separate from the school feeding that is already supported by the World Food Program (WFP) and a number of NGOs.

For all students in basic education, deworming took place in early 2007; a second round of deworming will occur in 2008.

REACHING THE EXCLUDED AND DEPRIVED: THE NEED FOR PARTNERSHIPS

The MoESS acknowledges the need to collaborate with education partners and key players in other sectors to attract the most excluded and deprived children to school. Abolition of school fees is making a big difference, but additional measures are needed. Collaborating and establishing new partnerships are helpful in addressing sociocultural barriers to education, for example, in girls' education. A special girls' education initiative has been initiated in partnership with the Ministry of Women and Children's Affairs in 15 districts with the worst gender parity indexes. In these cases, education officials collaborate with NGOs, traditional and religious leaders, and other ministries. Strategies include sensitization of and by traditional and religious leaders, use of community radio programs, and the establishment of community-based monitoring systems.

Strengthening existing partnerships and building new ones with other ministries and civil society are key to a holistic approach to reaching the most vulnerable. The initiation of the social protection strategy by the Ministry of Manpower, Youth and Employment will increase access to education for the most vulnerable, including children affected by HIV/AIDS. The strategy consists of a set of formal and informal mechanisms that provide social assistance and capacity enhancement to those who are vulnerable and excluded by society. In broad terms, such measures target extremely poor individuals, households, and communities, including those who need special care but lack access to basic social services and social insurance to protect themselves from the risk and consequences of livelihood shocks, social inequities, social exclusion, and denial of rights.

STRENGTHENING CAPACITIES FOR IMPROVED EDUCATION INFORMATION AND PLANNING

The basis of education planning and management for the medium and long term is the ability to forecast enrollment in basic education and its related resource requirements. To this end, more reliable population projections and related enrollment projects, including different scenarios based on policy choices, have been undertaken.

In addition, decentralization of EMIS was initiated in the latter part of 2006. In 50 out of the 138 districts, EMIS data collection, processing, and analysis will take place at the district level. Districts have been equipped with requisite computer equipment, and training of all district education planning officers took place in October 2006. It is expected that decentralization of education will improve planning and management capacities at the district level. By placing the core of the EMIS data collection at the district level, it is also expected that data quality and coverage will improve, especially the coverage of private schools.

The lack of reliable district-level population projections is a major challenge for medium- and longer-term education planning models. The MoESS, with the technical support of development partners, has developed a model to forecast teacher supply and demand. The model will enable the ministry to make better-informed decisions and to provide better medium- and long-term financial support. The model will also provide a better basis for estimating the long-term recurrent costs of school education, since the salaries of education staff (personnel) constitute about 90 percent of the total, and for reassessing the funding requirements to achieve the MDGs of universal primary enrollment and gender parity in primary and secondary education.

All district education directors and planning officers received continued training to strengthen their skills in education planning and management, including training in monitoring and evaluation in 2006 and preparation of district education plans in January 2007.

Kenya

CHAPTER 4

Abolition of School Fees and Levies in Kenya

Since Independence, the Kenyan government has placed education at the center of national development. In this regard, as early as 1964, the government established the Ominde Commission to chart the course of the development of the sector. The commission emphasized Kenya's need for universal primary education. Partial implementation of this recommendation started in 1974 and covered standards 1–4; it was extended to standards 5–7 in 1978. The initiative resulted in massive enrollments in primary schools; the gross enrollment rate (GER) level increased from 50 percent in 1963 to a peak of 105.4 percent in 1989. However, the high enrollments were negatively affected by the Cost Sharing Policy introduced in 1989 as part of the Structural Adjustment Programs (SAPs). The policy hindered many children, especially those from economically marginalized groups, from accessing primary education.

COST SHARING IN EDUCATION

The government continued to appoint commissions and presidential working parties to look into various issues in education and particularly into issues of access, equity, relevance, and quality. Thus, the Presidential Working Party on Education and Training for the Next Decade and Beyond (popularly known as the Kamunge Committee) was set up in 1988. This committee focused on issues of quality, relevance, cost, financing, devolment, and the management of education services. In its discussion of financing, the Kamunge Committee Report recommended cost sharing in the financing of the education sector. This policy, which was immediately implemented by the government, stipulated that local communities, including parents, were to construct schools and finance other projects in both primary and secondary public schools. They were also required to pay nonteaching staff salaries at the schools. For its part, the government trained and employed teachers in primary and secondary public schools. The task of mobilizing funds for schools was left to school management committees (SMCs) and the boards of governors, who in turn were supported by local politicians. Parent-teacher associations (PTAs) were also formed; projects approved by the school boards and PTAs were implemented without further reference to the government.

After this major policy shift in education financing, many schools were constructed through *"harambees"* (fundraising efforts) organized by PTAs and SMCs with the help of community leaders. Schools set up their own fees and levies for projects, which included staff wages, construction, purchase and maintenance of school buses, and swimming pools for the high-class public schools. Fee structures differed according to the "needs" of individual schools. Levies, in Kenya shillings (K Sh), ranged from K Sh 500 (US$6.60) to K Sh 10,000 (US$132) per parent per year. These included fees for admissions, examinations, activities, the building fund, and the District Education Board Levy. Some schools charged levies for textbooks and other instructional materials, while others asked parents to buy textbooks for their children. In addition, parents were required to meet extra tuition fees and salaries for school workers, watchmen, and PTA-paid teachers. However, the new policy did not cushion poor households, who could not raise the money to meet fees and the countless other levies imposed by schools.

As a result of the well-intended policy of cost sharing, many children dropped out of primary schools. Education became the preserve of the well-to-do members of Kenyan society. By December 2002, GER had fallen to 88.2 percent, compared with the 1989 level of 105 percent. Declining enrollment heightened concern among leaders; therefore, the provision of free education became the main agenda during the general election of December 2002. The National Rainbow Coalition (NARC) won the elections, breaking the 40-year rule of the Kenya African National Union Party.

There are other factors that contributed to declining enrollments in the 1990s and early 2000s. These include the increase in poverty, the availability of food, the prevalence of HIV/AIDS, and the use of child labor.

- The inability of households to shoulder the high cost of education is mainly the result of deepening poverty in Kenya. The *Second Report on Poverty in Kenya* (Ministry of Finance and Planning 2000) revealed that 56 percent of Kenyans live on or below the poverty line; 30.7 percent of children out of school cite cost as the main reason for nonattendance. The overall cost of education for parents includes teaching and learning materials, fees, extra levies, capital development projects, and other miscellaneous charges.

- In poverty-stricken areas where household food security is precarious, school attendance is severely compromised. For example, in Marsabit District, if transportation problems constrain the availability of food under the World Food Program, schools are closed. In Turkana District, the synthesis report on education for nomads in Eastern Africa (Carr-Hill et al. 2005) reveals that one school's enrollment dropped from 300 to 40 pupils at the end of term because of lack of food. This means that the supply of food and water to these areas is critical for enrollment and retention. Worse still, these areas are also beset with natural calamities like floods and strong winds that occasionally destroy classrooms.
- During the past 10 years, HIV/AIDS has emerged as a major cause of school dropouts in Kenya. Parents affected by the pandemic become too sick to provide for their children's basic needs, including education. Children also leave school to care for sick parents or because they are orphaned. By the year 2020, it is estimated that 11.8 percent of all children below 15 years of age will be orphaned mainly because of AIDS.
- Child labor critically affects school attendance in Kenya and is common in parts of Nyanza, Eastern, Coast, and Central Provinces. Primary school dropouts work in coffee and sugarcane plantations, sand harvesting, the fishing industry, quarrying, the *Jua Kali* small-scale enterprise sector, or as "beach boys" (prostitutes). Street children in major urban areas also collect garbage and wash cars, instead of going to school. Predominantly, children seek employment to supplement household incomes.

The initiation of free primary education (FPE) was itself reflective of a growing international consensus shared by governments, donors, and international agencies, such as the World Bank, that cost sharing in the health and education sectors—which had been highly encouraged through structural adjustment programs of the 1980s and 1990s—often produced highly adverse social outcomes. There were thus regional precedents, as well as widespread international support, for the NARC campaign promise to make primary education free for all pupils. NARC ran on a social reform platform that prominently featured the promise to abolish school fees and levies.

In its manifesto, published before the December 2002 election, NARC made the following pledges:

- To provide free and compulsory primary education to all children
- To undertake a comprehensive review of the current system of education
- To design a new system that guarantees all children the right to education and a competitive edge in a global job market.

RATIONALE FOR FREE AND COMPULSORY PRIMARY EDUCATION

Since independence, Kenya has articulated the need to attain universal primary education. To demonstrate its conviction, the government ratified the recommendations of the 1990 Jomtien World Conference on Education for All and the Dakar Framework for Action adopted at the 2000 Dakar World Education Forum and endorsed the goals of the Millennium Summit (2000). The Dakar Forum reiterated the right of every child to education and emphasized the duty of the Kenyan government to provide education to all its citizens. Furthermore, the Children's Act of 2001 grants every Kenyan child the right to education. It is therefore incumbent upon the government to take deliberate policy measures and actions to fulfill this obligation.

Expanding access to primary schooling is of fundamental importance to the government's development strategy for various reasons. First, universal primary education is central to the implementation of the Poverty Reduction Strategy since the acquisition of basic literacy skills will expand Kenyans' access to employment opportunities and sustainable livelihoods. Second, human resource development is key to sustaining the country's economic growth. Kenya's labor force can only participate in the competitive global economy if it has skills that come with education. Third, universal access to primary school education is the most effective strategy for creating equity in education and in opportunities for survival and development. Ensuring that all children are able to enroll in school presents new opportunities for disadvantaged children, including children from underprivileged regions and communities and girls.

OBJECTIVES OF FREE PRIMARY EDUCATION

The objectives of free primary education include the following:

- To reverse the declining enrollments at primary level
- To enhance access, retention, quality, and relevance at the primary level
- To improve participation, progression, and completion rates at the primary level
- To implement sector policy goals, including universally accepted conventions on the provision of education (to which Kenya is a signatory)
- To reduce the cost of education, previously borne by parents in the provision of primary school education
- To streamline and rationalize the use of educational resources
- To implement the provisions of the Children's Act of 2001
- To improve on learning achievements.

PROCESS OF PLANNING AND IMPLEMENTATION OF FREE PRIMARY EDUCATION

Upon winning the December 2002 election, the NARC government implemented one of its preelection pledges to provide universal primary education. It declared that as of January 4, 2003, all Kenyan children were entitled to enroll in public primary schools. Following the initiation of FPE, the new minister for Education, Science and Technolgy clarified that no child would be required to pay fees or levies to any public primary school and that every child regardless of age should report to the nearest public primary school for admission. As schools were to open on January 6, 2003, the minister summoned senior officials from the Ministry of Education, Science and Technology (MoEST) to a crisis meeting on January 3, 2003, to strategize on the challenges in implementing FPE in Kenya. Of primary concern was the call for immediate implementation of FPE. Since the announcement for FPE was made in the middle of the financial year, there was no plan or budgetary allocation in place for its implementation. Hence, the planning process had to start forthwith. The majority of ministry officials, who were in turn expected to mobilize other stakeholders, feared that the quality of education would be compromised. The policy was seen as a mirage and the wishful thinking of a new and inexperienced government.

On Monday, January 6, 2003, when schools across the country opened, the response to the FPE policy was overwhelming. Some public primary schools, especially in urban slum areas, found it difficult to cope with the large numbers of pupils seeking admission. A good example was Kibera's Olympic Primary School, where the head teacher had serious problems trying to restrain children and parents from breaking the school gate to gain entrance and admission. Reports from districts and provinces across the country presented similar scenarios. In one instance, Kimani Maruge Ng'ang'a, an 82-year-old man, took advantage of the FPE policy and enrolled in standard 1 at Kapkeduiwo Primary School in Uasin Gichu District. He became the world's oldest student to enroll in primary school; in 2006, he was still in school, enrolled in standard 4.

For its part, the ministry continued to strategize and devised free primary implementation guideline circulars for field officers and head teachers. In response to the initial implementation problems, the minister for Education, Science and Technology convened an urgent meeting for stakeholders at the Kenya Institute of Education in Nairobi on January 10, 2003. The meeting was attended by senior ministry officials, development partners, the private sector, civil society organizations (CSOs), and international agencies. The outcome of the meeting was the appointment of the Free Primary Education Task Force, chaired by Dr. Eddah Gachukia, a prominent educationist. The main objective of the FPE Task Force was to assist the government develop appropriate strategies to implement FPE and to identify concrete guidelines for smooth and effective implementation.

The task force was mandated to identify the immediate and long-term issues inherent in the implementation of FPE, including rationalization of the curriculum. The task force membership was drawn from a cross section of stakeholder groups (CSOs, education professionals, media, development partners, and MoEST officials). The FPE Task Force used a participatory approach to develop a plan incorporating short-term strategies. The ministry also sent out its officers to all the districts to carry out a rapid assessment of the situation on the ground and to collect data to inform the implementation process. Simultaneously, curriculum materials were developed and teachers advised on the modalities of coping with the various challenges.

RESOURCE MOBILIZATION

Immediately after the initiation of FPE, the government and other stakeholders embarked on a rapid resource-mobilization exercise for the program. A technical team of officers from the MoEST, the Ministry of Finance, and the Kenya Institute of Public Policy, Research and Analysis were instructed to come up with an acceptable unit cost for financing FPE. The task was to identify the legitimate and necessary expenses for primary schools to determine a unit cost. Items identified as key expenses included instructional materials; support staff wages; repairs, maintenance, and improvement of school structures; and others, indicated in table 4.1. The net effect was to remove the financial burden from households.

The team came up with a capitation grant of K Sh 1,020 per child per year. The grant was considered the minimum possible requirement at that time for running the schools and for providing teaching and learning materials. The funds for instructional materials were meant to achieve a textbook-pupil ratio of 1:2 in the upper primary and 1:3 in the lower primary over a period of time. The capitation grant was by no means a replacement for the loss of revenue to schools resulting from the abolition of fees, as most of the fees had been unnecessary.

Once the team had agreed upon the unit cost, a cabinet memorandum was drafted seeking approval for the release of additional funds under the supplementary estimates to facilitate the financing of the program for the financial year ending June 2003. The additional funds were necessary, as

Table 4.1 Breakdown of Expenses Financed by the Capitation Grant

Expense	Cost (K Sh)
Account I: School Instructional and Materials Bank Account (SIMBA)	
Textbooks per pupil (1.5:1)	360.00
Exercise books per pupil (21:1)	210.00
Supplementary readers and reference materials per pupil	55.00
Pencils per pupil (3:1)	15.00
Dusters, chalk, registers	5.00
Charts and wall maps	5.00
Total for tuition	650.00
Account II: General Purpose Account (GPA)	
Support staff wages	112.00
Repairs, maintenance, and improvements	127.00
Activity	43.00
Quality assurance	29.00
Local traveling and transport	21.00
Electricity, water, and conservancy	10.00
Postage/box rental/telephone	22.00
Contingency	6.00
Total for other expenses	370.00
Grand total	1,020.00

Source: Ministry of Education, Science and Technology, Textbook Management Unit (TMU).

the FPE was declared in the middle of the government financial year, which runs from July to June.

Some of the initial sources of FPE funds (2002/03 fiscal year) were as follows:

- The government disbursed K Sh 519 million (US$6.8 million) in emergency grants for use in public primary schools to meet immediate school needs. Of the total, each school received a capitation grant of K Sh 28,871 (US$380) for basic needs such as chalks, dusters, and exercise books.
- The Treasury disbursed a further K Sh 2.4 billion (US$31.6 million) under the supplementary estimates for the financial year 2002/03.
- The Department for International Development (DFID) provided a grant of K Sh 1.6 billion (US$21.1 million).
- UNICEF provided K Sh 192 million (US$2.5 million) to purchase teaching and learning materials, train primary teachers in child-centered interactive methods, supply materials for makeshift classrooms, and provide water and sanitation facilities in schools.

During the 2003/04 financial year, additional support came from the following sources:

- World Bank—K Sh 3.75 billion (US$50 million) for instructional materials and capacity building over a two-year period
- DFID/Swedish International Development Agency—K Sh 809 million (US$10.6 million)
- World Food Program—K Sh 1.056 billion (US$13.9 million)
- Organization of Petroleum Exporting Countries (OPEC)—K Sh 753 million (US$9.9 million)
- Other contributors, including Oxfam (U.K.) and Action Aid.

In response to the willingness of well-wishers to support the FPE initiative, an account was opened at the Kenya Commercial Bank, Kenyatta International Conference Centre (KICC) Branch, under the name Universal Primary Education Fund to receive donations from individuals and the private sector. There was overwhelming support for the program by Kenyans living in Kenya and abroad, who contributed generously: a total of K Sh 798,000 (US$10,500) was raised through this account. However, ministry officials were too preoccupied with FPE implementation to cultivate the wider support of the private sector and other well-wishers.

To meet school expenses, the government adopted a strategy for direct transfer of funds (excluding teachers' salaries) to individual school accounts. The decentralized funding system had been pioneered in a pilot project in Laikipia and Machakos Districts in 1996 with support from the Dutch Government. From 1999 until 2006, the pilot project initiatives, (which also produced the current national primary textbook policy of 1998) were further developed by the government/DFID Strengthening Primary Education (SPRED) 3 Project, which extended the same basic principles to every district in Kenya. Accordingly, each public primary school was directed to open two bank accounts. To ensure consensus among stakeholders for the direct transfer mechanism, the ministry persuaded banks to levy minimal charges on FPE accounts. Large commercial banks signed a Memorandum of Understanding with the MoEST to waive most of the tariffs to ease operation of FPE accounts.

Since that time, capitation grants have been based on enrollment: K Sh 1,020 (US$14) was allocated per pupil per year (see table 4.1 for details). Funds were disbursed to schools through the two accounts managed by the school management committee (SMC), which consisted of the head teacher (as secretary) and elected parent members. The SMC also formed a subcommittee of teachers and parents, which made all the purchase orders on behalf of the SMC. The first of the two accounts (account I) was the School Instructional Materials Bank Account (SIMBA). One parent who was not a member of SMC was made a signatory to that account to ensure transparency and accountability in the use of funds. The second account (account II) was the General Purposes Account, which met operational and maintenance expenses of the school, excluding teachers' salaries.

Thus, the MoEST transfers funds electronically twice a year. Funds must reach individual school accounts within 48 hours of being received in the MoEST account from the Treasury. Apart from the SMC, each primary school was instructed to form a School Instructional Materials Selection Committee (SIMSC) to direct the procurement of instructional materials. This committee was composed of a teacher from each standard, the head of the school, the deputy head teacher, the chairman of the SMC, and an elected parent representative. Before releasing the bulk of FPE funds to schools, the government engaged in rigorous capacity building in April 2003 through sensitization of primary school head teachers, chairmen, and treasurers of respective SMCs. The training was focused on financial management and procurement procedures, and relevant manuals were provided to all schools. The government enhanced the school audit unit by employing additional auditors and, for the first time, required an annual audit of primary school account books. To ensure effective FPE implementation, the government institutionalized the monitoring of fund and other resource use. Under this arrangement, monitoring was done at four levels: national, provincial, district, and school. In addition, parents and school committees could demand information on the use of funds. Accounts were displayed for stakeholders.

DEFINITION OF *QUALITY OF EDUCATION*

A quality education is a programmed form of instruction that seeks out learners and assists them to learn using a wide range of strategies and approaches. It recognizes that learning is linked to experience, language and cultural practices, gifts, traits, the external and internal school environments, and interests. Within the learning experience, there are several components that affect quality: the learner, content, processes, and environment. The government is committed to providing quality education to all Kenyans on the understanding that education is a critical and effective medium for achieving sociocultural-political transformation and overall economic growth and development. Recent policy initiatives in education have focused on the attainment of Education for All (EFA) and

Millennium Development Goals (MDGs) related to universal primary education, gender parity, and adult literacy.

The key concerns are access, retention, equity, quality, and relevance. The implementation of FPE is a move toward the attainment of gender parity and toward the realization of EFA goals and the MDGs through enhanced internal and external efficiencies. The overarching objective of FPE is to promote learning and life-skills development for young people and adults; to increase adult literacy by 50 percent; to achieve gender parity by 2010 and gender equality by 2015; to improve transition rates to the post-primary level up to 70 percent; and also to foster partnerships in education.

The main determinants of quality education include provision of adequate textbooks and teaching staff, a conducive learning environment (including water and sanitation facilities and classrooms), as well as a broad-based curriculum that is implemented through child-centered interactive teaching methodologies.

SUCCESSES OF ABOLITION OF SCHOOL FEES AND LEVIES

The abolition of school fees and levies removed one of the major barriers to access to education for children of parents with limited resources and reversed a trend of declining enrollment rates. The number of pupils in public primary schools increased from 5.9 million in December 2002 to 6.9 million in January 2003 and to 7.1 million in December 2004. In 2006, there were about 7.6 million pupils enrolled in public primary schools, nonformal schools (NFSs), and nonformal education centers (NFECs). This translates to an increase of over 29 percent in a span of three years. Other indicators of success include provision of quality education, improved completion rates, reduced repetition and dropout rates, improved textbook-pupil ratio, and enhanced supply of instructional materials.

Table 4.2 illustrates enrollment figures in public primary schools by province. It is evident from the table that the surge was notable between 2002 and 2003, when enrollment grew by 17.6 percent.

Primary Gross Enrollment Rate. After the introduction of FPE in 2003, the gross enrollment rate increased from 88.2 percent to 102.8 percent in 2003, rising to 104.8 percent in 2004 (table 4.3). The GER for boys and girls increased considerably from 88.9 and 87.5 percent, respectively, in 2002 to 108.0 and 101.6 percent, respectively, in 2004. In 2004, Western Province recorded the highest GER of 134.2 percent, followed by Nyanza Province (121.8) and Eastern Province (119.0). North Eastern and

Table 4.2 Impact of Free Primary Education Policy on Public Primary School Enrollment by Province, 2002–04

Province	2002		2003		2004	
	Boys	Girls	Boys	Girls	Boys	Girls
Central	398,683	399,773	429,366	420,106	430,670	420,677
Coast	199,414	165,344	251,194	208,091	285,455	241,183
Eastern	572,082	574,437	652,555	636,123	685,811	663,127
Nairobi area	72,611	72,668	96,366	96,466	101,044	102,017
North Eastern	33,200	15,034	43,244	21,194	46,188	21,249
Nyanza	514,524	499,554	654,575	626,789	651,151	607,739
Rift Valley	756,571	720,321	889,003	834,884	920,177	853,704
Western	430,433	450,127	527,501	518,898	554,690	537,525
Subtotal	2,977,517	2,897,259	3,543,804	3,362,551	3,675,186	3,447,221
Total for both	5,874,776		6,906,355		7,122,407	

Source: Ministry of Education, Science and Technology, Statistics Section.

Table 4.3 Primary Gross Enrollment Rate by Gender and Province, 2002–04
(percent)

Province	2002		2003		2004	
	Boys	Girls	Boys	Girls	Boys	Girls
Central	92.2	93.3	102.3	100.9	102.2	99.9
Coast	70.3	59.4	86.9	73.7	97.3	83.7
Eastern	103.0	105.2	116.3	114.9	120.6	117.4
Nairobi area	32.3	36.2	39.1	43.9	41.0	45.8
North Eastern	25.3	13.3	32.4	18.8	33.5	18.5
Nyanza	104.8	102.3	127.8	122.8	126.2	117.4
Rift Valley	92.3	88.1	109.5	102.7	113.0	104.2
Western	112.6	108.0	137.4	123.2	143.3	125.9
All Kenya	88.9	87.5	105.0	100.5	108.0	101.6
All Kenya, both	88.2		102.8		104.8	

Source: Ministry of Education, Science and Technology, Statistics Section.

Nairobi Provinces recorded the lowest GER of 26.6 and 43.2 percent, respectively. The low enrollment in Nairobi can be attributed to the high number (60 percent) of Nairobi Province residents who live in slum areas. The majority of children in these slum areas attend nonformal schools as their particular socioeconomic background puts multiple demands on their time. Pressure to supplement family incomes prevents these children from attending formal schools. Enrollment in nonformal schools is estimated at 300,000 pupils, the majority of whom are in

Figure 4.1 Primary School Gross Enrollment Rates, 1999–2004

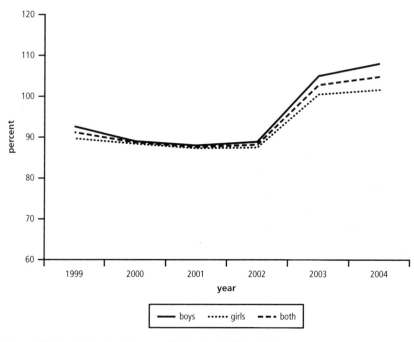

Source: Ministry of Education, Science and Technology, Statistics Section.

Nairobi. For this reason the abolition of fees has not had a greater impact on the enrollment rate in formal primary schools in Nairobi. Figure 4.1 illustrates the provincial trend in GER for the years 1999 to 2004.

Primary Net Enrollment Rate. Table 4.4 shows that the net enrollment rate (NER) increased from 76.4 percent in 2002 to 80.4 percent in 2003, further rising to 82.1 percent in 2004. In 2004, the highest NER was recorded in Western Province with boys and girls registering 99.3 and 97.2 percent, respectively, followed by Nyanza Province at 96.9 for boys and 96.2 percent for girls. North Eastern Province registered the lowest NER of 23.6 for boys and 14.9 for girls.

Primary Completion Rate. After the introduction of FPE in 2003, the primary completion rate (PCR) increased to 68.2 percent from 62.8 percent in 2002 and rose further to 76.2 percent in 2004, as shown in table 4.5. Provincial analysis shows that most provinces witnessed an increase in the PCR between 2002 and 2004. In 2004, the province with the highest PCR was Central Province at 91.8 percent, followed by Eastern Province (81.2), Rift Valley Province (80.1), Western Province (79.9), and Nyanza Province (79.1). The provinces with the lowest PCR were North Eastern at 27.7 percent; followed by Nairobi, 44.9 percent; and Coast, 57.6 percent.

Table 4.4 Primary Net Enrollment Rate by Gender and Province, 2002–04
(percent)

Province	2002 Boys	2002 Girls	2003 Boys	2003 Girls	2004 Boys	2004 Girls
Central	83.5	87.8	83.6	84.2	81.4	81.8
Coast	58.2	53.2	66.9	60.1	72.8	67.7
Eastern	87.7	91.6	90.4	90.3	91.4	91.5
Nairobi area	25.4	29.5	35.5	40.3	35.9	41.1
North Eastern	19.6	14.1	26.1	16.2	23.6	14.9
Nyanza	88.9	89.6	96.2	95.4	96.9	96.2
Rift Valley	81.1	81.5	84.1	82.0	87.8	85.4
Western	95.4	91.7	97.5	93.2	99.3	97.2
All Kenya	76.5	76.3	80.8	80.0	82.2	82.0
All Kenya, both	76.4		80.4		82.1	

Source: Ministry of Education, Science and Technology, Statistics Section.

Table 4.5 Primary Completion Rate by Gender and Province, 2002–04
(percent)

Province	2002 Boys	2002 Girls	2003 Boys	2003 Girls	2004 Boys	2004 Girls
Central	78.7	80.0	82.5	84.4	91.5	92.1
Coast	54.0	36.6	59.5	40.2	69.2	47.3
Eastern	65.8	65.2	73.2	71.3	83.5	79.1
Nairobi area	37.4	40.1	39.3	42.5	43.3	46.6
North Eastern	28.5	11.3	32.7	14.2	39.0	14.8
Nyanza	73.6	59.3	80.2	63.7	88.0	69.8
Rift Valley	69.1	64.0	75.1	69.8	84.1	76.6
Western	65.3	60.3	72.2	66.9	84.5	75.5
All Kenya	65.5	60.1	71.3	65.2	80.3	72.1
All Kenya, both	62.8		68.2		76.2	

Source: Ministry of Education, Science and Technology, Statistics Section.

Primary Repetition Rate. The repetition rate at the primary level declined from 13.2 percent in 1999 to 9.8 percent in 2003, as shown in table 4.6. Analyses show that in 2003 more boys repeated than girls at 10.1 percent and 9.4 percent, respectively. The Rift Valley had the highest repetition rate in 1999 at 15.2 percent, and the Coast had the highest rate in 2003 at 11.5 percent. The lowest repetition rate in 2003 was reported in Nairobi (0.6 percent) and North Eastern (4.7 percent).

Table 4.6 Primary Repetition Rate by Gender and Province, 1999 and 2003
(percent)

Province	1999			2003		
	Boys	Girls	Both	Boys	Girls	Both
Central	11.6	10.5	11.0	6.8	6.2	6.5
Coast	14.7	15.1	14.9	11.6	11.2	11.5
Eastern	13.2	13.1	13.2	8.5	7.9	8.2
Nairobi area	3.0	2.4	2.7	0.7	0.6	0.6
North Eastern	6.5	9.3	7.4	4.5	4.9	4.7
Nyanza	12.7	12.2	12.5	10.3	9.3	9.8
Rift Valley	15.6	14.9	15.2	11.0	10.0	10.5
Western	15.4	13.8	14.6	12.3	11.4	11.9
All Kenya	13.5	12.9	13.2	10.1	9.4	9.8

Source: Ministry of Education, Science and Technology, Statistics Section.

Table 4.7 Primary Dropout Rate by Gender and Province, 1999 and 2003
(percent)

Province	1999			2003		
	Boys	Girls	Both	Boys	Girls	Both
Central	3.1	2.6	2.9	1.0	0.8	0.9
Coast	5.2	5.0	5.1	1.9	1.8	1.8
Eastern	6.4	5.7	6.1	1.9	1.4	1.6
Nairobi area	1.6	1.3	1.5	1.6	1.3	1.5
North Eastern	5.5	6.9	6.0	2.3	3.1	2.6
Nyanza	5.5	6.2	5.8	2.8	3.1	2.9
Rift Valley	4.9	4.7	4.8	2.3	2.2	2.2
Western	5.1	5.0	5.1	2.4	2.4	2.4
All Kenya	5.0	4.8	4.9	2.1	2.0	2.0

Source: Ministry of Education, Science and Technology, Statistics Section.

Primary Dropout Rate. As illustrated in table 4.7, the dropout rate declined from 4.9 percent in 1999 to 2.0 percent in 2003. In 2003, the highest rate was recorded in Nyanza Province (2.9 percent), followed by North Eastern Province (2.6 percent) and Western Province (2.4 percent). The provinces with the lowest dropout rates were Central Province (0.9 percent) and Nairobi Province (1.5 percent). Generally, more boys were reported to have dropped out than girls in all the provinces except Nyanza and North Eastern Provinces.

The increased completion rate can be attributed to MoEST's ban on forced repetition of standards and the abolition of fees and levies, which had hitherto caused children from poor families to drop out of school. Further, the FPE program encouraged parents to send children to school and also motivated children to learn by its provision of instructional materials.

Textbook-Pupil Ratio. One of the key achievements of FPE is the provision of learning materials, particularly textbooks in primary schools, which has improved the quality of education. Children now receive textbooks, exercise books, pencils, and geometrical sets, items they had previously not known that are essential inputs in the provision of quality education. By the year 2004, public primary schools had approximately 9 million textbooks for the five core subjects, as shown in table 4.8 and figure 4.2.

An analysis of table 4.9 indicates that English, mathematics, and science subjects had an overall textbook-pupil ratio (TPR) of 1:2, 1:3, and 1:3, respectively, as compared with 1:4 and 1:71 for Kiswahili and GHCRE (geography, history, civics, and religious education), respectively. The results show that, on average, most of the schools had attained the target of 1:3 TPR in lower primary for English and science subjects.

Although guidelines existed on the ideal TPR prior to the introduction of free primary education, there was no effort to structurally implement these targets and achieve a productive TPR. Parents continued to shoulder the costs of books depending on their financial ability within and across schools.

Number of Teachers and Pupil-Teacher Ratio. The number of teachers in public primary schools remained fairly constant since the introduction of

Table 4.8   Number of Textbooks in Primary Schools by Subject and Standard, 2004

Standard	Subject					Total
	English	Math	Science	Kiswahili	GHCRE	
1	520,909	424,653	437,226	321,731	7,620	1,712,139
2	249,057	210,662	216,733	123,410	4,138	804,000
3	312,779	247,883	255,883	146,730	3,283	966,558
4	284,705	251,992	265,783	181,547	9,212	993,239
5	408,983	370,776	381,344	359,087	15,979	1,536,169
6	224,064	198,891	207,268	147,281	14,349	791,853
7	271,384	245,306	249,628	183,523	17,797	967,638
8	266,722	229,268	251,666	187,611	18,209	953,476
All standards	2,538,603	2,179,431	2,265,531	1,650,920	90,587	8,725,072

Source: Ministry of Education, Science and Technology, Statistics Section.
Note: GHCRE = geography, history, civics, and religious education, a composite subject.

Figure 4.2   Number of Textbooks by Subject and Standard, 2004

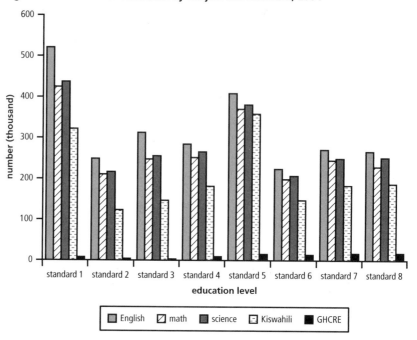

Source: Ministry of Education, Science and Technology, Statistics Section.
Note: GHCRE = geography, history, civics, and religious education, a composite subject.

Table 4.9   Textbook-Pupil Ratio by Subject and Standard, 2004

Standard	Subject				
	English	Math	Science	Kiswahili	GHCRE
1	1:2	1:3	1:3	1:4	1:164
2	1:4	1:5	1:4	1:8	1:234
3	1:3	1:4	1:4	1:6	1:273
4	1:3	1:3	1:3	1:5	1:95
5	1:2	1:2	1:2	1:2	1:51
6	1:3	1:4	1:4	1:5	1:53
7	1:3	1:3	1:3	1:4	1:41
8	1:2	1:2	1:2	1:3	1:29
All standards	1:2	1:3	1:3	1:4	1:71
Lower primary	1:3	1:4	1:3	1:5	1:207
Upper primary	1:3	1:3	1:3	1:3	1:49

Source: Ministry of Education, Science and Technology, Statistics Section.
Note: GHCRE = geography, history, civics, and religious education, a composite subject.

Table 4.10 Number of Teachers in Public Primary Schools and Pupil-Teacher Ratio, 1999–2004

Province	Number of teachers						Pupil-teacher ratio					
	1999	2000	2001	2002	2003	2004	1999	2000	2001	2002	2003	2004
Central	26,280	26,867	26,619	24,176	23,709	23,303	31.9	31.4	31.0	33.0	35.8	36.5
Coast	11,139	10,784	10,426	10,398	10,527	10,783	32.9	33.5	34.6	35.1	43.6	48.8
Eastern	37,745	37,779	37,510	36,386	36,815	36,573	29.2	28.7	29.3	31.5	35.0	36.9
Nairobi area	4,721	4,521	3,710	4,117	4,007	4,189	31.9	32.2	34.4	35.3	48.1	48.5
North Eastern	1,131	1,182	1,118	1,262	1,288	1,478	40.3	40.8	41.1	38.2	50.0	45.6
Nyanza	32,815	33,217	32,429	29,467	30,611	31,205	30.9	30.5	30.7	34.4	41.9	40.3
Rift Valley	47,781	46,603	47,150	44,685	46,897	46,603	29.9	30.2	31.0	33.1	36.8	38.1
Western	24,128	23,707	22,885	21,933	22,718	22,753	34.9	35.0	36.3	40.1	46.1	48.0
All Kenya	185,740	184,660	181,847	172,424	176,572	176,887	31.2	31.0	31.6	34.1	39.1	40.3

Source: Teachers Service Commission.

free primary education. As shown in table 4.10, the total number of primary teachers in public primary schools rose marginally from 172,424 in 2002 to 176,887 in 2004, an increase of 2.6 percent. On the other hand, the utilization of teachers improved over the same period as depicted by the trend in the pupil-teacher ratio (PTR). The national PTR rose from 31.2 in 1999 to 40.3 in 2004. However, it is evident that the annual rise in PTR was highest between 2002 (34.1) and 2003 (39.1) following the introduction of free primary education. In 2004, the provinces with PTR above the national average of 40.3 were Coast (48.8), Nairobi (48.5), Western (48.0), and North Eastern (45.6), while the Central and Eastern Provinces recorded the lowest rates, at 36.5 and 36.9, respectively.

However, there are wide regional disparities in enrollments in Kenya resulting from economic and sociocultural factors. This makes it practically impossible to maintain a national average PTR of 40:1. In the high population areas, there are schools with very large classrooms that are unmanageable. Similarly, the arid and semiarid lands (ASALs) face unique teacher imbalance problems. These remote and climatically hostile areas are not favored by teachers. The situation is particularly bad in areas prone to insecurity, such as West Pokot and East Baringo zones. Because these areas are highly unpopular destinations for teachers, it is still common to find primary schools with only one teacher for all classes. The average PTR in these areas is 20 compared to an average of 45 in the highly densely populated areas.

Kenya Certificate of Primary Examination Performance from 2002 to 2005. The MoEST has been monitoring the performance of primary education through the Directorate of Quality Assurance and Standards and

Table 4.11 Analysis of Trends in Kenya Certificate of Primary Examination, 2002–05

District	Performance (mean standard score)				Performance trends Improved/ not improved/ fluctuated after FPE 2003–05	Remarks on FPE
	2002	2003	2004	2005		
Garissa	208.6500	206.9111	219.5600	227.6200	Fluctuated	Gains
Gucha	236.8038	242.8771	250.2462	250.9750	Improved	Gains
Kilifi	279.3048	280.4105	273.4018	263.3105	Not improved	Gains not apparent
Kisii	209.4794	216.5971	217.7156	223.7039	Improved	Gains
Kisumu	261.2143	265.5443	268.8707	273.5371	Improved	Gains
Kwale	263.3974	241.9125	230.7395	226.2500	Not improved	Gains not apparent
Machakos	257.4500	263.6397	255.9242	251.3078	Not improved	Gains not apparent
Makueni	288.1486	289.2657	288.5482	284.6771	Fluctuated	Gains
Mandera	167.7867	192.3400	213.4444	218.2125	Improved	Gains
Mbeere	229.0450	239.1858	231.8970	231.9195	Improved	Gains
Meru Central	211.9830	223.0455	218.9500	211.9026	Fluctuated	Gains
Meru North	233.9425	237.5895	232.6305	238.9560	Fluctuated	Gains
Meru South	249.633	254.9611	250.0107	249.551	Fluctuated	Gains
Mombasa	255.9789	257.7344	241.7411	234.6611	Not improved	Gains not apparent
Mt. Elgon	240.6242	236.6417	243.7208	226.4958	Not improved	Gains not apparent
Nyamira	238.8111	236.1772	244.3450	234.3872	Not improved	Gains not apparent
Rachuonyo	253.6218	256.3372	264.9961	259.3472	Improved	Gains
Suba	237.0932	255.4289	249.3355	243.1995	Fluctuated	Gains
Teso	249.5235	240.9129	239.3435	224.8915	Not improved	Gains not apparent
Trans Mara	220.8488	217.9732	219.9563	222.9004	Improved	Gains
Vihiga	220.2624	224.6033	221.4853	225.9956	Improved	Gains

Source: Kenya National Examinations Council (KNEC).
Note: FPE = free primary education.

the Kenya National Examinations Council (KNEC). The directorate has been carrying out national quality assurance and standards assessments in all districts. The assessment of February 2006 illustrates that there has been a steady improvement in the Kenya Certificate of Primary Examination (KCPE) performance in 21 out of the 35 low-achieving districts. Low-achieving districts are defined as those that attained a mean standard score (MSS) below 250 out of a possible 500.

An analysis of the KCPE performance trends (see table 4.11) in 21 out of the sampled 35 districts assessed for the period 2002 to 2005 reveals the following:

- Only seven districts failed to record steady improvement.
- Six districts demonstrated a fluctuating performance, that is, occasional drop or rise in the mean standard score.

- Eight districts registered remarkable improvement from 2002 to 2005.
- A total of 80 schools were included in the sample.

The quality of education depended on multiple factors that existed in any one district. Although there was an adequate supply of books, there remained an uneven distribution of teachers throughout the country. There was also a sizable number of orphaned pupils in several schools. This led to noticeable dropout rates in such schools. Other reasons for static or fluctuating performance included the following:

- Absenteeism of teachers because of illness
- Absenteeism of pupils because of the effects of HIV/AIDS
- Inadequate physical facilities
- Dilapidated structures
- Inadequate coverage of the syllabus or the use of old-fashioned teaching methods, which yield poor results
- Inadequate teaching and learning aids and ineffective internal supervision
- Poor bookkeeping and maintenance of professional records.

Some districts in ASALs or marginal areas, including Garissa and Mandera, performed better than some districts in high-potential areas, for example, Meru North and Meru Central. Urban districts such as Mombasa experienced high enrollments and overcrowding in classrooms, leading to reduced teacher-pupil contact and, therefore, decline in KCPE performance. Schools in districts with a high human dependency index (HDI) or poverty level had dilapidated infrastructure. The disrepair of the schools demonstrated diminished parental support to repair, maintain, and improve tuition blocks and other physical facilities. Consequently, KCPE performance was generally low in these areas over the years 2002–04. A good example is Machakos District.

Based on data from the 80 schools sampled from the 21 low-achieving districts, it is evident that the supply of adequate instructional materials has had a positive impact on learning.

Further Analysis on KCPE Performance Trends. The KNEC analysis on KCPE performance indicates a similar trend. The national mean score for KCPE declined from 247.91 in 2002 to 247.76 in 2003 but increased marginally to 247.89 in 2004, a rise of 0.13 points as shown in table 4.12. This illustrates that upon implementation of FPE in 2003, performance in the primary examinations (KCPE) initially declined, an indication of decline in the quality of education. However, the situation was reversed in 2004, when performance started improving. Over the years, males recorded higher performance than females, both at the national and at

Table 4.12 Mean Score of Kenya Certificate of Primary Education by Gender and Province, 2002–05

Province	2002		2003		2004		2005	
	Female	Male	Female	Male	Female	Male	Female	Male
Central	234.12	243.78	236.29	248.81	235.53	244.95	234.31	243.79
Coast	248.01	263.23	245.52	262.31	243.33	256.84	238.01	253.32
Eastern	239.90	253.07	238.93	253.36	240.27	251.33	237.60	248.67
Nairobi area	267.21	269.98	267.58	273.03	267.67	269.46	259.29	266.39
North Eastern	167.87	198.42	180.50	205.32	194.32	218.88	190.20	216.07
Nyanza	227.02	246.79	227.80	250.00	233.40	254.32	233.07	253.54
Rift Valley	249.88	263.41	243.70	260.61	242.64	257.98	243.48	259.05
Western	244.60	260.04	243.23	260.94	246.60	262.00	250.34	265.99
All Kenya	241.02	254.39	239.62	255.38	240.79	254.43	240.14	254.01
All Kenya, both	247.91		247.76		247.89		247.44	

Source: Kenya National Examinations Council.

the provincial levels. Further analysis shows that KCPE 2005 performance in ASAL districts and specifically in Rift Valley Province improved significantly as compared with high-potential districts or municipalities. For instance, 9 districts in the province were among the top 20 out of 76 in the country. Out of these 9, 5 were from ASALs (Baringo—position 6, Koibatek—position 9, Keiyo—position 10, Kajiado—position 11, and Turkana—position 14).

Additional Resources to the Education Sector. Implementation of the FPE initiative was accompanied by the allocation of additional funds to the education sector. The total budget of the ministry was increased from K Sh 53.4 billion (US$702.6 million) in 2001/02 to K Sh 63.4 billion (US$834.2 million) in 2002/03 and further increased to K Sh 72.3 billion (US$951.3 million) in 2003/04 financial years. This reflects an annual increment of about K Sh 10 billion (US$131.6 million) to cater to the program and other related services. In 2004, 33.46 percent of the public sector recurrent budget was devoted to education. Additional resources were mobilized from donor agencies, although over 90 percent of funding for primary education continues to be mobilized from domestic sources.

CHALLENGES

The *immediate challenges* that emerged in 2003 include the following:

- The immediate announcement and implementation of FPE was done without prior consensus building and consultation among the relevant stakeholders on the mechanics of rolling it out. In addition, there was lack of preparedness by both implementers and stakeholders on how best to manage the immediate demands of the program. The government required additional time to release the emergency grants to schools.

- Many opposition politicians had campaigned against FPE as an impracticable and far-fetched proposal.
- A majority of Kenyans were anxious about the success of FPE. It was felt that the troubled economy would not be able to sustain the demands of the program. Many were also fearful that the lack of prior budgetary provision would lead to failure.
- The FPE was launched in the middle of a financial year by a new government; there were no funds allocated to the program in the 2003/04 budget.
- Transferring large sums of money directly to school accounts was risky. School managers had no prior knowledge, capacity, or skills to handle large sums of money at the school level. Indeed, most primary schools did not operate functional bank accounts. There was no established accountability system at that level, and many feared resource mismanagement given the low capacity of school management committees (SMCs).
- Some SMCs were apprehensive about adopting the FPE policy. School heads and SMC members had previously benefited from school fees and levies. They had used these at their own discretion without proper accounting as there was no mandatory bookkeeping in schools prior to the introduction of the FPE. For this reason, most opposed the abolition of levies. Members of SMCs strongly believed that the capitation grants received from the government would not meet all the school requirements. Consequently, committee members at some schools resigned.
- Affluent parents were fearful that FPE would badly compromise the quality of education at all levels of the primary cycle. As a consequence, the initial reaction of the well-to-do was to transfer their children to private schools, thereby raising the enrollments in these schools from 187,966 in 2002 to 253,169 in 2003, an increase of 34.7 percent. However, in some provinces, such as Central and Rift Valley, some private schools closed after parents transferred their children to public primary schools following the declaration of FPE.
- Although the Kenya National Union of Teachers was supportive and even participated in the FPE Task Force, they opposed the larger class sizes, arguing that the government should have first hired more teachers to handle the increased workload rather than burden head teachers

and classroom teachers with increased teaching and bookkeeping responsibilities. At the same time, the teachers' union demanded the immediate implementation of the negotiated increase in teachers' salaries in lump sum. The government therefore faced a dilemma as to what it should implement first. Even before the declaration of FPE, the country had faced a teacher shortage caused by a public sector–employment freeze ordered by the government in 1997. This shortage of teachers was, however, aggravated by massive enrollments in public primary schools after the declaration of the free primary education policy.

- Parents in some schools expected the government to buy school uniforms although it was not mandatory to have uniforms as a precondition for entry into school.
- Some schools were charging levies for miscellaneous expenses and using these to bar enrollments for those unable to afford them.

However, there are *ongoing challenges,* and they include the following:

- Despite its popularity, implementing the FPE policy has proved to be a difficult task. Absence of prior planning led to crowded classrooms with too many children sharing few and inadequate facilities, especially in ASALs and urban informal settlements. As enrollment rates soared, class sizes increased significantly. Other facilities including water and sanitation were also stretched to the limit. Construction of additional schools and classrooms was not part of the initial FPE initiative, and enrollment surges placed a similar strain on other physical infrastructure of schools. In some schools, multishift or multigrade classrooms were created in response to the shortage of teachers and classrooms.
- High pupil-teacher ratios in some schools because of increased enrollment were not matched by an increase in the number of recruited teachers. The PTR increased from a national average of 34:1 in 2002 to 40:1 in 2003. Besides overstretched resources, which threaten the quality of education, other difficulties include teacher shortages in some areas, which mean that pupils receive fewer assignments as teachers have no time to mark papers. Increased enrollment at the primary school level has created serious understaffing in a majority of schools, forcing SMCs in some areas to hire untrained teachers.
- High cost of special equipment, facilities, and materials required for children with special needs hinders access to education for those categories of learners. Even in some primary schools where few physical facilities were available, these were not disability-friendly.

- Low transition rates from primary to secondary or to technical, industrial, vocational, and entrepreneurship training programs result in high wastage of primary school graduates. The current transition rate stands at 57 percent, denoting a high wastage rate. In the Kenyan context, basic education now means 12 years of continuous learning in school. However, Kenya also faces budgetary constraints so that all standard 8 graduates cannot be transitioned to secondary schools. Expanding access at the secondary level has not taken center stage after FPE.

- High prevalence of HIV/AIDS has led to increased numbers of orphans in schools. The pandemic also forces many out-of-school pupils to work and care for affected and infected relatives. They cease being care receivers and become caregivers. The pandemic has also robbed the country of trained and experienced teachers.

- Limited sensitization to the free primary education policy among communities has led to diminished parental support in the provision of requisite physical facilities. The FPE declaration created the perception that parents no longer had any obligation to provide for school needs.

- Is the FPE program financially sustainable? In 2006, over 90 percent of FPE funding came from domestic sources; the balance was covered by development partners. The education sector consumes the largest share of the annual government budget (28 percent in 2006). This high allocation must be weighed against competing demands from other critical sectors, including health, physical infrastructure, and agriculture. The need to engage communities and the local private sector is, therefore, urgent.

- For professional growth, primary school teachers also need regular and in-service training to effectively deliver the 2002 revised curriculum, undertake school-based assessment of learning achievements, and learn alternative approaches to curriculum delivery such as multigrade, multishift, and mobile schools. The existing preservice training program in primary teachers' colleges should be reviewed to make it relevant to the 2002 revised syllabuses. The ministry should also organize large-scale training sessions for practicing teachers, Teacher Advisory Centre tutors, and core teachers from cluster schools to help them master subject content and upgrade their skills.

- Quality was also affected in schools where head teachers lacked sufficient managerial skills to handle multiple tasks such as bookkeeping, supervising curriculum implementation, and teaching at the same time. Head teachers' heavy workloads left them insufficient time to effectively supervise class teachers on preparation and maintenance of professional records, work schemes, lesson plans, and actual teaching.

- There was further need for quality monitoring and teacher-support visits to schools. Headquarters' staff, field quality assurance and standards officers, key resource teachers trained in subject-based teacher development, head teachers, and Teacher Advisory Centre tutors would be involved in the effort.
- The government has yet to establish strategies and modalities to reach out-of-school children, including the children of pastoralist communities; to develop and implement a comprehensive communication strategy to generate massive public awareness on the Kenya Education Sector Support Program (KESSP); to build partnerships among the private sector; to develop and operationalize district and school development plans; and to cooperate with other line ministries and agencies.
- A national system is required that effectively monitors learning achievements at all levels and not only at the end of the primary school cycle. To this end, numeracy and literacy competency instruments that gauge learner achievements and competencies at every level of the primary education cycle must be developed.
- Although introduction of FPE has increased primary-level access and completion rates, expanding access at the secondary level to cater to primary-level graduates remains a major challenge. In 2006, the transition rate from primary to secondary stands at 57 percent. The massive wastage (43 percent) must be amended to guarantee the investment that has been made in free education.

COPING STRATEGIES AND MECHANISMS

The MoEST issued circulars on guidelines of FPE implementation mainly to field officers and heads of schools. It also produced manuals on financial management and procurement procedures for use in primary schools. An FPE Task Force was formed and was mandated to identify the immediate and long-term issues on the implementation of FPE.

Rigorous internal sensitization and consensus building took place among senior ministry officials at the headquarters and field offices. A sustained public-awareness campaign was conducted through the print and electronic media and the public *barazas* (public community gatherings where announcements are made, key information is shared, and important issues are discussed). In addition, an open door policy was established whereby stakeholders and other well-wishers were encouraged to play a key role in supporting the FPE. To allay apprehension of failure, the government embarked on a rapid resource-mobilization exercise. To that end, it disbursed emergency grants of approximately

K Sh 28,871 (US$380) to each public primary school as it continued to mobilize more resources for the program. The government has also increased support to special needs learners. An additional K Sh 153,660 (US$2,022) per school was disbursed to special schools and units to procure special needs equipment. Further, every school was given K Sh 10,000 (US$132) to create a disability-friendly environment at school. An additional budget has been provided to the Kenya Institute of Special Education to expand training of special needs education teachers and thus achieve the goal of an all-inclusive educational system.

To ease direct money transfers to schools, as a first step, the government instructed all public primary schools to open two bank accounts: one account for instructional materials and the other for general purposes. In the meantime, all school heads and school management committees were instructed not to spend the disbursed funds until they were sensitized on the management of those funds. Sensitization workshops were conducted for school heads, chairmen, and parent representatives on financial management and procurement procedures. In addition to sensitizing participants on the operation of the accounts, these workshops also advised on the formation of SIMSCs and the election of bank signatories. Within the same period, commercial banks entered into a partnership with the MoEST whereby they agreed to give concessionary services to all 18,000 public primary schools. The arrangement entailed waiving certain bank charges and included free issuance of bank balances to the MoEST to monitor and oversee the drawdown of these accounts. As a further control measure, the MoEST in conjunction with the commercial banks disallowed cash withdrawals from the SIMBA account. Rather, payments drawn on this account would be by check to all concerned merchants. These combined efforts had the effect of ensuring credibility and transparency in the use of FPE funds.

To allay the fear that FPE would lower the quality of education in public primary schools, the ministry intensified quality monitoring and standards assessment visits to all schools to ensure that disbursed funds were used prudently to meet the needs of curriculum implementation. The Directorate of Quality Assurance and Standards also received a supplementary allocation to facilitate its extensive audit on quality and standards. This included the training of quality assurance and standards officers and the allocation of motorcycles and vehicles to facilitate monitoring.

In response to the aforementioned concerns of the Kenya National Union of Teachers, the government engaged the teachers' union in a structured negotiation that led to a five-year phased implementation of salary awards. To cope with the increased workload for teachers and to deal with the existing shortage of teachers in certain areas, the government embarked on a countrywide staff-balancing exercise by deploying teachers from overstaffed regions, districts, and schools to those that had been understaffed. On the basis of this, the Teachers Service Commission deployed one teacher to teach 45–50 pupils in urban and high-potential areas. Meanwhile, for smaller classes with lower enrollments, especially in ASALs with sparse pupil catchments, teachers will be trained to use alternative delivery modes such as multigrade teaching. As a way of linking teacher promotions to performance, the government has instated teachers' proficiency courses as an ongoing program. A study on teacher staffing norms to establish criteria for training, recruitment, deployment, and more equitable distribution and efficient use of teachers has been completed but has yet to be implemented. In 2006, the staffing norm for a given district was one teacher per class plus 2.5 percent of the total number of classes in the district. Intensive staff training and sensitization have been carried out since 2003. The training has extended to all stakeholders at all levels.

Under the FPE capitation grant, most schools have procured sufficient stocks of textbooks in the ratio of 1:3 for lower and 1:2 for upper primary levels. Devolving grant management and procurement of textbooks to the school level has increased the availability of textbooks, which, in turn, has enhanced access and retention.

Implementation of the revised curriculum commenced in January 2003 and is now complete. It was examined for the first time in the 2006 Kenya Certificate of Primary Examination. The number of examinable subjects was reduced from seven to five.

Many children in ASALs, areas with pockets of poverty, and urban slums are out of school because of a lack of boarding schools or day schools within walking distance. To correct this shortfall, the government has increased grant disbursement to low-cost boarding primary schools. The government is also offering capitation grants to nonformal schools to improve the quality of education. These funds are for the purchase of instructional materials; they support children from poor households who enter through NFS. The government is also developing criteria for the distribution of FPE grants to NFECs, especially those catering to orphans. The government also plans to launch the newly developed accelerated NFEC curriculum. Under the KESSP infrastructure program, USAID and the World Bank have taken a lead role in providing additional classrooms and adequate water and sanitation facilities, particularly to schools in the ASALs. The KESSP has laid the foundation for FPE in Kenya and emphasizes that the provision of free primary schooling must be sustained. To improve access and participation of children of nomadic communities, particularly in North Eastern Province and parts of northern Kenya, the MoEST is establishing mobile schools there.

In addition to providing instructional materials and infrastructure, the government will continue in-service training for teachers and review the various testing and assessment systems (KNEC efforts) that are in place and integrate them into a national assessment system to monitor learning achievements (for instance, MALP—Monitoring Achievements in Lower Primary and SACMEQ—Southern African Consortium for Monitoring Educational Quality). Under the MALP initiative, the numeracy and literacy instruments for assessing learner competencies have been developed by the technical team for all 10 examinable subjects taught in standards 1 to 4. Once data from pretesting are cleared, MALP will be pilot tested in three selected districts before it is scaled up in the whole country. Under the SACMEQ initiative, preparatory work was done for the commencement of the SACMEQ III Project in November 2006. To improve quality of teaching, learning, and performance, the government has reviewed the existing preservice training program with a view to rationalizing current programs of primary teacher colleges and, in the long run, upgrading primary school teachers' colleges to diploma level. The Directorate of Quality Assurance will also initiate a national accreditation system to ensure continuous professional development, upgrading, and skills development in conjunction with private in-service training providers.

Other interventions for quality assurance include establishing and operationalizing item banking and procuring printing equipment for KNEC. KNEC will also conduct basic adult education and nonformal education examination review to serve the interests of adult learners. Meanwhile, the Kenya Institute of Education plans to produce curriculum-support materials that boost Hindu religious education, sign language, and various mother tongue languages, areas where commercial publishers have not yet ventured. Further, KIE will launch an educational broadcasting channel that is accessible nationwide to reach adult learners and out-of-school children as well as those in the mainstream education system.

Schools must provide a healthy, clean, and secure environment from which to address the urgent need for life skills education for young people and equip them with knowledge and skills for survival. To this end, the government continues to strengthen HIV/AIDS education and health and sanitation in all schools and to ensure that these initiatives are mainstreamed in school programs. The information on drug abuse, HIV/AIDS, and school health and sanitation will be included in the Orange Book, the list of school instructional materials, with appropriate instructions for purchasing. The lessons learned from ongoing pilots and enhanced guidance and counseling programs in schools will benefit the implementation of HIV/AIDS education. Primary school teachers will continue to receive regular and in-service training for professional growth to enable them to deliver the new curriculum effectively, undertake school-based assessment of learning achievements, and use alternative approaches to curriculum delivery.

To confront other challenges arising from the abolition of fees and levies, the government convened a National Conference on Education and Training in November 2003 that produced a blueprint for the development of FPE and, more broadly, for education and training for the country. The conference outcomes were used to develop "Sessional Paper No. 1 of 2005" (MoEST 2005), stipulating certain policies and strategies. To operationalize this policy framework, the ministry in collaboration with development partners, CSOs, and other stakeholders developed a five-year investment program, the KESSP, as a road map to implement the policy guidelines of the sessional paper. The development of KESSP is guided by the broad principles stipulated in the Economic Recovery Strategy, the Millennium Development Goals, and Education for All. Of the 23 investment programs listed in the KESSP document, the following 18 directly or indirectly support the implementation of FPE:

1. Primary School Infrastructure Program
2. Early Childhood Development and Education Program
3. Nonformal Education Program
4. Special Needs Education Program
5. Adult Basic Education Program
6. HIV/AIDS Program
7. School Feeding Program
8. School Health and Nutrition Program
9. School Instructional Materials Investment Program
10. Support to Low-Cost Boarding Primary Schools
11. Primary Teacher Training Investment Program
12. Primary Teacher In-Service Training Investment Program
13. ASAL Mobile Schools Investment Program
14. Capacity Building Investment Program
15. Education Management Information System (EMIS)
16. Information and Communication Technology (ICT)
17. Guidance and Counseling Program
18. Quality Assurance and Standards Investment Program.

It is important to note that the theme of the KESSP program is "Delivering quality education and training to all Kenyans."

LESSONS LEARNED

As 2006 was the fourth year of implementation of the FPE program in Kenya, we can conclusively say that it has so far been a success story. This initiative has, however, had certain limitations and raised some challenges. Thus, many lessons can be learned from this undertaking, including the following:

- Capacity building entails organizing sensitization workshops. From the onset of FPE, the MoEST embarked on rigorous basic training for head teachers on financial management and procurement procedures. The training involved basic bookkeeping and financial reporting. Capacity building is critical for effective implementation of a program of this magnitude of scale and expenditure. There is consequently greater confidence in the people implementing the program and less fear of mismanagement of funds.
- In addition to capacity building, there is a critical need for continuous reassurance and confidence building among stakeholders to prevent them from giving up under extreme pressure. A critical asset in Kenya was that the minister and permanent secretary for Education, Science and Technology were viewed as honest and trustworthy by all parties.
- Political commitment and goodwill are critical to the successful implementation of an FPE program. The program has enjoyed goodwill from the highest offices—the president, cabinet ministers, assistant ministers, and members of parliament, including the opposition, who now realize that resistance to the program would be political suicide. It is, however, the unflinching commitment of the minister for Education, Science and Technology and the dynamic leadership of the permanent secretary in the administration of FPE that have been singularly important.
- A clear policy on FPE implementation that defines the roles and responsibilities of different stakeholders must be stipulated. For the program to succeed, there must be continuous dialogue with stakeholders such as parents, school committees, and local communities to inform them from the onset of their specific roles in supporting the policy.
- Intensive and sustained public information and a communication strategy to educate all stakeholders on their various roles are needed.

- The drawdown reports by commercial banks to the ministry assist in expenditure tracking, which in turn enables policy makers to determine whether the program is on target. Commercial banks give balances of individual school accounts to the ministry, enabling it to track expenditures at the schools. Cases of large unspent balances require immediate action. This mechanism has contributed positively to the sustained and successful implementation of the program and is a case of public-private partnership enhancing transparency and accountability in the handling of public funds.

- Upward revision of the capitation grants to schools is required in keeping with the rising inflationary rates. The capitation grant has remained constant at K Sh 1,020 (US$14) since 2003 while inflationary levels have continued to rise over time, thus undermining the purchasing power for schools. The capitation grants should, therefore, be reviewed from time to time in keeping with the prevailing inflationary trends.

- Consistency and commitment in program leadership are necessary. The FPE program has benefited greatly from the consistency in the top-level management, which includes the minister and the permanent secretary. The two have sustained a very high commitment to the process from its inception. Key professionals who were in the initial planning process are still on board and hence have kept the pace and development on track.

- Eliminating the bureaucracy in the disbursement of FPE resources facilitates the effective disbursement of funds directly to the schools. Removing the middlemen minimizes leakages.

- A functional adult basic education system is a prerequisite to successful implementation of an FPE program.

- Partnership at every level of implementation is vital to the success of the program. The involvement of all stakeholders, including parents, development partners, communities, and school management committees, has contributed immensely to the success of the program. Close consultation and consensus building have enhanced ownership.

- Public account keeping at the school level has ensured transparency and accountability for the program's resources. It is mandatory that all schools display on their notice boards all receipts of FPE funds as well as expenditures within a given period of time.

- There has been intensive financial monitoring of the program by the minister and permanent secretary for Education, Science and Technology and by MoEST staff both at the headquarters and at field offices, including quality assurance and standards officers, National Audit Office staff, internal auditors, and external auditors. These internal and external checks have contributed greatly to the efficient use of FPE resources, thus reducing mismanagement to the bare minimum.

- Operational manuals to guide teachers and school management committees must be provided. After launching the program, the ministry embarked on the production and dissemination of operational manuals to guide implementation of the program with respect to financial management, procurement of instructional materials, and general accountability principles.

- In the wake of the massive enrollments, no immediate steps were taken to maintain the standard of quality except to remind parents to provide funds to expand physical facilities and buy uniforms for the increased number of pupils. The challenges to quality should be dealt with before declaring an abolition of fees and levies so that the quality of schools is not compromised. However, it is stated government policy that no child should be denied access to school merely because the parents have not provided funds for expanding physical facilities or buying a school uniform.

- As illustrated by the variation in enrollment rate by province shown in table 4.3, school fees and levies are not the only determinants of enrollment. Other critical factors include cultural practices, religious inclinations, and the level of understanding about the value of education within a given community, as demonstrated in the case of urban slums.

CONCLUSION

The FPE program has been an opportunity for countless Kenyan children who would not otherwise have had access to education. The smooth implementation of FPE may be attributed to various factors, including sustained political goodwill, foresightedness in leadership, and consistency in the application of rules of implementation. Pragmatism is essential to the success of such a program. The government is determined to use all alternative teaching and learning approaches to reach all children and in particular those who are hard to reach. The success of FPE can only be guaranteed if disbursements are divorced from political considerations and manipulations. Since the government cannot implement FPE alone, it has provided an institutional framework for enabling others to participate in the program; this is key to the program's sustainability. As a result of the bold move, Kenya has earned a place in the history books as having enrolled the oldest primary school student on earth. Despite encountering some teething problems such as shortages of teaching staff and other necessary education inputs, FPE has significantly boosted Kenya's chance of realizing universal primary education as stipulated in the Education for All and the Millennium Development Goals.

REFERENCES

Carr-Hill, Roy A., Almaz Eshete, Charlotte Sedel, and Alba de Souza. 2005. *The Education of Nomadic Peoples in East Africa: A Synthesis Report.* Paris: UNESCO-IIEP (United Nations Educational, Scientific and Cultural Organization International Institute for Educational Planning).

Ministry of Finance and Planning. 2000. *Second Report on Poverty in Kenya.* Nairobi, Kenya: Ministry of Finance and Planning.

MoEST (Ministry of Education, Science and Technology). 2005. "Sessional Paper No. 1 of 2005 on a Policy Framework for Education, Training, and Research." Available at www.un-kenya.org/ThemeGroups/**SessionalPaper**Finaljan.doc.

Malawi

CHAPTER 5

Review of the Planning and Implementation of Free Primary Education in Malawi

The overall objective of the study was to assess the planning and implementation of free primary education (FPE) in Malawi and to devise lessons learned from this experience. It looks first at the process of policy formulation, planning, and implementation of FPE in Malawi, by examining the following:

- The extent to which the planning and implementation of FPE took into account quality, access, equity, socioeconomic, cultural, management, governance, and financial issues
- The extent to which the planning and implementation of FPE was informed by earlier studies, reviews, and evaluations
- The strategies that were put in place during planning and implementation to minimize costs
- The extent to which the process of planning and implementation was well documented
- The lessons learned from the process of planning and implementation of FPE
- The extent to which objectives in terms of output, outcomes, and impact of introducing FPE were achieved.

The study then examines the impact of FPE reforms in Malawi and highlights the successes and challenges that arose during planning and implementation, identifying the coping strategies and mechanisms adopted to deal with them, and comparing the overall performance of the primary education sector before and after the introduction of FPE. The study concludes with some of the lessons learned from the Malawi experience.

METHODOLOGY

The information for the study was collected mainly through interviews with key stakeholders from the Ministry of Education (MoE)[1] and the Ministry of Finance (MoF) who were involved in the planning and implementation of FPE in 1994 (see annex 5A). These included senior- and lower-level personnel; for the latter, semistructured interviews and focus group discussions (FGDs) were held and included primary education advisers (PEAs), teachers, and head teachers from two selected schools in Lilongwe Rural West Education District. Data were also collected through a review of documents and related literature on primary education, specifically on FPE, as well as an analysis of a large quantity of contextual data on enrollment, efficiency, and quality indicators obtained mainly from the MoE Education Management Information System (EMIS). Among the key documents reviewed were the Ministry of Education, Sports, and Culture (MoESC)/UNICEF policy analysis study on the experience of free primary education in Malawi (1998), as well as recently completed studies on the implementation of FPE and on the performance of the primary education sector, and project documents from donor agencies such as the World Bank, United States Agency for International Development (USAID), and the Department for International Development (DFID).[2]

PLANNING AND IMPLEMENTATION OF SCHOOL FEE ABOLITION

Malawi was one of the first countries in Sub-Saharan Africa to take the bold initiative of abolishing primary school fees in 1994 and opening the doors of primary school to all children of primary school age. The public response to the initiative was both overwhelming and unprecedented: an additional 1 million children entered school, an overall increase of over 50 percent from the previous year.

THE CONTEXT OF FREE PRIMARY EDUCATION REFORM IN MALAWI

Until 1994, primary education was not free in Malawi. User fees were collected at both primary and secondary schools as a cost-recovery measure to supplement public expenditure. The fees and other educational expenses constituted a major financial burden for the majority of rural households, most of whom were poor. The situation in Malawi at that time was in sharp contrast to regional trends of most African countries. Others advocated universal primary education (UPE) and introduced free primary education upon attaining independence. Although Malawi was a signatory, it did not implement the 1961 declaration of UNESCO's Pan-African Conference on Education, which set the target of achieving universal primary education by 1980 and advocated the introduction of free and compulsory primary education.

In 1987/88 school fees collected in Malawi amounted to about 11 percent of the primary recurrent expenditure and were used mainly to cover the costs of instructional materials such as exercise books and textbooks, with over 80 percent of the fees being used for this purpose alone. The fees charged were lower in rural than in urban areas and were also lower for standards 1–5. Though the fees were low, for the majority of rural households, most of whom are poor, the fees together with other educational expenses constituted a major financial burden.

In 1982 the school fees, which had remained unchanged since 1975, were increased substantially, following the advice of the World Bank (Thobani 1983), especially for rural schools where fees increased by 75 percent for standards 1–5 compared with 29 percent for urban schools, and 38 percent for standards 6–8 compared with 15 percent for urban schools (Rose 2002). From 1982 until the fees were abolished in the early 1990s, the fees for rural schools were 3.50 Malawi kwacha (MK) for standards 1–5 and MK 5.50 for standards 5–8, and for urban schools, MK 4.50 for standards 1–5 and MK 7.50 for standards 5–8.[3]

In addition to fees, schools also levied various forms of charges for the payment of telephones, electricity, and water bills, and for sports and examination expenses. Parents also bore the cost of other nonfee expenditures, such as textbooks, exercise books, writing materials (mainly because government provision was inadequate), and school uniforms. During the same period, parents and local communities were also largely responsible for the construction and maintenance of primary schools through their provision of labor and materials. Thus, parents incurred substantial expenses, both direct and indirect, for their children's education; school fees constituted only a small proportion of that total expenditure.

The decision to increase school fees in 1982 had disastrous consequences on enrollment at the primary level. Overall absolute primary enrollments fell by 1.6 percent in 1982/83 from the previous year following the increase in school fees. The impact was greatest in standard 1 enrollment, which declined by almost 10 percent. The fees remained unchanged until the 1990s. In the 1990s, largely as a consequence of the Jomtien World Conference Declaration on Education for All (1990), a number of policy reforms on tuition and school fees were introduced. Most notably, the World Bank, which had, in the 1980s, advocated the increase in school fees on the grounds that the measure would increase efficiency and equity (Thobani 1983; Tan, Lee, and Mingat 1984), retracted its earlier position, and from the 1990s, supported efforts toward the abolition of fees.

THE MOVE TOWARD FREE PRIMARY EDUCATION

The 1990s saw a shift in government and donor policies regarding school fees; between 1991 and 1993 the government with support from donors introduced new measures to abolish school fees. In 1991/92, the government with World Bank support introduced tuition fee waivers beginning in standard 1 and phased in standards 2 and 3 over the next two years. This, however, was a partial abolition of school fees, as parents were still required to pay a book fee and to contribute to the school development fund. From 1992/93, a school fee waiver program for nonrepeating girls in standards 2–8 was introduced under the USAID-supported Girls Attainment in Basic Education and Literacy (GABLE) Program.

There were significant increases in enrollments following the changes in the tuition and school fee policy between 1990 and 1993, though far less than the increases after the introduction of FPE. For example, following the tuition fee waivers introduced in 1991/92, enrollments increased by as much as 19 percent compared with 6 percent in the preceding year, with the gross enrollment rate (GER) increasing significantly from 75 percent in 1990/91 to 86 percent in 1991/92. The enrollment increase was quite substantial in the first four years of schooling, with standard 1 enrollment increasing by 40 percent, suggesting that many children were encouraged to enroll as a result of the tuition fee waivers.

The school fee waivers under GABLE had a more limited impact, with enrollment increasing by 8 percent. However, the school fee waivers had a greater impact on girls' enrollment, which increased twice as much as boys' (12 percent and 5 percent, respectively); for the first time, the net enrollment ratio (NER) for girls surpassed that for boys. Enrollment increases exerted pressure on the limited resources, and there are indications that performance and quality indicators did in fact worsen as a result. For example, the proportion of unqualified teachers in the system increased as the demand for teachers grew. There were changes to the existing preservice teacher-training program with the introduction of an in-service program for untrained teachers under the World Bank–supported Malawi Special Teachers Education Program (MASTEP) and the introduction of a one-year teacher-training program in one of the teacher-training colleges. Pupil-teacher ratios (PTRs) also increased significantly during this period (see annex table 5B.4).

However, as discussed later, it appears that planning for FPE did not borrow much from its earlier experience of implementing school fee waivers. These earlier initiatives undoubtedly created the impetus for FPE, as was evident in the run-up to the first multiparty election between 1993 and 1994 when FPE became highly visible on the political agenda. School fees were abolished altogether in 1994 when free primary education was introduced. Apart from eliminating all fees, the government committed itself to providing all required learning materials for all primary pupils; it also removed the requirement for the wearing of uniforms.

MAIN FEATURES OF FREE PRIMARY EDUCATION REFORMS

The main objectives of introducing FPE were to increase access to primary education, to eliminate inequalities in enrollment, and to build a strong socioeconomic base within society and enhance civic understanding of the social and economic benefits of education at the community level (MoESC and UNICEF 1998). The main emphasis of FPE was to increase access. Initially, very little attention was paid to quality issues. Under FPE, the government promised to do the following:

- Abolish all forms of fees, including contributions to the school development fund
- Take responsibility for the provision of teaching and learning materials, teachers, classrooms, furniture, teachers' houses, sanitation facilities, and boreholes
- Assume the financing of all primary schools, including the previously unsupported community junior primary schools (unassisted schools), by merging them with government-assisted schools and thereby creating a unified primary school system
- Introduce community schools
- Encourage the participation of girls in primary education.

In theory, FPE implied an entirely free system of education for households, with the government shouldering all the cost of education. Though quality was one of the objectives of FPE, in practice more emphasis was placed on access and quantitative aspects; so initially quality issues were largely ignored.

To ensure effective implementation of FPE, a number of strategies and policies were introduced, including the following:

- Eliminating the requirement for school uniforms at primary school
- Using mother tongue or vernacular languages as the medium of instruction in standards 1–4

- Shifting from an inspection-based system to one based on teacher support and development (the post of primary education adviser was established to replace school inspectors; primary schools were grouped into 315 zones, each under the supervision of a primary education adviser)
- Increasing budgetary allocation to the education sector with priority for primary education, which received the largest share of the education recurrent budget.

THE PLANNING PROCESS FOR FREE PRIMARY EDUCATION

In Malawi it is widely accepted that the main drivers of the FPE policy were politicians (all the stakeholders interviewed from both central and lower levels of the government indicated that FPE was on the political agenda). As Avenstrup, Liang, and Nellemann (2004) observe for Kenya, Lesotho, Malawi, and Uganda, "the adoption of universal free primary education was triggered by political demand rather than by rational planning processes." FPE was high on the agenda of the main political parties that contested the first multiparty election in 1994. Both the Malawi Congress Party (MCP), whose government implemented the phased abolition of school fees, and the United Democratic Front (UDF) used FPE as a campaign strategy to win the election. Both parties' manifestos included the introduction of FPE. While the MCP manifesto proposed a phased approach for FPE, UDF was silent on the mode of implementation (MCP 1993; UDF 1993). Upon winning the election, the UDF immediately fulfilled its electoral pledge, declared the introduction of FPE in May 1994, and announced that implementation would start in September of the same year with the beginning of the new school year.

Thus, the government had exactly four months to plan the implementation of universal primary education. To expedite the implementation of FPE, a number of activities were undertaken (see table 5.1). Within the ministry, systems had to be developed to respond to the decree. In this regard, the Ministry of Education, the main implementing agency of the policy, created a task force headed by the chief planning officer to oversee and coordinate the planning and implementation of FPE. More important, that officer was charged with the task of determining the resource requirements and planning for resource mobilization. At a higher level, a ministerial task force was formed to coordinate activities of key ministries that would be involved in the implementation, such as the Ministries of Education and Finance and the Office of the President and the Cabinet.

One of the first activities of this task force was to convene a National Policy Symposium a month after FPE was declared. At the symposium, a

Table 5.1 Timeline for the Planning and Implementation of Free Primary Education, May 1994–February 1997

Time period	Activity
May 21, 1994	• FPE declared
June 1994	• Creation of MoE task force to coordinate planning and implementation of FPE and plan for resource mobilization • Creation of ministerial task force to coordinate activities of key ministries involved in FPE
June 27–28, 1994	• National Policy Symposium
July 1994	• Planning for implementation • Mass media campaign to mobilize the public
July 25–30, 1994	• Preregistration of pupils
August 1994	• Recruitment of 20,000 school leavers as untrained teachers and orientation of trainers to train them • Establishment of Supplies Unit for procurement and distribution of learning materials • Briefing of regional and district personnel and college professionals on the FPE policy
September 1994	• Two-and-one-half-week orientation of untrained teachers • Deployment of untrained teachers to schools
September 25, 1994	• Schools open
1995	• MoE issues directive on new language policy
April 1995	• Distribution of teaching and learning materials
June 9, 1995	• Consultative conference on national campaign strategies for keeping children in school
August 17–18, 1995	• Two-day seminar on status of FPE
September 1995	• World Bank–funded Malawi Social Action Fund (MASAF) pilot phase concentrating on school construction launched
November 1995	• Establishment of Education Development Management Unit (EDMU) within MoE to facilitate coordination of development projects • DFID-supported Primary Community Schools Project set up within MoE
December 1995	• Teacher Development Unit (TDU) established within MoE
January 1996	• Teacher development symposium held to establish Malawi Integrated In-service Teacher Education Programme (MIITEP) for training untrained teachers
May 1996	• MASAF launched with focus on education • World Bank Primary Education Project (PEP) launched
January 1997	• Training of teachers under MIITEP commences
February 1997	• Malawi School Systems Support Program (MSSSP) launched with support from British Government

Source: Ministry of Education, Sports, and Culture and UNICEF 1998; interviews with stakeholders.

cross-section of stakeholders met to discuss policy issues relevant to FPE and their resource implications. The symposium recommended that the government increase budgetary allocations to the education sector and recruit more teachers.

The symposium was followed by a preregistration exercise in July 1994 to determine potential enrollment, which was then used to establish resource requirements. Other activities that were carried out before schools opened included the creation of a new supplies unit to oversee procurement and distribution of teaching and learning materials to schools, briefing of all regional and district personnel on FPE policy, recruitment of untrained teachers, and orientation of trainers who would be used to train the newly recruited untrained teachers. The training of these teachers was done shortly before schools opened and, given time constraints, lasted only for two-and-one-half weeks, after which teachers were immediately deployed to schools. Schools opened at the end of September 1994.

Malawi organized a successful campaign using radio, newspapers, and politicians from the ruling party to mobilize the public and encourage parents to send children to school. However, most of the stakeholders interviewed for this study felt that the government did not adequately consult with all key stakeholders during FPE planning. In particular, key stakeholders such as head teachers, teachers, and parents were hardly ever consulted during FPE planning, which may not be very surprising given the little time that was available between declaration and implementation.

There was little time to develop policy, plan implementation, mobilize resources, and institute necessary structural changes and capacity development required for effective implementation to meet the demands created by the enrollment surge after FPE declaration. Most stakeholders interviewed felt that the government responded to the enrollment surge with a crisis-management approach, characterized by crash programs for teacher training, as the following observations suggest:

- After FPE was declared, the mode of planning in the ministry became planning after the fact.
- After the declaration of FPE, the challenge for planners was to balance thorough planning, which is essential for such a major policy reform, with the rapid results demanded by politicians, which did not give the ministry adequate time for planning. Thus, planning was largely a response to challenges created by FPE rather than a rational process aimed at achieving well-thought-out objectives and strategies.

The preregistration exercise had revealed that an additional 1.3 million children would enroll at the beginning of the school year, representing about a 68 percent increase in enrollment. This surge created unprecedented demands on resources such as infrastructure, teachers, and teaching and learning resources. The MoE responded by recruiting an additional 20,000 teachers. The majority (90 percent) were untrained secondary school leavers who were deployed after a two-and-one-half-week orientation; the intention being that they would provide professional support as well as continue their training on the job. The large number of teachers that needed orientation in a short time required an equally large number of trainers, but they were not available in sufficient numbers. To fill the gap, secondary school teachers in addition to primary teacher college tutors were employed to conduct the training. Thus, there were concerns about the quality of teachers who had been oriented in such a haphazard manner.

The initial plan was to continue teacher training during the school year through school-based supervision and professional support. However, as necessary structures and systems were not in place, this was not possible. A teacher development symposium for the Malawi Integrated In-service Teacher Education Programme (MIITEP) was held little over a year after FPE was implemented, in January 1996. An emergency teacher-training program to address the crisis was eventually developed. MIITEP was essentially a mixed-mode training program consisting of college-based and distance school–based training, replacing the preexisting conventional full-time preservice college-based training. The actual training of teachers started a year later in 1997.

However, as has been observed, the early phases of the program faced a number of serious setbacks. The problems sprang largely from the absence of an absorptive capacity within the sector to handle a large-scale and complex program, thus affecting the quality of teachers (MoESC and UNICEF 1998; Kunje, Lewin, and Stuart 2003). The MIITEP assumed the existence of certain supportive mechanisms in the schools, for example, that head teachers and senior teachers would supervise and mentor the recruits in the schools. However, these teachers did not necessarily have supervision and mentorship skills, and in some schools, trained teachers who could provide that support were greatly outnumbered by untrained teachers. Alternatively, some schools were staffed entirely by untrained teachers so that it was impossible to realize the objective of school-based training. To impart these skills, the Malawi School Systems Support Program (MSSSP) was established in 1997, one year after the MIITEP was launched and after the training had already begun and untrained teachers had been in schools for almost four years. If there had been better planning for FPE, the MSSSP should have preceded MIITEP.

Most aspects that were critical to the effective implementation of FPE were initiated and carried out after FPE was introduced. The sudden influx of pupils into the system led to what Avenstrup, Liang, and Nellemann (2004) have termed "access shock," as the massive enrollment increases resulted in overcrowded classrooms and acute shortages of teachers and of teaching and learning materials. As shown later, the resource requirements for FPE implementation were enormous, and it was obvious that the government alone could not meet these. In fact, resource mobilization was initiated after implementation and not before, partly because there was inadequate time for planning, but also because some donors were reluctant at first to provide support in the absence of a sector plan (MoESC and UNICEF 1998). As one of the stakeholders interviewed observed, "Donors were at first reluctant to support . . . , they wanted us to plan adequately first before implementation."

Only UNICEF supported the government in its initial declaration of intention to introduce FPE in the new school year. Later, after schools had opened for the new year, the private sector was also supportive. Most other donors joined in after UNICEF had provided support. Programs such as the World Bank–funded Malawi Social Action Fund (MASAF) and Primary Education Project (PEP) and the DFID-funded Community Schools Project, which were critical to the effective implementation of FPE, only started in 1995. Thus, school and classroom construction lagged behind enrollment increases. Inadequate time for planning also affected the procurement and distribution of teaching and learning materials. Nationwide distribution of teaching and learning materials came into effect in April 1995, seven months after the schools had opened.

Moreover, the urgency to meet resource requirements forced the MoE to adopt shortcut measures for procurement of teaching and learning materials, creating opportunities for fraudulent and corrupt practices. Interviewed stakeholders cited the 1995 Fieldyork scandal in which the government paid exorbitant prices for notebooks and was involved in related irregularities in the procurement and distribution of instructional materials for FPE between 1998 and 2000. They also cited the 1998 education scam in which the government lost almost US$2 million for the construction of ghost schools and from the breakdown in fiscal discipline and general decline in standards of public management that resulted in poor utilization and wastage of resources. Lack of resources led to disillusionment with the school system. The lack of instructional materials and other teaching and learning resources dampened high expectations and caused the exodus of nearly 300,000 pupils from the system as enrollment dropped from 3.2 million at the beginning of the school year to about 2.9 million by its end.

FREE PRIMARY EDUCATION AND THE CULTURAL AND SOCIOECONOMIC CONTEXT OF SCHOOLING

The stakeholders interviewed generally agreed that since FPE arose from a political agenda and was implemented to fulfill an electoral pledge, little time and thought were given to its planning. The perception was that politicians were in a hurry and therefore did not allow technocrats sufficient time to plan for FPE. The new government was under intense political pressure and had to be seen to be fulfilling its promises. FPE was seen as the easiest of the electoral pledges to fulfill and one that would bring immediate political gains.

Thus, political expediency dominated decisions that followed the declaration of FPE. It is now generally accepted that at the time FPE was introduced, the country was ill prepared. FPE was introduced at a time of severe macroeconomic instability. Drought had brought negative growth in the economy. There was a budget deficit resulting from expenditure overruns by the MCP government in the run-up to the first multiparty elections. Additionally, Malawi experienced rising inflation, depreciation of the currency, lower revenues, and the suspension of development aid by its major donors because of the MCP government's violation of human rights (Kadzamira, Nthara, and Kholowa 2004). At the time of FPE implementation, it was clear that the government did not have sufficient resources and capacity to absorb the massive expansion. It was also clear that the government was banking on the goodwill of donors.

Though the government and donors provided greater resources to education, and particularly, primary education, the resource implications of implementing FPE were enormous so that the resources made available were not adequate to maintain current standards or prevent deterioration in the quality of provision. For example, in the first year of implementation, the increased budgetary allocation to the sector did not prevent a decline in real per pupil expenditure, which is estimated to have slumped by 26 percent from MK 53 in 1993/94 to MK 39 in 1994/95 after the introduction of FPE, suggesting that the massive increase in enrollments was not matched by a proportionate increase in expenditure (Kadzamira and Chibwana 2000). Thus planning of FPE took neither prevailing economic conditions nor financial constraints into account. It was clear that at the time FPE was being planned and implemented, the government did not have enough resources to ensure effective implementation and outcomes.

No comprehensive analysis was undertaken beforehand to assess the impact of policy reform on the education sector and determine resource implications. The haste with which FPE was introduced suggested that the government did not learn from the experiences of ongoing reforms such as the GABLE Program and the tuition fee waiver program or that the government had not been informed by earlier studies, reviews, and evaluations. For example, the GABLE Program began implementation with quality reforms, which would improve the learning environment, and then introduced the quantity reforms, which would increase enroll-ments. Thus classroom construction and rehabilitation, curriculum reforms, and teacher training were sequenced before the social mobiliza-tion campaign, which was expected to increase enrollment.

At the time FPE was introduced, it was quite obvious that the existing Education Development Plan (EDP II 1985–95) had become outdated and needed revision in light of the major changes in the sector, especially after the 1990 Jomtien Conference. Thus, FPE was introduced in the absence of a major sector framework. To make matters worse, the govern-ment took a long time to develop a new sector plan. The Policy Invest-ment Framework (PIF), which factored in the impact of FPE, was con-cluded in 2001, seven years after FPE had been in place. All other national development frameworks such as the Poverty Alleviation Program and the Malawi Poverty Reduction Strategy Paper (MPRSP) were designed after FPE was introduced. Nevertheless FPE had good linkages with these national plans that sought to increase literacy and reduce levels of poverty. Thus, FPE became integrated into national plans after it was implemented.

FPE demanded a shift in the education paradigm, from one accessible only to the few who could afford to pay user fees to one that offered an inclusive education for all social strata. This required consideration of the cultural issues that prevented children from enrolling in school. Unfortu-nately, it does not appear that these considerations influenced, in any great detail, the planning and implementation of FPE. FPE did, however, address some cultural constraints that girls face in accessing school. By abolishing school fees, the government removed a major barrier to the enrollment of girls; previous studies indicated that families strongly preferred educating sons rather than daughters when school fees were charged.

The conflict between the demands of the school calendar and those of the livelihood systems of rural households has always been a problematic issue in Malawi. Previously the school calendar mirrored the agricultural calendar (which also influences the timing of initiation ceremonies) and ran from October to July, conflicting with peak times that required chil-dren's labor in assisting with household activities. The calendar was changed in 1997 and now runs from January to November. Reasons for the change remain controversial as they were not directly related to the needs of the primary education sector. Apparently, the calendar was adjusted to respond to problems affecting the secondary and tertiary edu-cation sectors: because of prolonged drought, boarding institutions were persistently affected by water shortages. In some years, institutions were closed for much of the first term. Since the new calendar was not designed to respond to the challenges faced by the primary education sector, the sector's calendar still conflicts with the peak agricultural periods and with the social calendar, which closely follows the agricultural calendar. During the implementation of FPE, it was thus necessary to extend the second-term recess for the primary-level calendar to avoid conflict with initiation ceremonies.

To further universalize education, it was felt that the language policy should be changed to accommodate children from different ethnic groups. Prior to 1994, the language policy required that Chichewa, the national language, should be the language of instruction in the first four standards. This policy was revised in 1995; the current policy states that children should be taught in the vernacular language or their mother tongue. In practice, however, implementation of the new language policy in schools has been difficult as textbooks are still only available in Chichewa, the previous language of instruction. Moreover, teachers have not received any training or practical guidance on how to use the local language as the medium of instruction. Deployment of teachers to schools does not consider their ability to speak the local language. The policy has become politically sensitive as it would be tantamount to asking teachers to teach in their district of origin, which was a politically unpopular policy during Hastings Kamuzu Banda's regime.

COPING STRATEGIES AND MECHANISMS

To address the challenges brought about by the enrollment surge, the government adopted a number of coping strategies. To manage the rising demand for teachers, it introduced two measures. First, it increased the official class size from 50 to 60. This was done mainly to reduce the demand for teachers: expanding the size of the teaching force would create a great deal of stress on the budget. Second, the government recruited untrained teachers and, after short inductions, deployed them in schools and also recalled retired teachers.

To ease the pressure on existing infrastructure, the government issued a circular in 1994, advising all schools with inadequate classroom space to introduce multishift schooling. Existing community structures such as churches were used as classrooms. In addition, temporary shelters were constructed in some areas.

To cope with the expansion, the structure of the MoE was reorganized. Six divisions were created; then, at the district level, schools were grouped into zones. There were a total of 315 zones, and each zone was managed by the newly created primary education adviser, who replaced the previous inspector and had both supervisory and advisory responsibilities.

IMPACTS OF THE FREE PRIMARY EDUCATION POLICY

Implementation of the free primary education policy has markedly increased enrollment. Additionally, it has increased gender equity as well as equity in enrollment between socioeconomic groups. However, access to primary education has been achieved at the expense of quality, and the quantitative gains made through FPE have been undermined by the failure of the system to retain pupils once they have enrolled.

EFFECT ON ACCESS

The introduction of FPE led to a massive increase in enrollments. Primary school enrollments increased dramatically in all standards (see figure 5.1). An additional 1 million children entered school, a 51 percent increase in enrollment from the previous school year. There was a remarkable increase in enrollment across all standards, with phenomenal growth rates in standard 8 (76 percent) and standard 1 (59 percent) in particular. The increase suggests that many children who had dropped out of school for lack of capacity to pay school fees reenrolled after the fees were abolished (see table 5.2).

Table 5.2 Enrollment Growth Rate by Standard following the Fee Waivers, 1991/92–1994/95

(percent)

Standard	1991/92			1992/93			1994/95		
	Girls	Boys	Both	Girls	Boys	Both	Girls	Boys	Both
1	43.3	37.6	40.4	9.3	0.1	4.6	54.0	64.6	59.2
2	16.0	21.0	18.7	18.5	3.8	10.4	31.1	41.4	36.3
3	7.1	14.4	11.0	18.7	4.2	10.7	48.8	54.6	51.8
4	21.9	5.3	12.3	11.1	8.1	9.4	45.8	52.7	49.4
5	10.0	9.3	9.7	7.8	7.2	7.5	45.6	47.0	46.3
6	12.0	7.8	9.6	4.5	7.2	6.0	45.5	44.7	45.1
7	12.3	8.1	9.9	0.1	3.6	2.1	51.8	43.7	47.1
8	−1.8	−12.8	−8.9	6.8	24.0	17.4	81.2	72.9	76.0
All standards	21.0	16.8	18.7	11.5	5.1	8.0	47.5	54.1	50.9

Source: Ministry of Education.

The government adopted an open door policy that allowed children to enroll or reenroll in any grade irrespective of age. This policy resulted in an influx of children, many of whom were overage, into the primary school system. The rate of enrollment growth following FPE was higher for boys than for girls in every standard except for the last three grades of primary school. Overall, boys' enrollment grew at a faster pace than did girls', reversing the trend in enrollment growth that was evident before the universalizing of primary education, when girls' enrollment grew at a faster rate than boys' (see table 5.3). However, the majority of those who entered school enrolled in standard 1 alone, suggesting that school fees were an important determinant of nonparticipation in school. Other factors such as the elimination of the uniform requirement and the re-admittance policy for pregnant girls may have contributed to increasing enrollments, but there is no doubt that the impact of the school fee waivers was the major reason for enrollment increase.

Absolute primary school enrollment increased from 1,400,682 (44.9 percent for girls) in 1990/91 to 1,895,423 (48 percent for girls) in 1993/94, an increase of 35 percent over the period (see table 5.3 and figure 5.1). The immediate impact of the enrollment increase was, however, a decrease in the proportion of girls enrolled in primary school from 48 percent in 1993/94 to 47 percent in 1994/95, as more boys enrolled

Table 5.3 Primary School Enrollments by Gender, 1990/91–2005

Year	Total	Girls (percent)
1990/91	1,400,682	44.9
1991/92	1,662,583	44.8
1992/93	1,795,451	47.2
1993/94	1,895,423	48.1
1994/95	2,860,819	47.0
1995/96	2,887,107	47.0
1997	2,905,950	47.7
1998	2,805,785	48.6
1999	2,896,280	48.2
2000	3,016,972	48.4
2001	3,187,835	48.4
2002	3,164,191	49.0
2003	3,067,843	49.6
2004	3,166,786	49.8
2005	3,200,646	49.8

Source: Ministry of Education.

Figure 5.1   Trends in Primary School Enrollments, 1990/91–2005

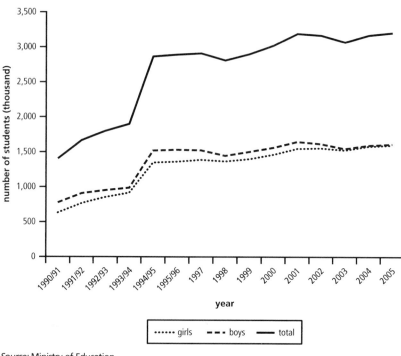

Source: Ministry of Education.

after FPE was introduced. Girls' enrollment, however, picked up again after 1995/96. By 2005 half of primary school enrollment was for girls. Even though Malawi is close to reaching full gender parity (see figure 5.1), the gender parity index (GPI) masks differences throughout the cycle. The number of girls who drop out after standard 4 increases compared to boys; and by standard 8, girls represent 43 percent of enrollment.

EFFECT ON EQUITY

One of the objectives of FPE was to encourage the participation of girls in primary education (MoESC and UNICEF 1998). This was achieved largely through the abolition of school fees, which previous research had shown were a real barrier to school access, particularly for girls. The majority of stakeholders interviewed felt that FPE increased gender equity. However, empirical evidence suggests that this was not the case immediately after the introduction of FPE; gender equity improved later, after enrollments stabilized. As indicated earlier, initially boys' enrollment grew faster than girls' because more overage boys took advantage of the open door

Table 5.4   Trends in Gross Enrollment Rates by Household Expenditure Quintile and Gender, 1990/91–2004

(percent)

House-hold expen-diture quintile	1990/91			1994/95			1997			2002			2004		
	Girls	Boys	Both	Girls	Boys	Both	Girls	Boys	Both	Girls	Boys	Both	Girls	Boys	Both
1 (poorest)	51	65	58	69	100	74	109	125	117	103	110	106	89	97	93
2	69	83	76	88	117	102	111	132	121	101	112	106	97	101	99
3	83	88	86	98	118	114	118	121	119	118	114	116	105	113	109
4	89	104	97	104	134	131	118	133	125	114	122	118	111	115	113
5 (richest)	106	113	110	120	134	133	112	129	120	121	132	126	113	120	117
All quintiles	75	86	81	96	121	108	113	128	120	111	118	115	103	109	106

Source: Data for 1990/91 and 1997 are from Al-Samarrai and Zaman 2002; data for 1994/95 are from Castro-Leal 1996; data for 2002 are from the National Statistical Office and ORC Macro 2003; and data for 2004 are from the National Statistical Office and ORC Macro 2005.

policy and reenrolled in school. Consequently, gender disparities in gross enrollment rates increased immediately after FPE was introduced (see table 5.4). Gender disparities have narrowed significantly since then, and by 2004 there was near gender parity in GER; that is, 94 girls enrolled for every 100 boys, compared with 88 girls in 1990/91 and 79 girls in 1994/95.

FPE also improved equity in enrollment between socioeconomic groups. The policy improved access to education for the poor. For most households, many of whom were poor, school fees and other associated costs of education were a heavy burden. Access improved substantially for the poorest groups following the abolition of school fees in 1994; the poorest quintiles made substantial gains in enrollment, with gross and net enrollment rates more than doubling over the period (see table 5.4). The enrollment gap between the richest and the poorest quintiles has also narrowed considerably as a result of the enrollment increase. The share of public spending benefiting the poor increased as a result of the enroll-ment increase. In 1990/91 the GER for the poorest group was 58 percent, about half the GER for the richest group (110 percent). GER for the poor-est quintile increased to 74 percent in 1994/95 after the introduction of FPE and exceeded 100 percent in 1997; however, by 2004 it had dropped to 93 percent.

Table 5.5 compares the net enrollment rate of children enrolled in school between 1990 and 2004 by income group. Again, the table shows that the proportion of school-age children attending school among the

Table 5.5   Trends in Net Enrollment Rates by Household Expenditure Quintile and Gender, 1990/91–2004

(percent)

Household expenditure quintile	1990/91			1997			2002			2004		
	Girls	Boys	Both	Girls	Boys	Both	Girls	Boys	Both	Girls	Boys	Both
1 (poorest)	31	34	33	74	77	76	74	72	73	75	72	73
2	45	50	48	77	76	76	73	76	74	79	74	77
3	57	52	55	77	74	75	83	79	81	84	81	82
4	61	66	62	81	76	79	83	87	85	88	83	86
5 (richest)	75	76	75	81	80	80	91	92	91	94	92	93
All quintiles	50	52	51	78	76	77	81	81	81	84	80	82

Source: Data for 1990/91 and 1997 are from Al-Samarrai and Zaman 2002; for 2002, from the National Statistical Office and ORC Macro 2003; and for 2004, from NSO and ORC Macro 2005.

poorest quintile increased significantly after the introduction of FPE, more than doubling (from 33 percent in 1990/91 to over 70 percent), suggesting that the 1994 reforms benefited the poorest groups. However, subsequent national surveys indicate that the gap in NER between the richest and the poorest groups has widened again, probably because of economic shocks during the period.[4] The disparity in enrollment rates of school-age children between the richest and poorest groups narrowed significantly as a consequence of the educational reforms. Gender parity in NER has been achieved, indicating that there is an almost equal proportion of primary school–age boys and girls attending school. The gender gap in the net enrollment rate favors girls, but the poorest girls are still more likely to be out of school.

After the introduction of FPE, significant improvements for all subgroups were evident; however, disparities remain between income groups (see tables 5.4 and 5.5). This suggests that, despite some relaxation of financial constraints on primary schooling, there are other, mostly poverty-related factors that constrain the poorest households from sending all their children to school. Despite the massive increase in primary enrollment after 1994, the poorest are still most likely to be out of school and more likely to drop out before completing primary education. School-level stakeholders also felt that FPE had increased disparities between socioeconomic groups. During discussions with the school management committee (SMC) and the parent-teacher association from the two schools visited, it was argued that "it is only the poor who enrolled for FPE, but the rich preferred to send their children to private schools because they feel FPE is not valuable."

CONSEQUENCES FOR QUALITY

The rapid expansion of enrollment following FPE implementation resulted in further deterioration of an already overstretched primary education system, characterized by poor quality and low internal efficiency. Budgetary and other resource implications of implementing FPE were considerable. Although public spending (both government and donor) increased substantially, it was not sufficient to ensure universal primary schooling of minimally acceptable quality.

All key quality indicators of primary education worsened after the enrollment increase. For example, the pupil–qualified teacher ratio deteriorated from 81:1 in 1993/94 to 108:1 in 1995/96 as the proportion of unqualified teachers increased from 16 percent in 1993/94 to 42 percent in 1994/95 because of the recruitment of 20,000 untrained teachers to meet additional demand. The number of pupils per permanent classroom, desk, and textbook increased dramatically after the enrollment increase: pupils per desk from 19 to 27, pupils per classroom from 115 to 162, pupils per English textbook from about 3 to 5, and pupils per math textbook from 2 to about 4 (see table 5.6).

Table 5.6   Primary Education Quality Indicators, 1990/91–2005

Year	Pupil-teacher ratio	Pupil-qualified teacher ratio	Pupil-classroom ratio[a]	Pupil-desk ratio	Pupil-English textbook ratio	Pupil-math textbook ratio
1990/91	78.1	114.8	95.6	16.9	2.03	2.77
1991/92	71.4	83.0	115.7	18.0	4.41	3.69
1992/93	68.2	78.4	118.5	19.0	2.89	2.86
1993/94	67.8	80.9	114.7	19.4	2.63	2.36
1994/95	62.5	107.8	161.8	27.1	4.66	4.18
1995/96	58.8	87.8	189.4	—	2.95	2.90
1997	61.4	119.3	158.7	20.5	2.00	2.09
1998	67.4	133.7	211.7	17.4	4.66	1.28
1999	63.2	118.1	93.5	17.7	1.40	1.43
2000	63.0	122.7	114.3	15.2	1.78	1.80
2001	59.6	100.2	113.6	—	2.09	2.09
2002	—	—	—	—	1.15	1.13
2003	68.0	95.8	107.6	11.6	1.30	1.25
2004	72.0	92.0	107.0	9.0	1.44	1.21
2005	71.0	82.8	106.4	—	1.83	1.83

Source: Ministry of Education.
— Not available.
a. Permanent classroom.

The quality of schooling is also said to have deteriorated because of the poor quality of teachers recruited. As the MoE had to recruit a large number of teachers, proper screening procedures were not followed, and some teachers used fake certificates to gain employment.

A major reason for the deterioration in the quality of education was that the massive increase in enrollment was not matched by a proportionate increase in expenditure. Although the proportion of government expenditure on education increased from 11 percent in 1990/91 to 24 percent in 1997 and the share of primary education in the education budget increased from 45 percent to 65 percent, primary spending per pupil actually declined and stagnated for the rest of the 1990s. Before the abolition of fees, public education expenditure had been on an upward trend in Malawi, but in 1994/95 spending per pupil declined by approximately one-quarter, implying that the government was initially unable to cover the fees households had been paying (Al-Samarrai 2003).

Moreover the bulk of additional resources allocated to primary education after 1994 has financed the salaries of additional teachers recruited after FPE, leaving very little money for nonsalary quality inputs. In 1997, for example, 83 percent of the primary recurrent budget was spent on teacher salaries while only 6 percent was spent on teaching and learning materials. Thus, current levels of financing primary education leave very little room for improving quality, which has been severely compromised by the massive expansion in enrollment.

One of the head teachers interviewed observed that when school fees were charged, money was available for purchasing teaching and learning materials. However, after FPE the money was no longer available, there was a shortage for both teaching and learning materials in schools and funds for school development and maintenance. In particular, the government has not been able to replace the lost income in fees, such as for the school development fund, which were used for maintenance and purchase of sports equipment, paying for utilities in urban schools, and for other needs such as recruitment of support staff. Schools have been left with no option but to charge extra fees to cover these expenses.

The majority of stakeholders interviewed felt that although FPE increased access to primary education, this was achieved at the expense of quality. In other words, there was a quantity-quality trade-off when FPE was introduced. Their view was that quality was compromised largely because of the recruitment of untrained teachers who were not fit to teach and, to make matters worse, were not given adequate training. FPE was said also to have increased teacher workload, particularly in rural areas where PTR increased significantly. Though overall PTR decreased with the recruitment of untrained teachers, the deployment of teachers to schools was unsatisfactory as the remotest schools faced chronic teacher shortages. School personnel noted that teachers and schools did not have the capacity to deal with the FPE reform and could not manage the large numbers of pupils in class; as a result teachers lost interest in teaching.

Stakeholders, particularly those at the school level, also felt that pupil behavior changed after FPE because of misconceptions about democracy and basic human rights. In particular, teachers, head teachers, and members of SMCs/PTAs who were interviewed all claimed that pupil behavior had changed and that most pupils lacked discipline as a result of these misconceptions. They did not take school seriously since they no longer paid fees. Parents too were reported to have lost interest in school; they did not feel obliged to monitor their children's progress, as schooling was free. During focus group discussions with SMCs/PTAs, it was claimed that in the pre-FPE era, teachers and head teachers followed up on pupil attendance so absenteeism was low. Parents too made sure that their children attended school regularly since they were paying fees. It is alleged that after FPE, pupil absenteeism increased, and parents and teachers were less concerned about regular attendance. Misconceptions about the meaning of free primary education have been reported in the literature: pupils and parents interpret FPE to mean that they are free to decide when to attend school, resulting in high rates of absenteeism and erratic patterns of attendance (Kadzamira and Chibwana 2000).

All stakeholders interviewed at the school level felt that poor school quality had a disastrous impact on pupil achievement. Primary education advisers, head teachers, teachers, and SMC/PTA members said that performance and achievement levels were very poor as a result of the poor quality of schooling and the use of untrained teachers, among other factors.

Unfortunately, it is not possible to ascertain whether stakeholders saw a deterioration in pupil achievement following FPE because of the absence of reliable achievement measures in the pre-FPE era. However, studies conducted on achievement after FPE have documented very low levels of achievement among Malawian primary school pupils, which validates the observations made by parents. The 1998 Southern African Consortium for Monitoring Educational Quality (SACMEQ) study, which assessed standard 6 reading skills, found that less than 25 percent of the pupils had reached the minimum levels of mastery and less than 1 percent had attained the desired levels of mastery (Milner et al. 2001).

Similarly the Gender and Primary Schooling (GAPS) Survey of the same year found the literacy levels among standard 3 pupils to be very low; more than 50 percent of the pupils assessed were not able to read and write simple words commonly found in their textbooks (Kadzamira and Chibwana 2000). The Monitoring and Learning Achievement (MLA1) Survey compared standard 4 performance in literacy, numeracy, and life skills in several countries in Sub-Saharan Africa. The results for Malawi showed that only 3 percent of the pupils assessed in standard 4 proceeded to the next grade with the desirable competencies in mathematics and English. Malawi was about average in overall performance; below average in literacy, the lowest of all countries; and had the best performance of all countries in life skills (Chinapah, H'ddigui, and Kanjee 1999).

These results have been corroborated by the Improving Educational Quality (IEQ) study, which found that less than 1 percent of pupils in standard 3, who were tested at the beginning of the school year, attained full mastery levels in reading accuracy, while 3 percent reached partial mastery, and an alarming 97 percent were at the nonmastery level. Follow-up testing of the same students at the end of the school year showed that very little progress had been made in moving pupils from nonmastery to full mastery levels (IEQ 2003). In a related longitudinal study that used curriculum-based achievement tests to assess performance in English, Chichewa, and mathematics of a sample of standards 2, 3, 4, and 5 pupils, it was found that a majority of children entered subsequent grades without mastering the prerequisite literacy and numeracy skills that would enable them to cope with the work in the higher standard. Over 50 percent of the pupils in standard 3 could not read the Chichewa and English text taken from standard 2 textbooks, and less than 30 percent of the standard 3 pupils had mastered basic mathematics skills (Chilora 2001; Jere 2001). The most recent achievement study documents similar findings, with more than 50 percent of pupils at nonmastery levels, particularly in English and mathematics (Kishindo et al. 2004).

As a consequence of these low levels of achievement, more years of schooling are now required to achieve basic literacy and numeracy. Parents, pupils, and teachers in the GAPS Survey felt that more years of schooling were required to achieve basic literacy and numeracy because of the deterioration of school quality after FPE (Rose 2002). This perception is strongly supported by findings from the IEQ longitudinal studies, which showed that the number of children at mastery level in basic literacy and numeracy increased at each subsequent grade (Chilora 2001; Jere 2001).[5]

EFFECT ON MANAGERIAL CAPACITY

The impact of FPE on human resources was felt at all levels from headquarters to schools. FPE required a greater number of competent accountants and administrators to manage the system, but these were lacking at the time FPE was introduced. Officials from headquarters who were interviewed noted that the magnitude and complexity of their workload increased as a result of FPE so that the existing systems could not cope with the demands. For example, the quality of budget planning and implementation was seriously compromised because the system did not have the capacity to absorb additional enrollment and to increase the supply of teachers. Furthermore, poor systems of record management caused delays in salaries. There were also delays in procurement and distribution of supplies to schools. The significant increase in workload and the larger number of pupils frustrated teachers and created a dispirited and unmotivated teaching force.

The increase in the number of teachers was not matched by an increase in administrative and accounting support staff. As one official observed, there was no government structure at the district level to manage the large numbers of recruited teachers or to help them get started; thus, there were ensuing problems with the payroll, such as salary delays, and in the creation of ghost teachers. The ministry recruited too many teachers at once without proper management; this also contributed to the creation of ghost teachers. The ministry was plagued by such malpractices for a considerable time; resources, which could have been used to improve quality, were wasted through pilferage.

Schools also failed to cope with the large influx of pupils. The changes were so sudden that schools were unprepared to deal with the consequences of the reform. The ministry did not provide any training; it merely issued circulars on confronting the crisis. As these were often irrelevant to local contexts, schools ignored them. According to a head teacher, "the school received more pupils than we could cope with, resulting in overcrowding, and we did not know how to deal with the large numbers."

EFFECT ON RETENTION AND COMPLETION

Further, the impressive quantitative gains made through FPE have been seriously undermined by the failure of the system to retain pupils once they have enrolled. The primary education system is highly inefficient and results in high wastage rates. In particular, the system is grappling with problems of high repetition and dropout, which translate into low completion rates. The massive enrollment gains of 1994 after FPE have been seriously undermined as very few children in Malawi reach the last grade of primary schooling (see figure 5.2), and the majority of those who drop

Figure 5.2 Comparison of Standard 1 to Standard 8 Enrollments, 1990/91–2005

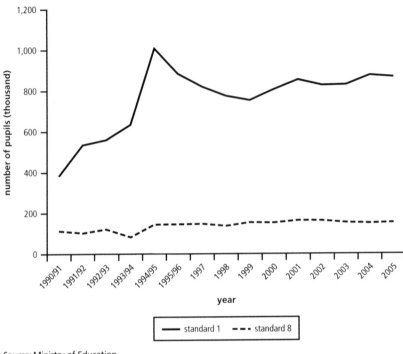

Source: Ministry of Education.

out do so before they have attained basic literacy and numeracy skills. Low internal efficiency was already apparent before the introduction of FPE and is a consequence of several factors relating to poverty and the poor quality of schooling.

Grade Repetition. Grade repetition has been considerably high in the primary system (see figure 5.3 and annex table 5B.1). The repetition rates, averaging about 20 percent in the period before FPE, increased substantially to nearly 30 percent in 1994/95 (the peak in figure 5.3) when the new FPE policy encouraged many pupils to reenter school as repeaters. The rates dropped significantly a year later, in 1995/96, to 15 percent and have remained fairly constant between 1995/96 and 2002 and below the pre-FPE levels. Since 2003 the repetition rates have shown an upward trend and have reached their pre-FPE levels again.

Dropout Rates. Dropout rates have also been considerably high, particularly in the first four years of schooling (see figure 5.4 and annex table 5B.2). Overall dropout rates, which were lower (8 percent) at the beginning of the 1990s, have been increasing since then. They have fluctuated between 18 percent in 1993/94, just before FPE was introduced, to about 20 percent in 2003; declining to 15 percent in 2005, still almost

Figure 5.3   Percentage of Repeaters in Primary School, 1990/91–2005

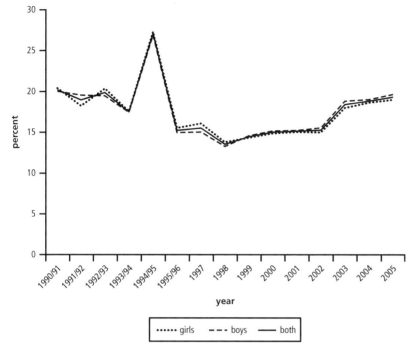

Source: Ministry of Education.

twice as high as they were at the beginning of the 1990s. Figure 5.4 shows a sharp decline in the dropout rate in 1994/95, corresponding to the period when an influx of pupils in all standards flooded the system. The negative dropout rates for this period imply that many children who had dropped out re-enrolled when FPE was declared.

As indicated in annex table 5B.2, there are wide variations in dropout rates by standard; they are generally higher in the lower standards than in the higher. For example, standard 1 dropout had decreased from 30 percent in 1995/96 to 23 percent in 2005, while standard 4 dropout decreased by 2 percentage points, from 15 percent in 1995/96 to 13 percent in 2005. In contrast, the trend in the upper standards suggests an increasing trend in dropouts. For example, standard 5 dropout rates increased from 15 percent in 1995/96 to 17 percent in 2005, with significant increase in 2002 when they peaked at 30 percent. Similarly, standard 7 dropout rates have increased considerably, from a low 4 percent in 1995/96 to 17 percent in 2005. A greater proportion of dropouts are from the first four years of schooling, particularly from standard 1, which has always registered the highest dropout rates. For example, although more than 1 million children entered the first grade in 1994/95, only 50 percent proceeded to the next

Figure 5.4 Trends in Primary School Dropout Rate, 1990/91–2005

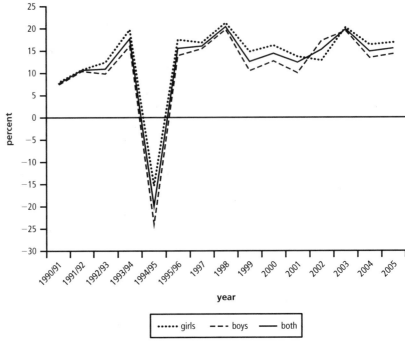

Source: Ministry of Education.

grade in the following year; over 300,000 (31 percent) dropped out of school, and the rest (19 percent) repeated standard 1.

The dropout rates for female pupils have been generally higher than for male pupils across all standards except in 2002, when the rates were higher for males. However, from standard 4 onward, the dropout rates have been consistently higher for girls than for boys. The net effect is that fewer females than males complete primary school.

Consequently, the impressive achievements in access have not been matched by improvements in internal efficiency: the increase in post-FPE enrollment has not led to any significant changes in the pyramidal structure of the education system (see figure 5.5). The progression of the first four FPE cohorts suggests that less than 20 percent of those who entered the first grade have so far made it to the last grade of primary school (see figure 5.6).

Research has identified several factors for high dropout rates. Economic factors have featured prominently in both the pre-FPE and the post-FPE periods. For example, the most common reason for dropout before free primary education was lack of money to pay school fees

Figure 5.5 Distribution of Primary School Enrollment by Standard, 1990/91–2005

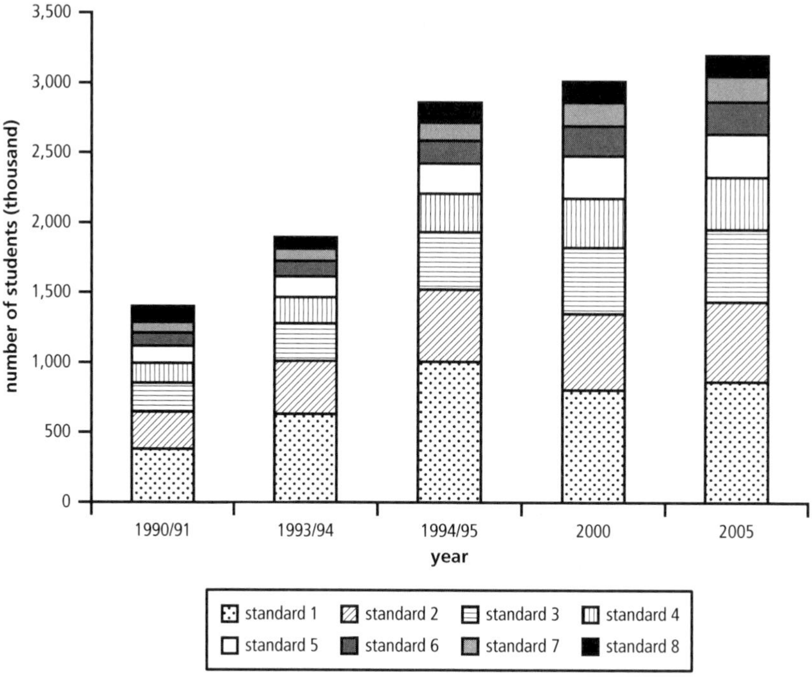

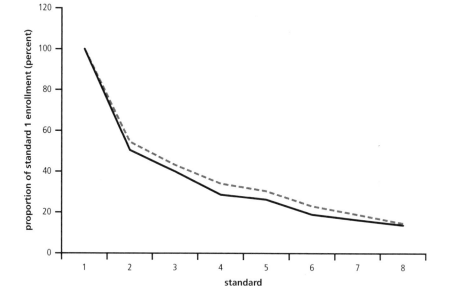

Source: Ministry of Education.

Figure 5.6 Progression of FPE Cohorts through the Primary School System

Source: Ministry of Education.

(Maganga and Mkandawire 1988; Kadzombe 1988; Kainja and Mkandawire 1989; Davidson and Kanyuka 1990; Hyde and Kadzamira 1994). Although primary education was made free and all forms of fees abolished in 1994, many poor households still find the cost of schooling prohibitive. Post-FPE literature identifies the lack of proper school clothes and of money to meet the cost of school essentials, such as learning materials, as significant causes of dropout among primary school children (see, for example, Burchfield and Kadzamira 1996; Chimombo 1999; Kadzamira and Chibwana 2000; Rose 2002). Although the government committed itself to meet all the costs of education, public spending has been insufficient, and Malawi households continue to bear a considerable share of both recurrent and capital costs of primary education (World Bank 2004).

Survival Rates. A major and persistent problem with Malawi's primary education system is its failure to retain pupils once they have enrolled in school. While the majority of children have access to school as a result of FPE, retention rates (which were already low before primary education was made free) have remained very low. Analysis of cohorts that entered school between 1990 and 2005 reveals that between 70 to 80 percent of each cohort did not complete the full eight-year primary education cycle; the majority dropped out during the cycle (see figure 5.5).

Approximately one-third of the 1990/91 cohort graduated from primary education; survival rates were higher for boys (32 percent) than for girls (27 percent) (see table 5.7 and annex table 5B.3). Between 1991/92 and 1993/94, survival rates declined from 26 percent to 16 percent. The decline is surprising as it occurred when targeted attempts to abolish school fees were introduced, including the GABLE Program school fee waivers, which should have improved access and retention of children in primary schools. In the period after FPE, survival rates have fluctuated between 14 percent and 28 percent. Given the pupil flow rates for 2005, it is expected that only 17 percent of children will complete primary school. Thus, the survival rates have not improved radically since the introduction of FPE; at worst, they have deteriorated from their 1990 levels and remained low despite the many interventions, such as improvements in infrastructure and teacher supply and curriculum reform. Though FPE has brought significant quantitative gains, very few children in Malawi complete primary schooling even in the fee-free schooling period, suggesting that quantitative gains are not sustained throughout the system.

Despite the low survival rates, the absolute number of children expected to complete primary education did increase after FPE, and

Table 5.7 Survival Rates by Standard and Gender, 1990/91–2005
(per 1,000 students)

Year/ gender	Standard								Graduate	Actual standard 1 enrollment	Expected number of graduates[a]	Actual standard 8 enrollment
	1	2	3	4	5	6	7	8				
1990/91												
Girls	1,000	703	596	464	409	329	278	341	274	178,679	48,958	39,516
Boys	1,000	746	622	492	444	370	330	393	318	197,972	62,955	72,210
Both	1,000	726	610	479	427	351	306	369	297	376,651	111,865	111,726
1993/94												
Girls	1,000	686	543	418	332	250	189	135	130	284,960	37,045	30,348
Boys	1,000	708	559	437	358	285	207	192	182	273,287	49,738	50,789
Both	1,000	697	551	427	345	268	214	165	157	558,247	87,645	81,137
1995/96												
Girls	1,000	603	499	378	307	248	205	176	166	496,857	82,478	55,814
Boys	1,000	630	528	414	342	282	247	249	235	509,337	119,694	87,879
Both	1,000	616	514	397	325	265	227	214	202	1,006,194	203,251	143,693
2000												
Girls	1,000	747	648	501	401	313	250	201	194	375,365	72,821	63,184
Boys	1,000	751	655	523	516	356	297	270	259	375,637	97,290	87,072
Both	1,000	749	652	512	459	335	274	236	227	751,002	170,477	150,256
2005												
Girls	1,000	664	589	449	364	278	216	160	153	447,073	68,402	66,042
Boys	1,000	701	617	477	386	299	222	201	191	425,993	81,365	84,714
Both	1,000	682	602	462	375	288	229	180	172	873,066	150,167	150,756

Source: Ministry of Education.
Note: The survival and completion rates in this table have been calculated using the reconstructed cohort method.
a. This number is obtained by dividing the number of graduates by 1,000 and multiplying the result by actual standard 1 enrollment, that is, (graduates/1,000) X standard 1 enrollment. The girls' and boys' rows do not add up to the total row because of rounding error.

standard 8 enrollment has increased by 35 percent, from 111,726 in 1990/91 to 150,756 in 2005 (table 5.7). The primary completion rate (PCR) is estimated to have increased from 30 percent in 1990 to 50 percent in 1995 (Bruns, Mingat, and Rakotomalala 2003). However, as Bruns and her cowriters have argued, the deterioration in school quality after elimination of fees in 1994 has slowed down if not reversed progress made in 1995. Since 1994/95, every year almost 800,000 children enter the first grade. However, enrollment for standard 8 has remained below 200,000 for the four cohorts that should have completed on time, bearing testimony to the system's failure to retain pupils until they complete their primary education. Furthermore, the decline in enrollment by standard is quite disturbing as it suggests that households have not been able to sustain their initial demand for schooling.

LESSONS LEARNED

The first major lesson from Malawi's experience is that FPE requires careful planning and strategizing. This was not the case in Malawi; planners and the entire education system did not have sufficient time to plan for and respond to the challenges brought about by FPE. In the short to medium term, coping strategies were adopted to mitigate the challenges: introducing multishift schooling, using existing nonschool buildings for classrooms, and increasing the official class size from 50 to 60. However, these did not prevent further deterioration of the system, and educational outcomes have remained dismal. Stakeholders interviewed averred that more time was required to plan for FPE and to make adequate consultations with all stakeholders. More time was needed to strategize on resource requirements, especially teacher and classroom needs.

Thus, most stakeholders favored a phased approach in which FPE would be implemented in stages, which would be less challenging than the big bang approach that Malawi adopted in 1994. The phased approach, it is argued, would have given them more time to plan, budget, construct classrooms, procure materials, and hire and train teachers. In addition, it would have allowed the continuous monitoring and evaluation of successes and failures of the implementation process and would thus have been more manageable. Although the MoE was already implementing a phased FPE program, it was definitely not ready for a full-scale one. The economic indicators were not favorable during the period FPE was launched. Even more critical, the government had not yet mobilized resources for the effective implementation of FPE. To make matters worse, no comprehensive analysis of the education sector was undertaken beforehand to assess financial and other implications of introducing FPE or even to learn from the previous year's experience of phased FPE implementation.

Strategizing policy reforms was necessary to ensure effective learning outcomes. For example, FPE adopted an open door policy and allowed children of all ages to enroll in school. As it turned out, children of all ages, including those who had dropped out in higher standards and those who were overage, were allowed to join the system, thereby escalating costs and creating serious age distortions and overcrowding in the lower standards. For example, standard 8 witnessed the highest growth (76 percent) as many repeaters anticipated that under the new dispensation they would be able to get a place in secondary school; standard 1 enrollment increased by over 50 percent. Given the resource constraints, the government should have given priority only to those within the primary school age. Enrollment to each standard should have been restricted to the specified age range as was done in Tanzania, and alternative systems of providing basic education developed for those who were too old to be enrolled in the first grade. A full-scale program was inadvisable; it made no sense to open access to all children when the government was not ready and systems were not in place.

Thus, there was a need to moderate demand for primary education by restricting the age of entry and by restricting new enrollment to lower standards, preferably only the first two grades. The secondary education sector was under a lot of pressure to expand as well. This forced the government to convert distance education centers into community day secondary schools without attending to the inherent problems of low quality and poor performance. Another consequence was the proliferation of private secondary schools, most of which have been of very low quality.

Indeed, an important lesson to be learned from Malawi's experience is that the introduction of FPE, while achieving an increase in access to education (quantity), adversely affected quality. The reason is that financial resources were simply insufficient to maintain the same quality of education. Already, just before the introduction of FPE, there had been growing public concern about the deterioration in the quality of education. Thus, the problem in primary education was not just access but quality as well. However, while more teachers were recruited after the introduction of FPE, they were not properly trained and their numbers were so large that, given the limited resources, they were not adequately remunerated. This, coupled with larger class sizes, means that teacher morale has generally been very low since the introduction of FPE. Thus, a gradual scaling up of the FPE program that had already been started before 1994 could have ensured that other sectors and programs were not adversely affected in financial terms, and also that quality was not compromised.

Another lesson that may be learned from Malawi's experience is that governments need to meet the minimum resource requirement before they undertake a major policy reform program. In Malawi, although government and donor spending increased significantly to accommodate enrollment increase, the increase was not sufficient to reverse the many years of underfunding or to maintain quality at current levels.

Another vital lesson is that strong political will is necessary to implement far-reaching reforms such as FPE and is particularly essential in overcoming bureaucratic bottlenecks and resistance. The Malawi experience clearly shows that political will played a critical role in the introduction of wide-ranging educational reforms. The objective of increasing access to primary education was in fact achieved in the first year of implementing the new policy. Malawi was able to adopt FPE because there was enough political will to introduce the program, regardless of the apparent capacity problems and the skepticism from other sectors of society. However, when the new government announced the introduction of FPE, the MoE was confronted with a crisis as it did not have the capacity to implement the policy effectively.

Malawi's managerial and financial management capacity for education was overstretched with the rapid expansion of the primary sector. As a consequence, the system has been particularly inefficient in handling teachers' salaries. The MoE has for several years been dogged by the problem of ghost teachers. It is argued that huge sums of money have been wasted as a result.[6] If the system had been efficient, the money could have been saved and used to better remunerate teachers. Undoubtedly, the problem of ghost teachers has been caused partly by the fact that the ministry has been overwhelmed by the huge expansion in the primary education sector after FPE. This only reinforces the recommendation for proper planning and strategizing before introducing FPE.

In conclusion, FPE in Malawi was underfunded and underresourced. There was inadequate planning because of time constraints. The primary education system remains seriously underfunded and mismanaged and requires extensive external financial assistance to lift it out of its present quagmire. In the case of Malawi, while more funds were allocated to the education sector in general, and to primary education in particular, these were simply not enough to achieve all the desired education outcomes. DFID estimates indicate that public expenditure on education is only about half of the total needed to achieve the minimum acceptable standard (DFID 2004).

THE WAY FORWARD

The FPE policy succeeded in dramatically increasing the net and gross enrollment rates in Malawi at the primary school level. Both NER and GER indicate that if they are slightly increased, Malawi can achieve EFA and MDG goals for access. However, the retention and completion rates, the quality and relevance of education, the achievement rates at all levels, and the low transition from primary to secondary education remain major concerns.

Two major policy documents, the Malawi Growth and Development Strategy (MGDS) and the National Education Sector Plan (NESP), 2007–11, seek to address these issues. Participatory planning that involves major stakeholders and development partners in education has received added emphasis recently, along with decentralization processes that herald the assignation of additional responsibilities and accountability at the local levels. As information and data are critical to planning and management, another area that has been highlighted for urgent attention includes the EMIS. Some key milestones for the next decade are listed below.

THE MALAWI GROWTH AND DEVELOPMENT STRATEGY

The MGDS provides a policy framework that balances the development of the productive and the social sectors of the economy. It is linked to vision 2020 and the Malawi Millennium Development Goals that represent the long-term development aspirations of the Malawians. The MGDS considers the limitations of the Malawi Poverty Reduction Strategy and the Malawi Economic and Growth Strategy in defining future strategic options. The MGDS identifies specific outputs related to increased equitable access to quality primary education, increased access and achievement by girls, vulnerable children, and children with special learning needs. It also addresses issues of financing, planning, and management of education. Education is seen as critical to poverty reduction and to the creation of a solid human resource base that is essential for Malawi's development.

THE NATIONAL EDUCATION SECTOR PLAN

The NESP provides the basis for investment in education by the government of Malawi and its development partners for the next 10-year planning period and beyond. Funding decisions will be based on this plan. The plan is structured around the following three main goals:

- Expand equitable access to education to enable all children to benefit
- Improve quality and relevance of education and promote effective learning
- Improve governance and management of the system to enable more effective and efficient delivery of services.

The plan takes a broad view of the sector, embracing primary, secondary, vocational, teacher, and university education. Technical working groups have been established: these comprise the government, development partners, civil society, and NGOs to ensure participatory planning and to follow up on implementation. The groups have been formed on the basis of major strategic themes. The plan is in advanced draft form and should be completed and costed by the end of 2008.

SECTORWIDE APPROACH

The finalization of the Sector Development Plan will herald the beginning of a shift toward a sectorwide approach (SWAP) to education management and delivery in Malawi. Discussions about these approaches have been on the agenda for the past few years, but are expected to pick up momentum when the plan is finalized and costed so that it becomes the basis for the SWAP. The Joint Sector Review, which brings together the government and its development partners in education, agreed that this would be the way forward.

Such collaboration will facilitate the review of policies and implementation strategies for key areas, such as teacher education, textbook production and supplies, in-service training and supervision, special needs education, and infrastructure development. Within this context, opportunities for vulnerable groups—in access, retention, completion, and performance—will be improved. Alternative and innovative ways of education delivery, such as satellite schools and distance and complementary education, will also be considered.

CURRICULUM REFORM

The curriculum reform process commenced in 2001 and will probably be completed in 2011, by which time the last two standards will be introduced to the new syllabi. Financing the primary school curriculum reform process could also provide an opportunity to initiate an embryonic SWAP when the three major partners (CIDA [Canadian International Development Agency], GTZ [Gesellschaft für Technische Zusammenarbeit], and DFID) pool their resources to fund the reform. The pool could be expanded through the inclusion of UNICEF.

RESOURCE MOBILIZATION

After years of a lukewarm approach to education, partly the result of the education sector's substandard performance, the Ministry of Finance now fully supports the current reform initiatives in the sector. This provides a good opportunity to seek alternative funding sources to enhance the resource base for education development. The minister of Finance has requested that the National Education Sector Plan be completed (including costs) expeditiously as it will provide the basis for generating additional funding to education at international forums.

The recently announced debt relief has been heralded as another opportunity to increase resources to education. At the same time, the dialogue between MoE and its development partners in education seems to be improving.

PLANNING AND MANAGEMENT

There are plans to strengthen the EMIS to provide timely, accurate, and gender-disaggregated data. This will facilitate planning and management of the system, which is envisaged to grow substantially at all levels. Management structures must also be strengthened, including the conditions for personnel.

CONCLUSION

Despite the numerous challenges outlined in this chapter, there is optimism about education development in Malawi. It is anticipated that the School Fee Abolition Initiative, which prompted this study, will contribute to the financing of education in Malawi and continue to provide technical inputs though experience sharing and other approaches.

(Chapter continues on the next page.)

ANNEX 5A: LIST OF PEOPLE INTERVIEWED

Interviewee	Affiliation
Government	
Mr. M. C. H. Jere	Former Principal Planning Officer, Ministry of Education
Mrs. M. Kabuye	Former Regional Education Officer, Ministry of Education
Mr. E. Ngaye	Former Chief Planning Officer, Ministry of Education
Mrs. M. Nkaonja	Formerly, Inspectorate Division, Ministry of Education
Mr. Kavinya	Former Principal Secretary, Ministry of Finance
Mr. P. Moyo	
Mr. N. Kapermera	Former Deputy Director, Malawi Institute of Education
School	
Head teachers	Mpingu Primary School, Lilongwe
Head teachers	Njewa Primary School, Lilongwe
Teachers	Mpingu Primary School, Lilongwe
Teachers	Njewa Primary School, Lilongwe
Primary education adviser	Lilongwe
SMC/PTA	Mpingu Primary School, Lilongwe
SMC/PTA	Njewa Primary School, Lilongwe

ANNEX 5B: ADDITIONAL DATA ON EDUCATIONAL OUTCOMES

Table 5B.1   Primary Repetition Rates by Standard and Gender, 1990/91–2005
(percent)

Year/ gender	Standard								
	1	2	3	4	5	6	7	8	All
1990/91	**21.0**	**19.3**	**17.5**	**14.3**	**15.5**	**15.5**	**18.3**	**40.0**	**20.2**
Girls	21.1	19.5	18.1	15.0	16.6	17.3	22.6	39.4	20.4
Boys	20.8	19.1	17.0	13.8	14.7	14.2	15.7	40.4	20.0
1991/92	**23.2**	**17.4**	**10.4**	**13.4**	**11.9**	**14.0**	**16.6**	**44.4**	**18.9**
Girls	23.1	14.3	10.7	15.2	12.7	14.6	18.1	41.8	18.2
Boys	23.2	20.0	10.2	12.1	11.3	13.5	15.5	45.9	19.5
1992/93	**20.9**	**20.8**	**20.7**	**14.6**	**15.0**	**13/6**	**13.8**	**35.5**	**19.8**
Girls	21.9	21.8	22.3	14.5	15.8	14.6	15.0	28.4	20.3
Boys	19.8	20.0	19.3	14.7	14.4	12.8	12.8	39.9	19.4
1993/94	**21.4**	**20.4**	**18.0**	**11.6**	**12.5**	**10.2**	**9.6**	**16.5**	**17.5**
Girls	21.9	20.1	17.6	11.0	12.1	9.9	9.2	14.8	17.5
Boys	21.0	20.6	18.3	12.1	12.7	10.5	10.0	17.4	17.4
1994/95	**28.6**	**24.5**	**27.2**	**26.8**	**26.2**	**26.0**	**26.4**	**31.6**	**27.1**
Girls	28.5	24.3	27.5	27.0	26.9	26.9	28.1	33.5	27.3
Boys	28.6	24.6	27.0	26.7	25.7	25.3	25.2	30.4	26.9

Table 5B.1 (*continued*)

Year/ gender	Standard								
	1	2	3	4	5	6	7	8	All
1995/96	**18.7**	**16.0**	**14.7**	**11.2**	**9.8**	**7.9**	**7.32**	**20.2**	**15.2**
Girls	19.0	16.2	14.8	11.3	10.2	8.4	7.78	19.5	15.5
Boys	18.5	15.8	14.6	11.0	9.5	7.4	6.96	20.7	14.9
1997	**17.3**	**16.1**	**15.7**	**13.4**	**12.4**	**11.3**	**10.61**	**20.3**	**15.5**
Girls	17.6	16.6	16.4	13.9	13.2	12.2	11.91	20.4	16.0
Boys	17.0	15.5	15.2	12.9	11.7	10.7	9.62	20.2	15.0
1998	**16.3**	**14.4**	**13.4**	**11.5**	**10.2**	**9.3**	**8.05**	**14.6**	**13.5**
Girls	16.5	14.6	13.6	11.7	10.4	9.8	8.67	14.4	13.8
Boys	16.2	14.3	13.3	11.4	10.0	8.9	7.56	14.7	13.2
1999	**17.4**	**15.9**	**15.6**	**12.1**	**10.2**	**8.7**	**7.61**	**15.9**	**14.4**
Girls	17.2	15.3	15.4	12.0	10.3	9.0	7.92	15.4	14.3
Boys	17.7	16.5	15.8	12.2	10.1	8.3	7.37	16.2	14.5
2000	**19.2**	**16.6**	**16.6**	**13.9**	**11.7**	**11.3**	**10.11**	**13.9**	**15.0**
Girls	18.7	16.2	16.0	13.7	12.6	11.6	10.21	13.3	14.8
Boys	19.6	17.0	17.1	14.1	11.0	11.1	10.03	14.6	15.1
2001	**19.5**	**17.6**	**17.0**	**14.1**	**12.0**	**11.4**	**9.85**	**13.7**	**15.1**
Girls	19.0	17.3	16.8	13.9	13.0	11.8	10.14	12.9	15.0
Boys	20.1	17.9	17.3	14.4	11.1	11.1	9.61	14.3	15.2
2002	**17.5**	**17.5**	**17.1**	**14.6**	**11.0**	**11.8**	**10.04**	**13.8**	**15.2**
Girls	17.0	17.7	17.3	14.6	12.4	12.5	10.69	13.4	14.9
Boys	17.9	17.3	16.9	14.5	10.0	11.2	9.54	14.1	15.5
2003	**21.3**	**19.1**	**19.8**	**16.3**	**14.8**	**12.6**	**10.90**	**13.5**	**18.4**
Girls	20.9	18.6	19.5	16.1	14.6	12.8	11.28	12.9	17.9
Boys	21.8	19.6	20.0	16.4	14.9	12.4	10.57	14.1	18.8
2004	**25.0**	**20.2**	**21.6**	**16.8**	**15.3**	**12.4**	**10.19**	**13.3**	**18.8**
Girls	25.1	19.8	21.2	16.4	15.1	12.1	10.33	12.1	18.6
Boys	24.9	20.6	22.1	17.2	15.5	12.7	10.05	14.3	19.0
2005	**24.7**	**20.8**	**21.7**	**16.5**	**15.1**	**12.3**	**10.45**	**14.3**	**19.3**
Girls	23.8	21.2	20.8	16.1	14.8	12.1	10.74	13.7	19.0
Boys	25.7	20.5	22.7	17.0	15.4	12.5	10.20	14.8	19.6

Source: Ministry of Education.

Table 5B.2 Primary Dropout Rates by Standard and Gender, 1990/91–2005
(percent)

Year/ gender	Standard							All
	1	2	3	4	5	6	7	
1990/91	**21.2**	**11.6**	**16.0**	**7.2**	**12.6**	**7.6**	**−22.8**	**7.6**
Girls	22.9	10.9	16.3	8.0	13.6	9.0	−25.7	7.8
Boys	19.6	12.2	15.7	6.5	11.7	6.5	−21.0	7.3
1991/92	**6.0**	**5.0**	**19.9**	**3.7**	**15.1**	**9.7**	**15.3**	**10.7**
Girls	8.5	10.8	21.3	−4.5	15.1	11.5	12.3	10.7
Boys	3.7	0.1	18.7	9.6	15.0	8.2	17.5	10.4
1992/93	**26.1**	**14.1**	**11.8**	**8.8**	**14.5**	**13.9**	**−12.9**	**10.9**
Girls	25.5	9.0	7.6	9.4	16.3	18.5	0.5	12.4
Boys	26.8	18.4	15.2	8.3	12.9	10.2	−23.0	9.8
1993/94	**23.3**	**15.3**	**16.6**	**15.6**	**17.6**	**16.5**	**18.9**	**17.7**
Girls	24.0	15.2	17.3	17.0	19.9	20.4	24.2	19.7
Boys	22.5	15.4	15.9	14.4	15.7	13.4	15.0	16.0
1994/95	**4.2**	**−12.9**	**−11.7**	**−22.0**	**−16.8**	**−20.7**	**−59.6**	**−19.9**
Girls	9.2	−8.1	−7.7	−17.6	−14.5	−19.1	−49.5	−15.3
Boys	−1.0	−17.6	−15.5	−26.0	−18.7	−22.0	−66.9	−24.0
1995/96	**30.8**	**13.1**	**18.4**	**14.9**	**15.3**	**12.3**	**3.9**	**15.5**
Girls	31.8	13.5	19.5	15.6	16.1	14.5	11.7	17.5
Boys	29.9	12.7	17.3	14.3	14.7	10.5	−2.0	13.9
1997	**28.3**	**15.7**	**18.3**	**14.6**	**15.2**	**13.8**	**6.3**	**16.0**
Girls	28.2	15.1	18.0	14.0	15.9	15.0	11.5	16.8
Boys	28.3	16.3	18.4	15.2	14.6	12.8	2.4	15.4
1998	**26.7**	**19.3**	**24.9**	**20.1**	**20.4**	**17.8**	**13.5**	**20.4**
Girls	24.9	19.0	24.9	20.0	21.0	19.1	19.9	21.3
Boys	28.4	19.7	25.0	20.2	19.8	16.7	8.5	19.8
1999	**24.0**	**13.3**	**16.6**	**6.9**	**13.2**	**11.0**	**2.7**	**12.5**
Girls	25.0	15.2	17.5	14.1	13.9	12.4	5.4	14.8
Boys	23.0	11.5	15.7	0.1	12.6	9.9	0.7	10.5
2000	**19.9**	**9.9**	**16.4**	**7.2**	**22.3**	**14.4**	**10.5**	**14.4**
Girls	20.1	10.3	17.7	15.8	17.4	16.2	15.7	16.2
Boys	19.6	9.5	15.2	−0.9	26.7	12.8	6.2	12.7
2001	**20.3**	**6.6**	**15.4**	**5.0**	**20.8**	**11.9**	**6.6**	**12.4**
Girls	21.2	7.6	16.4	13.3	14.0	13.3	9.9	13.7
Boys	19.3	5.7	14.5	−3.0	26.1	10.6	3.8	11.0
2002	**25.9**	**8.0**	**15.6**	**12.0**	**22.8**	**12.3**	**10.1**	**15.2**
Girls	26.4	5.9	13.9	10.4	13.2	10.5	9.3	12.8
Boys	25.4	9.9	17.2	13.5	29.9	13.8	10.7	17.2

Table 5B.2 (*continued*)

Year/ gender	Standard							All
	1	2	3	4	5	6	7	
2003	**25.9**	**12.9**	**20.0**	**19.0**	**21.6**	**20.5**	**18.9**	**19.8**
Girls	26.0	13.0	19.5	18.6	21.0	21.1	22.4	20.2
Boys	25.9	12.8	20.5	19.3	22.1	19.8	15.8	19.4
2004	**19.6**	**7.2**	**15.7**	**13.1**	**15.8**	**15.0**	**17.4**	**14.8**
Girls	19.6	7.3	16.1	13.9	16.6	18.4	22.4	16.3
Boys	19.7	7.1	15.2	12.3	15.0	11.7	12.8	13.4
2005	**23.2**	**7.4**	**15.7**	**13.2**	**16.9**	**15.6**	**16.6**	**15.5**
Girls	24.9	7.1	16.5	13.3	17.6	17.4	20.9	16.8
Boys	21.3	7.7	14.8	13.0	16.3	14.0	12.8	14.3

Source: Ministry of Education.

Table 5B.3 **Primary Survival Rates by Standard and Gender, 1990/91–2005**
(percent)

Year/ gender	Standard								Graduate
	1	2	3	4	5	6	7	8	
1990/91	**100**	**70.3**	**59.6**	**46.4**	**40.9**	**32.9**	**27.8**	**34.1**	**27.4**
Girls	100	74.6	62.2	49.2	44.4	37.0	33.0	39.3	31.8
Boys	100	72.6	61.0	47.9	42.7	35.1	30.6	36.9	29.7
1991/92	**100**	**91.1**	**84.1**	**64.6**	**60.5**	**49.1**	**42.2**	**32.8**	**25.7**
Girls	100	87.9	75.9	57.1	58.7	47.4	39.6	31.9	25.6
Boys	100	94.0	91.9	71.8	62.7	51.0	41.8	34.0	26.2
1992/93	**100**	**66.4**	**53.3**	**43.8**	**38.1**	**30.5**	**24.6**	**27.1**	**22.8**
Girls	100	66.7	57.5	49.8	42.9	33.2	24.9	23.6	20.7
Boys	100	66.1	49.9	39.3	34.5	28.3	25.4	29.4	23.9
1993/94	**100**	**69.7**	**55.1**	**42.7**	**34.5**	**26.8**	**21.4**	**16.5**	**15.7**
Girls	100	68.6	54.3	41.8	33.2	25.0	18.9	13.5	13.0
Boys	100	70.8	55.9	43.7	35.8	28.5	20.7	19.2	18.2
1994/95	**100**	**91.9**	**103.5**	**112.1**	**133.3**	**147.2**	**167.2**	**263.9**	**219.0**
Girls	100	85.1	90.7	93.5	106.0	113.7	126.4	183.7	148.8
Boys	100	99.0	117.4	132.9	164.6	186.0	149.0	358.0	299.1
1995/96	**100**	**61.6**	**51.4**	**39.7**	**32.5**	**26.5**	**22.7**	**21.4**	**20.2**
Girls	100	60.3	49.9	37.8	30.7	24.8	20.5	17.6	16.6
Boys	100	63.0	52.8	41.4	34.2	28.2	24.7	24.9	23.5

(*Table continues on the next page.*)

Table 5B.3 (*continued*)

Year/ gender	Standard								Graduate
	1	2	3	4	5	6	7	8	
1997	**100**	**65.5**	**52.6**	**40.5**	**33.0**	**26.6**	**22.0**	**19.9**	**18.7**
Girls	100	65.4	52.9	40.7	33.3	26.5	21.4	18.1	16.9
Boys	100	65.6	52.4	40.3	32.7	26.7	22.4	21.3	20.0
1998	**100**	**67.8**	**52.0**	**36.5**	**27.8**	**21.2**	**16.7**	**14.1**	**13.6**
Girls	100	69.8	53.8	37.7	28.7	21.6	16.8	12.9	12.4
Boys	100	65.8	50.3	35.4	26.9	20.7	16.9	14.9	14.4
1999	**100**	**70.5**	**58.7**	**46.3**	**42.0**	**35.2**	**30.4**	**29.0**	**27.8**
Girls	100	69.5	56.4	44.0	36.3	30.2	25.6	23.7	22.8
Boys	100	71.6	61.0	48.7	47.8	40.4	29.9	34.7	33.2
2000	**100**	**74.9**	**65.2**	**51.2**	**45.9**	**33.5**	**27.4**	**23.6**	**22.7**
Girls	100	74.7	64.8	50.1	40.1	31.3	25.0	20.1	19.4
Boys	100	75.1	65.5	52.3	51.6	35.6	26.9	27.0	25.9
2001	**100**	**74.2**	**67.2**	**53.5**	**49.2**	**36.7**	**30.9**	**28.0**	**26.9**
Girls	100	73.3	65.6	51.6	42.6	34.8	28.8	25.0	24.1
Boys	100	75.2	68.9	55.4	55.9	38.6	30.6	31.0	29.7
2002	**100**	**68.3**	**60.9**	**48.3**	**40.5**	**29.5**	**24.7**	**21.4**	**20.6**
Girls	100	67.9	62.2	50.6	43.4	35.9	30.7	26.8	25.8
Boys	100	68.6	59.6	46.3	38.0	24.9	26.7	17.7	17.0
2003	**100**	**66.4**	**54.7**	**39.8**	**29.8**	**21.5**	**15.9**	**12.1**	**11.6**
Girls	100	66.6	54.9	40.4	30.4	22.2	16.2	11.8	11.3
Boys	100	66.2	54.5	39.2	29.1	20.8	15.8	12.4	11.8
2004	**100**	**72.6**	**64.5**	**49.5**	**40.2**	**31.4**	**25.1**	**19.6**	**18.7**
Girls	100	72.7	64.5	49.4	39.7	30.7	23.4	17.0	16.4
Boys	100	72.6	64.5	49.7	40.6	32.1	24.4	22.2	21.1
2005	**100**	**68.2**	**60.2**	**46.2**	**37.5**	**28.8**	**22.9**	**18.0**	**17.2**
Girls	100	66.4	58.9	44.9	36.4	27.8	21.6	16.0	15.3
Boys	100	70.1	61.7	47.7	38.6	29.9	22.2	20.1	19.1

Source: Ministry of Education.
Note: For the school year 1994/95 from standard 3 to standard 8, the totals are above 100 percent because of reentrants after school fee abolition.

Table 5B.4   Primary Pupil-Teacher Ratio, 1989/90–2005

Year	Total enrollment	Total teachers	Pupil-teacher ratio
1989/90	1,325,453	20,580	64.4:1
1990/91	1,400,682	17,942	78.0:1
1991/92	1,662,583	23,294	71.4:1
1992/93	1,795,451	26,333	68.2:1
1993/94	1,895,423	27,748	67.8:1
1994/95	2,860,819	45,775	62.5:1
1995/96	2,887,107	49,139	58.8:1
1997	2,905,950	47,343	61.3:1
1998	2,805,785	41,634	67.4:1
1999	3,016,972	45,812	63.2:1
2000	3,187,835	47,825	63.0:1
2001	3,164,199	53,444	59.7:1
2003	3,067,843	45,100	68.0:1
2004	3,166,786	43,952	72.0:1
2005	3,200,646	45,075	71.0:1

Source: Ministry of Education.

NOTES

1. The Ministry of Education (MoE) is presently named Ministry of Education, Science and Technology. It used to be Ministry of Education, Sport and Culture (MoESC), and at some point also Ministry of Education. For purposes of consistency, MoE is used throughout this chapter, except for citations to the MoESC/UNICEF study.

2. These include Castro-Leal (1996); Minis (1997); Chimombo (1999); Kadzamira and Chibwana (2000); Chimombo (2001); Rose (2002); Kadzamira and Rose (2003); Kunje, Lewin, and Stuart (2003); Kadzamira, Nthara, and Kholowa (2004); and World Bank (2004).

3. The composition of school fees was as follows: MK 1 per student was specifically earmarked for the purchase of core textbooks and kept at the central level; MK 0.50 per student, contributed toward the school development fund, were kept at the school level and used for maintenance and payment of utility bills and other school expenses. The rest of the money was allocated for teaching and learning materials, including the purchase of chalk and notebooks by the district education office (DEO).

4. In 2001, Malawi experienced a devastating famine, which adversely affected children's participation in schooling.

5. The longitudinal study assessments were taken from texts one standard lower than the pupil's current standard as well as from the current standard in which the pupil was enrolled. Thus, standard 2 pupils were tested on material

based on standard 1 texts and part of standard 2 texts, while standard 3 pupils were tested on materials from standards 1, 2, and 3, and so on.

6. The amount of money wasted on ghost teachers has not been revealed publicly, but the problem was serious enough to prompt the MoE to carry out at least three headcounts of teachers on payday.

REFERENCES

Al-Samarrai, S. M. 2003. *Financing Primary Education for All: Public Expenditure and Education Outcomes in Africa.* Brighton: Institute of Development Studies.

Al-Samarrai, S. M., and H. Zaman. 2002. "The Changing Distribution of Public Education Expenditure in Malawi." Africa Region Working Paper 29, World Bank, Washington, DC.

Avenstrup, R., X. Liang, and S. Nellemann. 2004. *Kenya, Lesotho, Malawi and Uganda: Universal Primary Education and Poverty Reduction.* Washington, DC: World Bank.

Bruns, B., A. Mingat, and R. Rakotomalala. 2003. *Achieving Universal, Primary Education by 2015: A Chance for Every Child.* Washington, DC: World Bank.

Burchfield, S. A., and E. C. Kadzamira. 1996. "Malawi Girls Attainment in Basic Literacy and Education (GABLE) Social Mobilisation Campaign Activities: A Review of Research and Report on Finding of KAP." Follow-up study, Creative Associates International Inc. and USAID, Washington, DC.

Castro-Leal, F. 1996. "Who Benefits from Public Education Spending in Malawi? Results from the Recent Education Reform." Discussion Paper 150, World Bank, Washington, DC.

Chilora, H. G. 2001. "Literacy Development through Chichewa and English: Some Insights from IEQ Longitudinal Study in Mangochi and Balaka Districts." Paper presented at the Second National Seminar on Improving Educational Quality in Malawi, Mangochi, August 27–29.

Chimombo, J. P. G. 1999. "Implementing Educational Innovations: A Study of Free Primary Education in Malawi." PhD diss., University of Sussex, U.K.

———. 2001. "Educational Innovations in Developing Countries: Implications and Challenges for Policy Change in Malawi." *Journal of International Cooperation in Education* 4 (2): 39–54.

Chinapah, V., E. H'ddigui, and A. Kanjee. 1999. *With Africa for Africa: Toward Quality Education for All.* Pretoria: Human Science Research Council.

Davidson, J., and M. Kanyuka. 1990. *An Ethnographic Study of Factors Affecting the Education of Girls in Southern Malawi.* Zomba: Chancellor College.

DFID (Department for International Development). 2004. *Public Service Agreement (PSA) Country Annual Review 2004 (including Change Impact Monitoring Tables).* Lilongwe: DFID.

Hyde, K., and E. C. Kadzamira. 1994. "Girls' Attainment in Basic Literacy and Education (GABLE) Knowledge, Attitudes and Practice: Pilot Survey." Centre for Social Research, Zomba.

IEQ (Improving Educational Quality)/Malawi. 2003. *Exploring Factors That Influence Teaching and Learning: Collection of Selected Studies Using the IEQ/Malawi Longitudinal Data 1999–2002.* Vols. 1 and 2.

Jere, D. R. 2001. "Why Research Is of Value: IEQ/Malawi's Experience with Specific Reference to Pupil Performance in Numeracy." Paper presented at the Second National Seminar on Improving Educational Quality in Malawi, Mangochi, August 27–29.

Kadzamira, E. C., and M. Chibwana. 2000. "Gender and Primary Schooling in Malawi." Institute of Development Studies Research Report 40, Institute of Development Studies, Brighton.

Kadzamira, E. C., K. Nthara, and F. Kholowa. 2004. *Financing Primary Education for All: Public Expenditure and Educational Outcomes in Malawi*. Brighton: Institute of Development Studies.

Kadzamira, E. C., and P. Rose. 2003. "Can Free Primary Education Meet the Needs of the Poor? Evidence from Malawi." *International Journal of Educational Development* 23: 501–16.

Kadzombe, E. 1988. "Causes of Primary School Dropout." Paper presented at the National Seminar on Problems of Primary School Dropouts, Zomba.

Kainja, K., and F. Mkandawire.1989. *National Case Study on the Role of Female Teachers in the Enrolment and Persistence of Girls in Primary Schools*. Malawi: UNESCO.

Kishindo, E., W. S. Usuwere, L. J. Ndalama, and L. Mwale. 2004. "Pupils' Achievement in Malawian Primary Schools: A Case Study of 12 Districts." First draft. Ministry of Education/Malawi Institute of Education, Zomba.

Kunje, D., K. Lewin, and J. Stuart. 2003. *Primary Teacher Education in Malawi: Insights into Practice and Policy*. Multisite Teacher Education Research Project (MUSTER) Country Report 3. London: Department For International Development.

Maganga, J., and F. Mkandawire. 1988. "Report on Findings of the Pilot Survey on Causes of Primary School Dropouts." Paper presented at the National Seminar on Problems of Primary School Dropouts, Zomba.

MCP (Malawi Congress Party). 1993. *MCP Manifesto 1993: A Vision for the Future*. Blantyre: Malawi Congress Party.

Milner, G., J. Chimombo, T. Banda, and C. Mchikoma. 2001. "The Quality of Primary Education in Malawi: Some Policy Suggestions Based on a Survey of Schools." Malawi SACMEQ Policy Research Report 7, UNESCO/ International Institute for Education Planning, Paris.

Minis, J. R. 1997. "Moderating the Demand for Primary Education in Malawi." *International Journal of Educational Reform* 6 (3): 284–96.

MoESC (Ministry of Education, Sports, and Culture) and UNICEF. 1998. *Free Primary Education: The Malawi Experience 1994–98*. Lilongwe: MoESC.

Rose, P. 2002. "Cost Sharing in Malawian Primary Schooling: From the Washington to the Post-Washington Consensus." PhD diss., University of Sussex, U.K.

Tan, J-P., K. H. Lee, and A. Mingat. 1984. "User Charges for Education: The Ability and Willingness to Pay in Malawi." Staff Working Paper 661, World Bank, Washington, DC.

Thobani, M. 1983. "Charging User Fees for Social Services: The Case of Education in Malawi." Staff Working Paper 572, World Bank, Washington, DC.

UDF (United Democratic Front). 1993. *UDF Manifesto 1993: Toward a Better Malawi*. Blantyre: United Democratic Front.

World Bank. 2004. *Cost, Financing and School Effectiveness of Education in Malawi: A Future of Limited Choices and Endless Opportunities*. Africa Region Human Development Working Paper Series. Washington, D.C.: World Bank.

Mozambique

CHAPTER 6

Abolishing Fees and Reducing the Costs of Primary School: The Experience of Mozambique

This study is a review of Mozambique's experience in abolishing fees, reducing user costs, and providing incentives as steps toward achieving the Education for All (EFA) and the Millennium Development Goal (MDG) for universal primary education (UPE).

Obligatory school fees for the Social Action Fund (ASE—Acçao Social Escolar) were abolished by the government of Mozambique in 2004 as a step toward reducing cost barriers to access. The World Bank–funded Direct Support to Schools (DSS) program, which started in 2003, alleviates the cost of primary education for families and, at the same time, improves the quality of education by providing grants to schools for the purchase of materials. The DSS is one of the latest interventions in the ongoing improvement of access and quality of primary education in Mozambique, and through piloting, is being extended to include incentives for orphans and vulnerable children (OVC), especially girls.

THE MOZAMBICAN CONTEXT

Mozambique is one of the poorest countries in the world, in 168th place on the human development index (HDI), with an HDI value of 0.379 (average for Sub-Saharan Africa is 0.515). Out of a population of almost 19.9 million,[1] 54 percent live below the poverty line.[2] The gross domestic product (GDP) index is 0.30 (average for Sub-Saharan Africa is 0.63), and the gross national income (GNI) per capita is US$250 (average for

Sub-Saharan Africa is US$600).[3] Even so, the situation in 2006 was the result of considerable improvements in recent years. The GDP per capita has grown at a rate of approximately 6 percent in the past decade, and the percentage of the population living in absolute poverty has declined from 69.4 percent in 1996–97 to 54.1 percent in 2002–03.

However, HIV/AIDS is affecting both households and the national economy. Adult prevalence was estimated to be 16.2 percent in 2004 (Ministry of Health 2004)[4] and is projected to reach 16.8 percent by 2010 (INE 2004). Average life expectancy is just under 42 years (average for Sub-Saharan Africa is just over 46 years) and is likely to decline because of HIV/AIDS. The demographic impact calculation was 37 years in 2006 because of HIV/AIDS. It is also likely that HIV/AIDS is reducing per capita GDP growth by 1 percent per year. The implications for the educational system are that despite the overall economic improvements in recent years, household expenditure of the poor on education remains vulnerable to external factors and could become more so, especially for OVC. Both public income and expenditure on education will also be affected directly and indirectly by the impact of HIV/AIDS.

The policy context for achieving universal primary education is in place. The Constitution describes education as a right and a duty. The government has adopted the goal of achieving universal seven-year primary education by 2015. The Mozambique Poverty Reduction Strategy Plan (PRSP)—the Action Plan for the Reduction of Absolute Poverty (PARPA)—emphasizes access to and quality of basic education as crucial in reducing absolute poverty and for social development, economic justice, and gender equity, as well as in the fight against HIV/AIDS.[5]

> Education is one of the key sectors of the government to reduce absolute poverty. . . . (Priorities): increase access and learning at all levels, improve efficiency, give particular attention to girls and women, children with special learning needs, orphans and children in rural areas (Government of Mozambique 2006).

These policies are developed more fully within the Education Sector Strategic Plan II (ESSP II). The three key objectives of the ESSP are the expansion of access to basic education throughout all regions of Mozambique, the improvement of the quality of education services, and the strengthening of the institutions and the administrative framework for effective and sustainable delivery of education. Further, the ESSP states that its strategy is to support the three key objectives of the overall economic and social development policy: reducing absolute poverty, ensuring justice and gender equity, and fighting the spread of HIV/AIDS and mitigating its impact (MEC 2005b).

Having developed a PRSP and the ESSP (together with a costed plan), Mozambique met the criteria for inclusion in the EFA Fast Track Initiative (FTI) in 2002, making it eligible for funding from the FTI Catalytic Fund.

Since the cessation of the civil war in 1992, Mozambique has gradually developed its educational system in accordance with these policies. Factors such as the colonial legacy of a very poorly developed educational system, the impact of the civil war (loss of life, internal displacement, extensive destruction of infrastructure, lack of continuity in education, aggravation of poverty, and lack of highly educated human resources), and widespread and extreme poverty meant that Mozambique, with lower schooling and literacy rates, had a far worse starting point to achieve EFA than other countries in the Sub-Saharan region at that time. Despite major improvements since then, Mozambique still lags behind the average for Sub-Saharan Africa.

THE EDUCATIONAL SYSTEM

The formal education system of Mozambique is structured as follows: primary education with intended entry at age 6 (EP1, grades 1–5, and EP2, grades 6–7); secondary general education (ESG), divided into ESG1 (grades 8–10) and ESG2 (grades 11–12); technical and vocational training (TVT), divided into elementary, basic, and medium; teacher education for basic education (grade 7+3) and for middle school education (grade 10+2); and tertiary education. Adult literacy programs provide functional training in literacy and numeracy, up to a level equivalent to the end of EP2, giving access to skills (TVT) training.

Key indicators show that although Mozambique has some way to go, it is in the process of improving access and quality in the education system. The education component of the HDI is 0.45 (average for Sub-Saharan Africa is 0.56); adult literacy is 46.5 percent (average for Sub-Saharan Africa is 61.3 percent); and combined gross enrollment rate (GER) for primary and secondary schooling is 43 percent (average for Sub-Saharan Africa is 50 percent). Since 1997, primary and secondary education have expanded at a steady but rapid rate as shown in table 6.1 and figure 6.1. Enrollment at the EP1 level has more than doubled between 1997 and 2006, and EP2 more than tripled. ESG1 enrollment has increased by 6.54 times and ESG2 by just over 17 times. The gross enrollment rate for EP1 has risen by 57.5 percentage points and for EP2 by more than 26 percentage points. For ESG1 the increase is just over 12 percent and for ESG2 just over 3.1 percent.

Table 6.1 System Growth in Primary and Secondary Education, 1997–2006

Indicator/year	Level of primary and secondary education			
	EP1	EP2	ESG1	ESG2
Gross enrollment rate (percent)				
1997	74.8	20.7	4.8	0.6
1997 male/female	87.6/61.9	24.5/16.9	5.5/4.0	0.8/0.5
2003	112.7	36.9	12.0	2.9
2003 male/female	122.9/102.4	44.4/29.6	14.2/9.9	3.4/2.4
2004	121.2	42.7	13.8	3.4
2005	131.3	47.0	17.0	3.7
2005 male/female	140.1/122.5	55.5/38.5	19.8/14.2	4.4/3.0
Net enrollment rate (percent)				
1997	43.0	2.3	1.1	0.1
2003	69.4	4.5	2.7	0.5
2003 male/female	72.4/66.4	4.9/4.1	2.9/2.5	0.5/0.4
2004	75.6	5.6	3.0	0.5
2004 male/female	78.0/73.2	5.9/5.2	3.2/2.8	0.5/0.4
2005	83.4	6.7	5.6	0.6
2005 male/female	85.6/81.2	7.0/6.3	5.8/5.4	0.6/0.6
Number of learners				
1997	1,744,869	153,102	45,211	2,614
2003	2,884,111	365,590	164,213	23,502
2004	3,143,020	426,453	199,015	28,020
2005	3,471,140	469,593	247,787	32,803
2006	3,658,418	513,089	295,836	44,513
Number of schools				
1997	—	—	—	—
2003	8,077	950	125	29
2004	8,373	1,116	140	30
2005	8,696	1,320	156	35
2006	9,002	1,514	190	49

Source: Education Statistics.
— Not available.

Since 1997, the net enrollment rate (NER) has been improving, and there have been jumps in EP1 of 6 percent and almost 8 percent in successive years. Overall NER for primary education has continuously increased (to 83 percent in 2005), but 17 percent of primary-school-age children still do not enroll. In terms of gender equity, from 2003 to 2005, the rate of improvement in GER for girls in EP1 was slightly

Figure 6.1 Growth of EP1 Gross Enrollment Rate, 1981–2004 and 2005 Projection

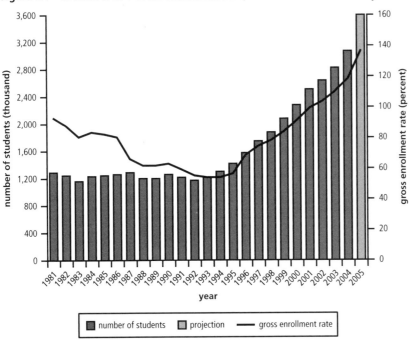

Source: Education Statistics.

greater than the rate of improvement for boys, and this is the case for EP2 as well.

Concerning system performance in terms of quality, although there are evident improvements over the years in repetition, dropout, and completion in EP1, a completion rate of 48 percent is still very low and gender difference is still notable (see table 6.2 and figure 6.2). Overall, this indicates high inefficiency in the system and a wasted investment if children do not stay long enough to become literate and numerate.[6] In EP2, repetition and completion rates, though they remain low, have improved despite an increase in the dropout rate. Compared to the completion rates for EP1, the completion rate for girls in EP2 is not as far behind that for boys but is also relatively low.

The average completion time for primary education is 18 years compared to the cycle time of 7 years. The pupil-teacher ratios (PTRs) have risen as the real numbers of enrollment and progression have increased. Table 6.2 shows that the distribution of teachers between EP1 and EP2 is very uneven and the percentage of unqualified teachers is rising. Less than one-third of EP1 and less than one-quarter of EP2 teachers are female; in EP2, less than one-quarter are female.

Table 6.2   Primary Education System Performance, 1997–2005

Indicator	EP1	EP2
Repetition rate (percent)		
1997	24.9	28.8
2003	21.9	19.5
2003 male/female	21.9/21.9	18.9/20.3
Dropout rate (percent)		
1997	8.8	6.9
2003	7.6	8.9
Completion rate (percent)		
1997	22.0	7.3
2003	40.8	17.8
2003 male/female	49.1/32.5	22.3/13.4
2004	48.0	28.9
2004 male/female	56.7/39.3	35.0/22.8
Completion time (years)[a]		
2003	18	
Efficiency coefficient	0.39	
Teacher supply		
Pupil-teacher ratio 1997	60.8:1	38.4:1
Pupil-teacher ratio 2003	66.0:1	38.7:1
Pupil-teacher ratio 2004	65.9:1	39.0:1
Pupil-teacher ratio 2005	74.0:1	41.1:1
Unqualified teachers 1997 (percent)	29.6	6.4
Unqualified teachers 2005 (percent)	42.0	31.6
Female teachers 2005 (percent)	31.3	23.3

Source: Education Statistics.
a. Completion time is the average number of years used by the grade 1 intake of a particular year to complete a cycle (in this case, primary education). It includes repetition and dropout. Cycle time is the number of years it should take to complete a cycle without any repetition.

All the statistics in figure 6.2 are national averages, and although these indicate the state of the system as a whole, including the overall gender gaps, they conceal considerable disparities between the 11 provinces. For example, overall GER (in percent) in EP1 ranges from 89.1 < 152.4 and in EP2 from 22.5 < 92.0. The overall NER (in percent) in EP1 ranges from 51.7 < 92.4, and in EP2 from 1.1 < 17.0. See table 6.3 for the wide range in difference disaggregated by province and gender. Figure 6.3 shows the rate of increase in GER by province between 2003 and 2005.

Even within provinces, between districts, and within districts, there are wide variations on averages and between the sexes. This is a clear

Figure 6.2   Gender Gap in Net Enrollment and Completion Rates in EP1, 1997/98 and 2004/05

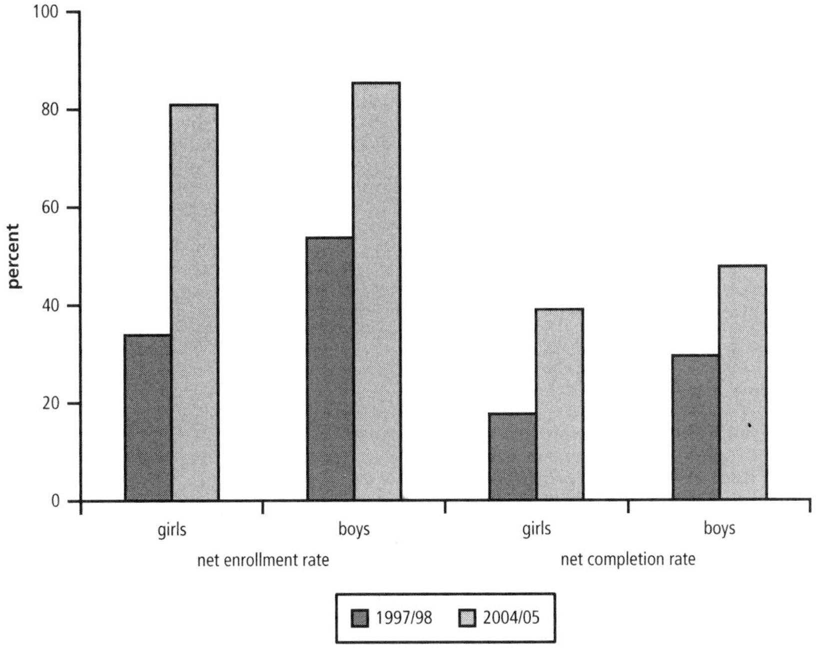

Source: Education Statistics.

Table 6.3   Range of Gender Differences between Provinces, 2004

(percent)

Indicator	EP1	EP2
Gross enrollment rate		
Boys	109.6 < 157.2	31.1 < 89.8
Girls	89.7 < 156.4	13.7 < 94.1
Net enrollment rate (2005)		
Boys	72.9 < 102.8	—
Girls	67.3 < 108.0	—
Repetition		
Boys	15.9 < 27.7	13.8 < 23.3
Girls	16.1 < 26.4	15.6 < 24.9
Completion		
Boys	32.1 < 94.2	15.5 < 45.8
Girls	14.6 < 96.7	6.0 < 46.2

Source: Education Statistics.
— Not available.

Figure 6.3 Increase in Gross Enrollment Rate by Province, 2003–05

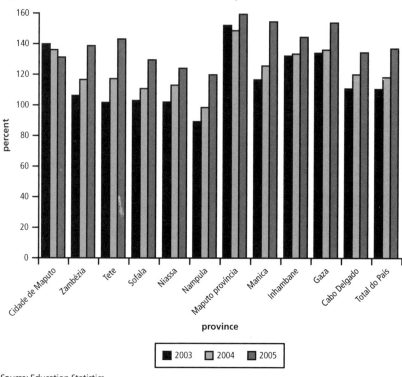

Source: Education Statistics.

indication that there is no one solution to improving access and quality: specific interventions or combinations of interventions need to be worked out for each context.

THE COST OF EDUCATION

As elsewhere, both direct and indirect costs affect access to education, particularly for poor families. Until January 2005, direct costs included school fees for ASE. The ASE was originally meant to provide school materials, uniforms, and essential personal items for learners whose families could not afford them. The amount to be collected was prescribed by the Ministry of Education and Culture (MEC) as 150 Mozambican meticais (Mt) for EP1 and Mt 250 for EP2. In addition to the ASE, boarding fees were also demanded. The boarding fee for EP2 was set at Mt 500.[7]

Direct costs alone made it difficult for very poor families to send more than one or two children to school. In addition to the ASE and boarding fees, schools could charge their own fees for materials, sporting, and cultural events. Indirect costs included opportunity costs, lunches, and school uniforms. In all, average fees came to Mt 21,410 per child per year for EP1 and Mt 60,013 for EP2; books were Mt 43,000 and uniforms were Mt 73,000.[8] In addition, textbook expenses at the EP2 level averaged Mt 114,249 per year. Expenses could quickly mount to an average of over Mt 137,000 for EP1 and over Mt 290,000 for EP2. Poor households have larger families than nonpoor (5.8 members compared to 4.5 members), and the cost of sending more than one child to school relative to household income increases considerably as the poverty level increases. According to the 2003 Public Expenditure Review (PER) on sectoral expenditures, the cost of one child in EP1 represented 12 percent of household consumption expenditure of the lowest decile and 10 percent in the second-lowest decile. Expenditure on EP2 was 34 percent and 29 percent, respectively (World Bank 2003).

The Poverty and Social Impact Analysis (PSIA) documented that regions and districts varied considerably in the amounts demanded, which, in the great majority of cases, was more than the MEC prescription (World Bank 2005). A district in one province could ask for more than three times the amount of another district in the same or another province for the same level of schooling. The example of Niassa Province showed that the difference in fees between EP1 and EP2 could vary from twice to four times as much in rural areas and up to four times as much in urban areas. Maputo City's costs are far higher than elsewhere.

The uses of school fees—ASE or other fees—vary from school to school and are almost entirely at the discretion of the school director. The percentage used for items that would give quick returns in quality of learning (notebooks, pens, chalks) or for other items that may be useful but not essential (sports equipment) is unknown. Evidence shows that there was considerable private investment in state education without much, if any, value to school effectiveness.

POVERTY AND ENROLLMENT

A series of studies provide information on the cost of education as a constraint to enrollment in Mozambique.[9] School fees were a major reason for not enrolling children in school, according to the 1996–97 Household Survey. The 2001 data by the National Institute of Statistics indicate three main reasons for dropping out: cost (29 percent), lack of relevance ("not useful"—29 percent), and distance to school (11 percent). Poverty was the main reason cited for not attending school: 38 percent of 6–12-year-olds and 27 percent of 13–17-year-olds not enrolled in school said school was too expensive. In 2003, approximately 12 percent of household income of the lowest-earning decile and 10 percent of the next lowest decile were used to meet the cost of education (World Bank 2003).

The 2004 PSIA (World Bank 2005) analyzed, among other things, GER and NER by consumption quintile (see tables 6.4 and 6.5). The combination of especially low NER with much higher GER for quintiles 1 and 2 clearly shows a relationship between the economic status of the family and the age at which children start school. The rapid decline of GER and NER shows that the poorer the family, the shorter the time spent in school. According to the 2004 PSIA, if the level of household consumption were to rise, especially in the lowest quintiles, school attendance would be likely to rise.

The 2003 Demographic and Health Survey (DHS) shows the correlation between the rate of school attendance by sex and wealth quintile (see

Table 6.4 Gross Enrollment Rate by Consumption Quintile and Level of Education, 2004

(percent)

Consumption quintile	EP1	EP2	ESG1	ESG2
1	98.8	50.3	13.2	2.3
2	95.6	54.6	15.4	3.7
3	98.1	46.5	22.1	6.2
4	104.3	54.2	20.5	5.4
5	106.1	86.6	46.9	22.6

Source: World Bank 2005.

Table 6.5 Net Enrollment Rate by Consumption Quintile and Level of Education, 2004

(percent)

Consumption quintile	EP1	EP2	ESG1	ESG2
1	59.4	8.0	2.2	0.6
2	59.8	8.3	4.6	0.4
3	60.2	6.0	4.6	0.9
4	66.6	9.8	7.1	0.6
5	72.2	15.2	9.9	3.6

Source: World Bank 2005.

Figure 6.4 Net Primary School Attendance Rate by Sex and Wealth Index Quintile

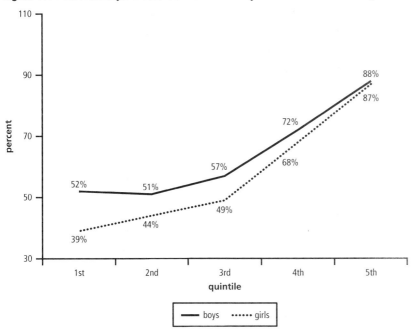

Source: Ministry of Education and Culture 2003.

figure 6.4)(see also MEC 2004). Undoubtedly, poverty affects school attendance, and the poorer the family, the greater the effect on girls. The 2003 DHS found that 49 percent of children are living in absolute poverty, 63 percent in rural areas and 20 percent in urban areas. Once again, regional disparities are evident: only 3 percent of Maputo City's children live in absolute poverty compared to 75 percent in Zambezia Province.

OTHER FACTORS AFFECTING ENROLLMENT

The 2004 PSIA identified other factors that seem to have a greater effect on enrollment and retention than cost in itself.[10] Proximity to school is a key variable. The greater the distance to school, the less probable it is that the child will be enrolled. The other most important factors are age and gender. The later a child starts school, the greater the likelihood that he or she will drop out; the likelihood is still greater for rural than for urban areas, and more so for girls than boys in EP1. In addition, the change of status from girl to woman through first menstruation and rites is an important factor in some provinces. The first PARPA (Government of Mozambique 2001) found that a poor child in an urban area is more likely to attend school than a nonpoor child in a rural area. In rural areas, a poor boy is more likely to attend school than a nonpoor girl. Finally, vulnerability (handicap) is a significant factor constraining enrollment in EP1.

Compared with long-standing poverty and inherited gender attitudes, HIV/AIDS is a relatively new factor that affects attendance. Additional analysis of the 2003 DHS found that maternal orphans had lower attendance than paternal orphans and nonorphans. However, paternal orphans had better attendance than nonorphans not living with their parents. A study conducted by the Ministry of Planning and Development (MPD) in 2005 found that children who are not direct biological descendants of the household head are discriminated against in terms of resource allocation within poor households. The discrimination is reflected in decisions about who should go to school and who should remain at home and work (Nhate 2005). Figure 6.5 shows that the role of the mother tends to be more important than that of the father in ensuring school attendance.[11] Greater HIV prevalence among women than men also lessens the likelihood of children's attendance in school.

Illness in the home also affects children's attendance. A 2003 study by Save the Children (U.K.) found that children often stop attending school when their parents become chronically ill. Illness also increases household expenditure on medicine, food, and other essential items. The study

Figure 6.5 Primary School Attendance Rate among Children Ages 10–14 Years

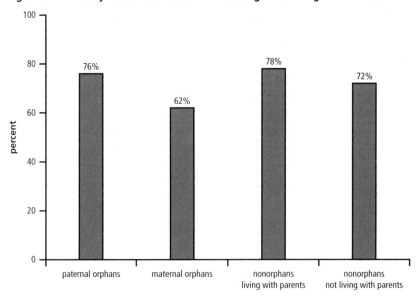

Source: Based on Nhate 2005.

also found high levels of discrimination from peers and neighbors, which resulted in children dropping out of school (Petty et al. 2003).

In the short to medium term, household income is dependent on developments outside the education sector, particularly agriculture, fishing, and forestry. Private as well as public expenditure on health is increasing, and productivity is weakened because of the impact of HIV/AIDS. If the demand for education is to be increased, replacing or subsidizing household expenditure on education should make a difference, especially since it is frequently mentioned by respondents in surveys. It is likely that free primary education (FPE) is not the only intervention needed to attain universal primary completion. Mozambique is attempting two interventions to reduce costs for the learner (strengthen demand) and several interventions to improve quality (strengthen supply).

THE ABOLITION OF ASE FEES

To keep pace with developments in other countries in the subregion (Kenya, Lesotho, Malawi, and Uganda), the MEC and the Ministry of Finance (MoF) decided in 2004 that all ASE fees should be abolished (see, for example, Avenstrup, Liang, and Nellemann 2004; MEC 2004b). Based on economic modeling, the 2004 PSIA study had argued that straightforward abolition of fees might not have a far-reaching effect. Rather, the key issue seemed to be on the supply side; the study suggested that other interventions would have greater impact, especially reducing the distance to school.

However, ongoing discussions continued within the MEC on ensuring children's attendance in school and the role of school fees in constraining attendance. Various options were considered on how to establish uniform practice in raising school fees so that individual schools did not charge fees that blocked access, whether exemption from school fees should apply after the second or third child, or whether school fees should be abolished for EP1. A campaign was launched in schools, encouraging them not to demand fees over and above the minimum and to apply the rules for exemption.

The MEC felt compelled to move ahead rapidly to get children to school. It agreed with the MoF that school fees should be abolished for grades 1–7 but that communities could make their own decisions about how to raise funds for schools as long as those decisions did not lead to the exclusion or dropout of learners.

The Direct Support to Schools (DSS) program (see below) started in 2003 and was already having an impact. To some extent, the DSS overlapped with the original intentions of the ASE, but as noted previously, the collection and use of school fees had shifted from the original stipulations. The DSS would replace some of the funding lost through the abolition of school fees. The minister of Education decided to abolish school fees for grades 1–7 in 2003, with effect from the 2004 school year.

The decision to abolish school fees is ultimately a political decision. In Mozambique, free primary education was introduced in an election year. In other countries that have abolished fees, the decision has come after extended negotiations with the donor community about the support needed to replace that income. Compensating for that loss is usually a combination of increasing efficiency in the system and ensuring increased funding until the system can become self-sustaining, or at least until the EFA goals and MDGs are met.

In the case of Mozambique, the donor community was not involved in decision making about the abolition of school fees, which was seen as an internal ministry decision. There were no negotiations with civil society to strengthen policy development and monitoring or to engage them in the process to support the system and meet potentially increased demand when ASE was abolished. In Mozambique, the private sector's role in education is very small (approximately 2.3 percent of EP1 and 4.2 percent of EP2 schools). Thus, unlike many other countries, there are no major proprietors to engage in negotiations. The DSS, however, was negotiated with donors.

As figure 6.1 shows, the overall growth of the system had been rising steadily since 1994. Enrollment in EP1 increased by 13 percent and in EP2 by almost 19 percent between 2005 and 2006. However, the increase cannot be attributed solely to the abolition of school fees, since 306 new EP1 and 206 new EP2 schools had been completed, and this would also have had a positive effect on enrollment. Even if the abolition of ASE fees did not have a massive and immediate impact on enrollment, which it had in other countries, it is likely to improve access for the poor who live within reasonable distance to a school.

Another perspective is that the abolition of school fees has symbolic if not monetary value. The abolition signals the government's willingness to reduce costs of education and can be meaningful to the public at large when combined with other interventions and awareness-raising campaigns.

THE DIRECT SUPPORT TO SCHOOLS PROGRAM

The DSS program was developed prior to the abolition of ASE fees and was not a substitute for them. The program seeks to overcome the cost barrier for poor families and to improve school quality at the same time. The program was discussed and planned by the World Bank and the MEC and discussed with other donors, but was implemented entirely by the ministry itself. It was launched in March 2003 and consists of small grants to schools. It has two main objectives: to promote the decentralization of decision making and resource management in the sector and to further the quality of education through the supply of basic learning materials and the involvement of the community in the life of the school.

By allowing school councils to ensure transparency and accountability in the use of the funds, the objective of decentralization was achieved. Quality was promoted by identifying basic materials for learners and teachers that could be purchased from the funds. The DSS has continued through four phases and in 2006, entered the fifth phase (MEC 2004a, 2005a, 2006).

PHASE ONE

The first phase was started with the training of all provincial and district directors of education in the objectives and operationalization of the program. Then special bank accounts, solely for the purpose of transferring DSS funds, were opened in the name of the district director.

Training and information materials were developed and printed, including manuals, brochures, posters, and wall and desk calendars. A wide range of communication strategies were used to reach the general public: these included newspapers and publicity and information spots introduced by the national anthem through all local media in Portuguese and local languages. Once the program was operational, funds were transferred to the accounts of the district directors of education. The amount of funds was based on the number of schools in the district.

In the first year, a total of Mt 37,721,840,000 (approximately US$1.7 million) was allocated. More than 8,100 EP schools could use up to Mt 240,000 (US$200) each in two half-yearly disbursements to cover the cost of school materials for learners and teachers (notebooks, textbooks, library books, pencils, pens, erasers, dictionaries, glue, chalk, blackboards, maps, and cupboards with locks to store books) chosen from a list prepared by the MEC.

The school management was trained in the necessary procurement and financial procedures, and a letter of authorization for the school to draw a check was countersigned. The school council, composed of teachers, representatives of the community, the school director, and the district director of education, decided on the most urgently needed items from the MEC list; a check was drawn and the items purchased directly by the school director and community representative.

The monitoring of the first phase was conducted in October and November 2003. The aim was to monitor the extent to which objectives were being realized, identify any obstacles to implementation in the different regions, and improve implementation mechanisms in the succeeding phases. Monitoring found immediate positive results. It was reported that learner participation in the classroom improved: students had pencils and notebooks, more students could do homework, participate in class, and come to the blackboard. Consequently, this improved motivation and reduced absenteeism and dropout.[12] The poorest children, whose families could not have afforded materials, benefited in particular.

The transfer of funds through the bank proved to be efficient. Further, links between school and community were strengthened though joint involvement and responsibility, and there were few delays between ordering and delivery. Generally speaking, the scheme was well administered. Apart from recommendations to strengthen managerial and administrative aspects, it was found that the amount available per school should vary according to school size and that additional criteria were needed to support orphans.

PHASE TWO

During the second phase, between Mt 3.5 million and Mt 90 million were allocated per school, according to the number of learners and the number of shifts. In addition, the district directorates of education (DDEs) received Mt 240,000 per school for the management team administrating the program. The total investment in this phase was just over the equivalent of US$2.5 million, benefiting more than 8,100 EP1 schools in the country.

The MEC developed and distributed a list of eligible schools in each district to the provincial and district directors. These lists specified the entitlement of each school and the goods each school received. The lists were available to all schools and could be reviewed by the general public.

The MEC extended the list of materials that could be purchased. Each school, through the school council, prepared its selection from the list of materials with the funds before the money was paid out from the bank. The ministry continued to strengthen the capacity of provincial directorates of education (DPEs) and DDEs to ensure the objectives of the program were being realized. In addition, regular auditing was carried out to ensure the efficiency of the program. The program's results led to the ministry's decision to continue the program in subsequent years.

According to the second phase monitoring report in February 2004, communities participated in all aspects of the program, and the increased funding benefited the children. The variation in disbursements (from Mt 3.6 million to Mt 90 million), depending on school size, was accepted as a fair criterion. Schools appreciated the extension of the list of items that could be purchased and were driven by a strong mix between school and learner needs. The DSS made it possible for the neediest learners to attend school; they were the direct beneficiaries of the program. The processes of information, selection, and decision making were usually conducted in a participatory manner. Although there was a general list of items that were eligible for purchase, the variation in schools' priorities was seen as positive. The improvements in learner motivation and classroom participation were evident, as were reductions in absenteeism and dropout. There was a high degree of satisfaction among all the actors.

PHASE THREE

In the third phase, a new component, deworming, was trialed in two selected provinces in EP1 and EP2 schools. To implement the deworming component, the Ministry of Health and the MEC decentralized planning of the entire process to a team activity (DDE staff and schools developed training and information materials). In this phase, EP1 schools received between Mt 4.2 million and Mt 70 million. Approximately 8,400 EP1 schools were involved. The program reached approximately 3,071,564 learners.

As in the other phases, the MEC took the following actions:

- Produced and distributed (through the DPEs) training and information and PR materials, namely, the manual for DSS procedures, brochures, lists of financial resource allocation by school, posters, manuals for deworming, and tape measures.
- Held the third capacity-building workshop throughout July 2004 for all personnel dealing directly with the DSS program. Altogether 400 personnel participated, including district directors of education or their representatives, departmental heads of administration and finance, and the secretariat. Depending on the availability of funds, the DPEs also attended along with the head of the Department of Administration and Finance.
- Publicized the DSS from July 23 through August 2004 throughout the country using national and eight regional Radio Mozambique channels. Information and publicity spots were disseminated in Portuguese

and 14 local languages. As for print media, the MEC solicited four major newspapers to publicize the third phase of DSS over a 10-day period in August.

- Completed the process of transferring funds to all DDEs in the country between September and November, a total of Mt 53,827,188,000 (US$2,242,800).

The primary objective of the DSS program was fully realized in that greatest efficacy and impact occurred at the level of the students. Materials from chalk, electrical plugs, paper, and locks to notebooks, maps, pens, and nails have all had an impact on teaching and learning. At a general level, it was found that vulnerable children, in particular, were able to enroll in EP1 and benefited directly from the DSS program. All primary schools received the funds allocated to them.

The information, selection, and decision-making processes and the beneficiaries of the identified materials from the DSS program were organized in a wide variety of ways at the school level. In most cases, the process was organized in a fully participative manner between the school director and the school council. At the classroom level, the increased motivation of learners resulting from the direct benefits of school materials was observable.

Through interviews, third-phase monitoring tested options for the continuation of the program. At the start, DSS had supplied funds to ease the cost burden on households and increase demand and improve quality (there is partial overlap here between the DSS and the original intentions of the ASE). At the end of the second phase, schools moved to direct or indirect incentives to improve the supply side. These included improving the provision of water, latrines, school-based health, HIV/AIDS interventions, and infrastructure. Many schools still have outside teaching spaces or leaky roofs over classrooms.

Particular attention was paid to gender issues. Pedagogical interventions that were mentioned as needing support included teacher professional development and improved supervision and special needs education. There was also mention of using funds for school sports although there was nothing in the studies to indicate that school sports were significant in improving attendance.[13] The monitoring report indicates that enhancing the sports program would not be a poverty-related intervention.

PHASE FOUR

The fourth phase was launched and implemented in 2005; funds were used from the International Development Association (IDA) credit. The program was extended to include EP2 in addition to EP1 schools, 9,500 schools in all. School allocation varied between Mt 5.25 million and Mt 78 million, depending on the size of enrollment and the number of shifts. The deworming activities continued at EP1 schools, and the inclusion of a school health and HIV/AIDS program was trialed for all EP1 and EP2 schools in three provinces (Sofala, Gaza, and Inhambane) with a view to informing strategies for national scaling up (see section on Combining DSS and Special Incentives for Orphans and Vulnerable Children below).

Implementation largely followed previous strategies. DPEs and DDEs produced training and information materials, brochures, and calendars. Capacity building of the MEC staff (the same target groups as before) was held throughout the country during February and March 2005, and again in August and September; radio broadcasting was used regularly for information spots in Portuguese and local languages.

In the fourth phase, almost Mt 98.8 billion (US$ 4.116 million) was transferred to schools. Of that total, over 71 percent was used for materials and almost 29 percent for school health and HIV/AIDS activities.

The monitoring of the fourth phase was conducted in April 2006 to verify the appropriate use of funds, including the decentralization of school health and HIV/AIDS activities.

COMBINING DSS AND SPECIAL INCENTIVES FOR ORPHANS AND VULNERABLE CHILDREN

A broad-based working group consisting of MEC officials and representatives from donor agencies took up the recommendations of the DSS monitoring report on support to OVC and developed a concept paper in June 2005 (MEC 2005c). The Dutch government contributed trust funds to the DSS (managed by the World Bank) for this purpose; these were matched by UNICEF funding for the elements of the project that were not covered by the school grant.[14] The DSS part of the program passed into sector-pooled funds in June 2006 to ensure greater sustainability. The objectives of this additional intervention were to increase EP1 enrollment in general and OVC enrollment in relation to the overall increase, and to increase the retention rate, particularly for OVC in EP1.

Orphans and vulnerable children are already exempt from all school fees. Nonetheless, this initiative focuses on OVC, especially vulnerable girls, as the social group most difficult to reach for schools. At the same time, the initiative realizes that the school is the widest-reaching public institution and may be a point of departure for other social services. Given the lack of certainty about interventions that will increase enrollment and retention, especially for OVC, two models will be tried in a longer pilot phase. One model doubles DSS funds per child for materials, and it funds an outreach program to identify OVC outside the school system, provide psychosocial support and monitoring of those at risk of dropping out, and link OVC with other social services (health, food and nutrition, and legal assistance). The model assumes that a combination of individually adapted interventions is needed to reach OVC and keep them in school. The other model is simply to double DSS funds per child for materials, based on the assumption that this alone will be enough to reach OVC and keep them in school.

Model 1 includes funding for the following:

- School materials (graphs, manuals, posters) and training
- Additional financial resources based on the increasing number of classes
- Birth certificates for all school children[15]
- School councils and other school-community link committees that support awareness of OVC issues
- Monitoring retention of OVC in schools throughout the school year
- Setting up a referral network for psychosocial support to children in need
- Material support to OVC, including school materials (books, writing materials) and clothes and shoes, according to individual needs
- Exemption from exam fees and any other financial contributions that may be required by schools
- Referral to psychosocial support when necessary.

Model 2 includes funding for the following:

- School materials (graphs, manuals, posters) and training
- Additional financial resources based on the increasing number of classes
- Material support to children, including school materials (books, writing materials)
- Exemption from exam fees and any other financial contributions demanded by schools.

This additional intervention to the DSS was piloted in the fifth phase (in Buzi, Angónia, Chokwé, and Mocímboa da Praia Districts) with a view to its expansion on a national scale to support OVC within the ESSP II and PARPA II frameworks. The MEC's intention was to expand the program in partnership with NGOs. To this end, a lesson-learning framework was put in place to combine NGO interventions in this area alongside the pilot to facilitate a future program based on partnership. There were concerns about the sustainability of those parts of the program supported by the Ministry of Women and Social Action, which has less capacity in general, less capacity to mobilize significant OVC resources from global funds in particular, and also a lesser share of the state budget than the MEC.

OTHER INTERVENTIONS TO IMPROVE ACCESS AND QUALITY

Abolishing fees and providing direct support to schools and incentives for OVC may go a long way in improving access and some way in improving quality. However, a range of other interventions is also needed if quality is to be raised substantially and the initiative is to become sustainable. Several interventions are currently being implemented.

NEW CURRICULUM

First, a new curriculum starting in grades 1, 3, and 6 was begun in 2004 in response to charges of "lack of relevance" and to claims that school was "uninteresting." This step meant that the EP cycle would be reformed quickly, over a period of only three years. Another challenge is that 20 percent of curriculum time will be used for locally relevant options, developed at the provincial level. Second, as of 2004, promotion has been automatic within subphases (grades 1–3, 4–5, 6–7), rather than grade by grade. This was meant to reduce repetition, improve flow-through, and decrease dropout.

The reforms indicate the need to improve cohort planning. Other countries that introduced free primary education experienced increased enrollment in the lower secondary level that was both greater and sooner than expected. There was a new access shock in secondary education, although not as massive as in primary education. Hence, there is a need to expand secondary schools and train more secondary teachers. Most countries have had to move qualified primary teachers up to the secondary level and put in teacher-upgrading programs, creating a vacuum at the primary level.

STRUCTURAL CHANGE

Second, EP1 and EP2 will be seen as a single cycle. Primary schools will be built as EPC grade 1–7 schools. Hence, the problem of proximity will be resolved and boarding costs will be reduced. In addition, teachers will be distributed evenly throughout the grades.

TEACHER TRAINING

The backlog of teachers increases each year. Enrollment in teacher-training colleges will be increased; the former 7+3 alternative will be phased out, and only the 10+1 will remain.

STRENGTHENING THE EDUCATIONAL PROCESS

Consideration is given to a range of issues that the ASE did not cover: provision of teaching and learning materials, equipment, and school libraries; improving supervision through the coordinators of the school cluster centers; revitalizing community mobilization for effective participation in the educational process; and monitoring the impact of initiatives to improve the quality of education.

MANAGING ACCESS SHOCK

A number of other countries in Sub-Saharan Africa have experienced or are experiencing access shock after the introduction of FPE. In access shock, education systems must adapt suddenly to a shift from a supply-driven system to a demand-driven one. The main features are as follows:

- Sudden or rapidly increased shortage of classrooms
- More double and triple shifts
- More overcrowded classes
- Acute shortage of teachers
- Acute shortage of textbooks
- Pressing need to make the system more efficient, effective, and responsive to demand; change procedures and bureaucratic behavior
- Need to sustain the confidence of the electorate in the education system.

These needs are not new to Mozambique. Despite the gradual and steady growth in Mozambique over the past decade, there is still a huge backlog in training teachers and building classrooms. Access shock has been chronic and is now also acute. Part of the explanation lies in the MEC's lack of capacity to mobilize resources and work efficiently. The 2002 Education Sector Expenditure Review noted that there were weaknesses in budget execution in the flow of funds to provinces and districts (Oxford Policy Management 2002). The 2003 review of the Economic and Social Plan indicated that the budget needed to be aligned with planned programs and activities (Government of Mozambique 2003).

The 2003 PER on sectoral expenditures revealed that the allocation of teachers did not follow efficiency criteria, a large number of ghost teachers existed, and classroom construction costs varied considerably. Off-budget support from cooperating partners was difficult to document, so actual budgets and expenditure could not be accurately presented, only approximated (World Bank 2003).

For some time the need for greater financial efficiency and efficacy had been identified as a prerequisite for universal completion of quality primary education. The report on an investment and implementation plan for ESSP II emphasized that detailed costing of all activities necessary to reach the targets must be the basis of budgeting, and expenditure must be linked to outcome indicators. The overall general issue is how to make the system itself a robust and effective framework for service delivery of quality basic education.

LEARNING FROM OTHER COUNTRIES

If the combination of interventions in Mozambique is successful, greater demands will be made on infrastructure, desks, the supply of textbooks, and the provision of teachers. To alleviate pressure, some interim measures, which other countries have adopted, may inform short- and medium-term implementation strategies in Mozambique. A few examples are noted here.

There is already a chronic and acute lack of classrooms, and ESSP II envisages building 2,000 per year with a US$10,000 limit per classroom. The low-cost construction policy was approved in 2005 and is now being implemented. However, that rate will still lag behind demand. Other countries have used different types of temporary solutions in such situations and been successful in keeping learners under shelter until proper classrooms are built. Lesotho set up tent classrooms in remote areas. Namibia built shelters using beams and corrugated iron sheets, which could be used when permanent construction catches up with demand, instead of exposing learners to the elements.

To improve quality, ESSP II plans will phase out the 7+3 teacher training and increase the output of 10+1 teachers. The output will still be less than required, and the supply will still lag behind demand. If the plans were tailored to actual need, there would be more grade 10 graduates to meet the intake. Other countries in a similar situation have also set up modular systems for training paraprofessionals near their homes, not least so that women with some education can be brought into the system.

This has been recommended in both the 2004 and the 2005 Joint Reviews of the ESSP (MEC and cooperating partners 2004, 2005).

The paraprofessional enters the system at a low level, but the training of paraprofessionals is not an endpoint in itself: it is the starting point of longer-term professional development to bring teachers up to full qualification. There are several programs in and outside the subregion that provide models. There are also several successful projects with localized on-the-job teacher development that start at low entry points. Other projects provide training to teach grade by grade progressively. In this way, teachers do not have to learn everything at once: in each year teachers learn only how to teach the next grade.[16] Mozambique has a school cluster network with resource centers (Zona de Influencia Pedagogica or ZIPs), which can bring modular training quite far out into the district. There are also lessons to be learned from using older learners, especially girls, to mentor younger ones.[17]

Other programs should be examined to improve the quality of existing teachers. For example, demand-driven, in-service training and local materials development, based on teachers' systematic analyses of pedagogical problems, were key features of the PPSE (Programme de Petites Subventions d'Ecoles, Guinea), now known as PAREEG—Programme d'Appui à la Rénovation Educative dans les Ecoles de Guinée), which was part of Guinea's effort at revitalization of basic education.

Given the social and economic context in Sub-Saharan Africa, reaching universal primary education begs many questions. One is whether the actual form of education is universally appropriate in the current phase. Formal primary education, as we know it, is inherited from colonial powers and developed under different social and economic circumstances in the colonial countries. It was not adapted to the exigencies of seasonal work or for overage learners. The system today still presupposes that all learners are of appropriate age for their grade and can follow a timetable, which applies to urban life.

This is not to imply that Africans should have a second-best education; however, it does imply that equally good alternatives should be considered. There is much to be learned and applied from the experience of nonformal and formal accelerated, alternative, and complementary basic education programs in several African countries such as Ethiopia and Tanzania. The structure and organization of such programs is often more flexible and conducive to the real-life situation of children from poor families and in rural areas.

In curriculum reforms across the subregion, there are major efforts to make curricula less expansive in content and more relevant to local contexts. However, in moving away from the encyclopedic approach, curricula are not necessarily less expansive. Instead, the emphasis is shifting to competencies, often a very detailed level of competencies, leading to assessment overload. Mozambique, a case in point, is moving to a competency-based curriculum, including local languages, and leaving two areas open for locally developed curricula. In the competency-based curriculum, the curriculum time is not reduced nor is a competency or outcomes-based curriculum easier to teach than a content-based curriculum—in fact, the reverse is true. On the other hand, the accelerated, alternative, complementary basic education curricula all have a more concentrated focus on core skills and readily assessable competencies, producing equivalent competence in less curriculum time than in formal education. Using such programs to move overage learners quickly through the system or to reach marginalized groups, as in other countries, may be considered.

Finally, large-class teaching will continue for some time. Curricula are not designed for large classes: the curriculum developer consciously or implicitly keeps certain parameters in mind of what a "normal" classroom should be. The teacher must decide how to adapt to classroom circumstances. If all the learners have the necessary textbooks and materials and these are well designed, then the teacher can function as an organizer of learning. Some specific methodologies can be applied in large classes, such as *pédagogie convergente*, even though it was developed only for language teaching. The classroom organization and lesson planning are highly structured to facilitate effective learning in large classes and can be used in a range of subjects.

There are many instructive experiences; however, a better flow of information is needed for countries struggling with the same problems. Also, although the interventions mentioned are intended as interim measures, parallel but equal systems of teacher education may need to stay in place for some time once the full impact of HIV/AIDS is felt on the teaching profession.

LEARNING FROM MOZAMBIQUE

Just as Mozambique can learn from the experience of other countries, so can Mozambique offer its experiences for comparison. The DSS is undoubtedly the success story in Mozambique's progress toward FPE. There is evidence that it is leading to quality improvement in the classroom under the most unlikely circumstances. Equally important, it is empowering communities and strengthening community-school links.

The schools and communities must decide how best to use funds to improve the quality of education for their children: the money is at the discretion of the end user. This arrangement has revitalized school councils and introduced local-level accountability and local-level solutions. The difference between the DSS and grants for construction is that in construction projects the community is quite often the cheap labor and provider of low-cost materials, sometimes also controlling the use of funds. Once the classroom or school is built, the community's involvement tends to end. The DSS, however, seeks to improve the quality of education, and is therefore an ongoing process.

It is a reasonable hypothesis that community and school empowerment not only contributes to quality enhancement and administrative efficiency, but also creates a stronger constituency for education. Some improvements are needed in the procedures and management system now that the program has been trialed, but there is also sufficient experience to expand the program to reach OVC and to adopt a more holistic approach to the learner's health and welfare.

The DSS cannot expand indefinitely. Sustainability can only be achieved if education reform is centered on system efficiency in delivery, the role of the school, and the importance of school-level capacity to generate local solutions. The role of the DSS is to reduce disparities through financial support (with formula funding similar to that in Uganda). PARPA is committed to poverty reduction; and the ESSP Joint Reviews strongly recommend supporting districts with the greatest disparities. Currently, there is no mechanism in place to achieve that end: the DSS is for the time being the only mechanism to reach all schools in the country.

THE WAY AHEAD

The DSS monitoring reports make some specific, practical recommendations. The list of items that may be purchased should be extended to areas not yet covered by DSS, especially a wider range for teaching and learning processes such as teaching materials, equipment, and school libraries. In terms of administration, support and supervision should be strengthened through the school cluster (ZIP) coordinators. Further, more is required in mobilizing communities to participate effectively in education. Finally, there are wider issues for consideration, such as the following.

KNOWLEDGE GAPS

Much is still unknown in the process toward universal primary completion in Mozambique, and questions for further exploration include the following:

- What financial and administrative systems are needed to steer budgeting and expenditure toward the targets of PARPA II and ESSP II?
- How much has the financial burden of education been reduced for poor families, and what difference does it make to their household consumption? What other areas demand increased expenditure?
- Who benefits most (added value) from the abolition of school fees, and from DSS?
- What is the impact of DSS on the self-esteem of school councils and communities? How has this affected their trust in the MEC to deliver quality education? How is the ministry responding to its obligation to meet the demand for quality?
- What skills have been developed in school councils and communities through DSS? Can these be transferred to other areas?
- What hard evidence is there that classroom learning is improving as a result of DSS?
- What evidence is there that improvements (for example, increased enrollment) are a result of DSS alone, or of combinations of factors?
- Which incentives take effect, and in which contexts; and which do not?
- What other factors besides cost influence school dropout (food security, health, push-out and pull-out factors, attitudes, values); and how are they best handled in each context?
- How can formal primary school systems adapt to a variety of local circumstances?
- What is the capacity of DSS to support disadvantaged schools with formula funding? What is the volume of funding for such a scheme?

THE DSS AND REFORM PROCESSES

So far, it is evident from program monitoring that the DSS program will be continued and will become a major vehicle to ensure that funds are moved as close to the end user as possible. However, the DSS must be connected to other reforms in the sector. The annual Joint Reviews of the ESSP make specific recommendations to improve sector development.

In 2005, it was agreed that the ministry should concentrate on the improvement of institutional capacity, prioritizing financial management and management of human resources (to avoid delays in the provision of salaries and textbooks). The potential impact of DSS will be enhanced if these and similar contextual issues are incorporated into implementation strategies. The 2005 Joint Review also saw the need for a decentralized system of pedagogical supervision in the field, both of the implementation of the new curriculum and the DSS, to efficiently support the processes of teaching and learning. In addition, the Joint Review recommends greater emphasis on achieving gender balance in primary education and on the inclusion of learners with special needs.

The government of Mozambique has allocated 9,103 additional posts in education, but these will be insufficient to lower the pupil-teacher ratio, which rose in EP1 from 66:1 to 74:1 in just one year (2004–05).[18] Whether the impact of DSS can be sustained must be assessed in light of these and other projections.

Although the DSS is well managed and accountable, it is only one part in the overall process of allocating funds to education. The 2006 budget was the first to include a large portion of external funds in the sector budget. Improvements in the overall planning, budgeting, and expenditure process and decentralization of responsibility provide a conducive financial management environment. With thorough evaluation, the DSS experience can inform other developments.

The PARPA II (2006–09) emphasizes the alleviation of absolute poverty among the poorest. Priorities in education include improving access and retention, especially among the poor, and improving quality and equity. The way ahead will, therefore, include a thorough impact evaluation of all aspects of the DSS, both to inform further developments of the program and to provide lessons learned for other ongoing reform processes.

TOWARD BETTER UNDERSTANDING

Much of the analysis done in Mozambique is based largely on economic models. The importance of human and social interactions tends to be relegated to the background in such models. Broader models are needed to capture all the factors that cause impact. The 2005 National Institute for Educational Development (INDE) study of barriers to girls' education in Zambezia Province uses a broader sociological model and identifies several issues that have not been given sufficient importance in other analyses. The study shows that barriers to girls' education are complex sets of interlinked causes. It confirms other findings that distance to school and an irrelevant curriculum are constraining factors on the supply side, but also reports that violence and abuse in schools or in connection with school are very important negative factors for girls.

Factors affecting girls' attendance and performance in school expressed in the study are already known but need special interventions not yet detailed in DSS. Some provisions can be changed nationally, such as regulations dealing with pregnancy and married girls, and educating more female teachers. Others—such as teachers' sexual exploitation of girls and use of violence as punishment, and tacit acceptance of these—require a concerted effort and specific interventions to change attitudes and behaviors.[19]

On the demand side, the study identifies three categories of barriers to girls' education: structural conditions, perceptions (of schooling), and dispositions (as used by Pierre Bourdieu). The structural conditions of poverty include having to work to support family or, in urban areas, finding and cultivating a "sugar daddy." Perceptions that affect schooling include the views that schools alienate girls from culture and tradition, treat them like children after the *ritos* (initiation into adulthood), or corrupt their morals by allowing contact with boys and men so their *lobolo* (dowry) is very small. In urban areas the money needed for *curtir* ("la dolce vita," or modernity) over and above basic things encourages girls to pursue sugar daddies and prostitution.

This study has been cited at length for two reasons. First, it shows that girls' situations need particular interventions that are determined by each context and that each context must be well understood. If school councils are made aware of the issues, DSS funds may also be used for community sensitization and teacher training in gender issues.

Second, this study demonstrates the need for a more nuanced understanding of all issues involved in achieving universal primary education. To gain better understanding, we must develop better and more comprehensive models for analysis. Universal primary education is more than achieving the statistics of universal completion: it must be a positive and meaningful process of learning for all. It is the right of the child.

NOTES

1. The 2005 calculation by National Institute of Statistics—Instituto Nacional de Estadistica (INE).

2. The 2002/03 Household Survey–*Inquérito aos Agregados Familiares* (IAF).

3. The 2005 Human Development Index (see UNDP 2005).

4. The original projection was that it would not reach 16 percent until 2010.

5. A new PARPA was finalized in 2006 (PARPA II).

6. Bruns, Mingat, and Rakotomalala (2003) set out a typology of countries that will struggle to reach universal primary education because of this inefficiency.

7. Both the ASE and the boarding fee increased in ESG1 and ESG2, and registration fees were added at those levels. Adult education required a registration fee and examination fees.

8. Mt 25,000 = approximately US$1.

9. See 2004 PSIA (World Bank 2005).

10. The PSIA statistical modeling for the significance of cost as a variable is limited by the fact that only official (verifiable) costs are included. The PSIA does note, however, that actual cost can be much more.

11. Among the many examples in the subregion, in Lesotho a greater amount of household income is spent on children's education by single female-headed households than by single male-headed households.

12. The monitoring reports do not define the difference between the terms *absenteeism* and *dropout* when referring to a period of only a few months rather than a whole school year.

13. In fact, gender studies from other countries show that girls often feel embarrassed if they do not have a change of clothes for sports and if they do not participate when they have menstruation. The embarrassment leads to demotivation for school.

14. The MEC wished to see all innovations channeled through the same program.

15. Birth certificates are not only a right but are also needed to register for examinations, to receive various welfare benefits, and as part of the documentation of right of inheritance.

16. The *écoles commuanitaires* in Francophone Africa, the Basic Instructional Skills certificate in Namibia, and the training of paraprofessionals in Lesotho are just a few examples. There is also much to learn from the way small teacher-training projects have been structured in Guinea Fôret and in the Ju/'Hoansi region in the Kalahari.

17. For instance, the experience of the Pestalozzi Children's Foundation project in alternative basic education in Ethiopia.

18. The pupil-teacher ratio has been included as a quality indicator for the system since 2007.

19. These findings are borne out by a DFID three-country study of abuse of girls in African schools (see Leach et al. 2003).

REFERENCES

Avenstrup, R., X. Liang, and S. Nellemann. 2004. *Kenya, Lesotho, Malawi and Uganda: Universal Primary Education and Poverty Reduction.* Washington, DC: World Bank.

Bruns, B., A. Mingat, and R. Rakotomalala. 2003. *Achieving Universal, Primary Education by 2015: A Chance for Every Child.* Washington, DC: World Bank.

Government of Mozambique. 2001. "Action Plan for the Reduction of Absolute Poverty (Plano De Acção para a Redução da Pobreza Absoluta—PARPA), 2001–5." Maputo.

———. 2003. "Review of the Economic and Social Plan for 2003." Maputo.

———. 2006. "Action Plan for the Reduction of Absolute Poverty (Plano De Acção para a Redução da Pobreza Absoluta—PARPA II), 2006–9." Maputo.

INDE (National Institute for Educational Development)/Copenhagen Development Consulting. 2005. *Multifaceted Challenges: A Study on the Barriers to Girls' Education, Zambezia Province, Mozambique.* Maputo.

Leach, F., V. Fiscian, E. Kadzamira, E. Lemani, and P. Machakanja. 2003. *An Investigative Study of the Abuse of Girls in African Schools.* London: Department for International Development (DFID).

MEC (Ministry of Education and Culture). 2003. "Supplementary Analysis of the Demographic and Health Survey 2003." Maputo.

———. 2004a. "Direct Support to Schools Report." Maputo.

———. 2004b. "Relatório Final Acçao Social Escolar (ASE), Phase 2." Maputo.

———. 2005a. "Direct Support to Schools Report." Maputo.

———. 2005b. "Education Sector Strategic Plan II (ESSP II)—Plano Estratégico de Educação 2. 2005–9." Maputo.

———. 2005c. "Support to Orphaned and Vulnerable Children under the Direct Support to Schools Program: Memorandum of Concept." Maputo.

———. 2006. "Direct Support to Schools Report." Maputo.

MEC (Ministry of Education and Culture) and cooperating partners. 2004. "Joint Review of the Education Sector—Análise do Setor da Educação do Reo Revisão Conjunta." Maputo.

———. 2005. "Joint Review of the Education Sector—Análise do Setor da Educação do Reo Revisão Conjunta." Maputo.

Ministry of Health. 2004. "Report on the Update of the HIV Epidemiological Surveillance Data—2004." Maputo.

INE (Instituto Nacional de Estadistica—National Institute of Statistics). 2004. *Impacto Demografico do HIV/SIDA em Mocambique.* Maputo.

Nhate, Virgulino. 2005. *Orphans in Mozambique: Vulnerability, Trends, Determinants and Programme Responses.* Maputo: Ministry of Planning and Development.

Oxford Policy Management. 2002. *Mozambique Education Sector Expenditure Review* (September). Oxford.

Petty, C., K. Selvester, J. Seaman, and J. Acidri. 2003. *Mozambique Assessment: The Impact of HIV/AIDS on Household Economy.* London: Save the Children (U.K.).

UNDP (United Nations Development Programme). 2005. *Human Development Report.* New York: UNDP.

World Bank. 2003. *Mozambique Public Expenditure Review, Phase 2: Sectoral Expenditures.* Washington, DC: World Bank.

———. 2005. *Mozambique. Poverty and Social Impact Analysis (PSIA): Primary School Enrollment and Retention—the Impact of School Fees.* Washington, DC: World Bank.

Index

Boxes, figures, maps, notes, and tables are indicated by *b, f, m, n,* and *t,* respectively.